The Theology of the Cross
and Marx's Anthropology

American University Studies

Series VII
Theology and Religion

Vol. 84

PETER LANG
New York · San Francisco · Bern
Frankfurt am Main · Paris · London

Winston D. Persaud

The Theology of the Cross and Marx's Anthropology

A View from the Caribbean

PETER LANG
New York · San Francisco · Bern
Frankfurt am Main · Paris · London

Library of Congress Cataloging-in-Publication Data

Persaud, Winston D.
   The theology of the cross and Marx's anthropology :
a view from the Caribbean / Winston D. Persaud.
      p. cm. — (American university studies. Series VII,
Theology and religion ; v. 84)
   Includes bibliographical references and index.
   1. Sociology, Christian.   2. Theology, Doctrinal —
Caribbean Area.   3. Marx, Karl, 1818-1883 — Contributions
in philosophical anthropology.   4. Man (Christian
theology)   5. Jesus Christ — Crucifixion.   6. Holy Cross.
7. Alienation (Philosophy)   8. Reconciliation — Religious
aspects — Christianity.   9. Caribbean Area — Church
history — 20th century.   10. Christianity and culture.   11. cc.
   I. Title.   II. Series.
BT738.P459   1991   230'.09729 — dc20   90-40423
ISBN 0-8204-1409-3   CIP
ISSN 0740-0446

© Peter Lang Publishing, Inc., New York 1991

Printed in the United States of America.

In loving memory
of
my father
and
my sister

ACKNOWLEDGMENTS

Excerpts are reprinted from *The Experiment Hope* by Jurgen Moltmann, copyright 1975 SCM Press. Used by permission of Augsberg Fortress Publishers.

Excerpts reprinted by permission of Augsburg Fortress Publishers from Wolfhart Pannenberg, *What is Man?* Philadelphia: Fortress Press, 1970. All rights reserved.

Extracts reprinted by permission of Augsberg Fortress Publishers from Walther von Loewenich, *Luther's Theology of the Cross*, translated by Herbert J.A. Bouman. Minneapolis: Augsburg Publishing House, 1976. All rights reserved.

Excerpts reprinted by permission of Basil Blackwell from Karl Marx, *Early Texts*, translated and edited by David McLellan. Oxford: Basil Blackwell, 1971. All rights reserved.

Excerpts reprinted by permission of Cambridge University Press rom Bertell Ollman, *Alienation*. Cambridge: Cambridge University Press, 1971. All rights reserved.

Excerpts reprinted by permission of Cambridge University Press from Charles Taylor, *Hegel*. London: Cambridge University Press, 1975. All rights reserved.

Excerpts from *The Crucified God* by Jurgen Moltmann, translated by John Bowden and R.A. Wilson. Copyright 1974 by SCM Press Ltd. Reprinted by permission of Harper and Row, Publishers, Inc.

Extracts reprinted by permission of International Publishers Co., Inc., from Karl Marx and Frederick Engels, *The Communist Manifesto*. New York: International Publishers Co., Inc., 1948. All rights reserved.

Excerpts reprinted by permission of Lawrence & Wishart Ltd. from *Collected Works*, Marx and Engels, 1976.

Excerpts reprinted by permission of Lawrence & Wishart Ltd. from *Pre-capitalist Economic Formations*, Karl Marx, translated by Jack Cohen, edited and with an introduction by E.J. Hobsbawn, 1978.

Excerpts reprinted by permission of Orbis Books and SCM Press from Gustavo Gutierrez, *A Theology of Liberation*, translated and edited by Sister Caridad Inda and John Eagleson. Maryknoll, N.Y.: Orbis Books, 1988, rev. ed. All rights reserved.

Excerpts reprinted by permission of Oxford University Press from Svetozar Stojanovic, *Between Ideals and Reality*, translated by Gerson S. Sher. New York: Oxford University Press, 1973. All rights reserved.

TABLE OF CONTENTS

PREFACE

This study, in its original form as "The Theology of the Cross and Marx's Concept of Man, with Reference to the Caribbean," was submitted, in 1980, to the University of St. Andrews, St. Andrews, Scotland, in fulfilment of the requirement for the degree of doctor of philosophy. Given the themes of *perestroika* and *glasnost* and the events of the 1980's, the relevance of this work has increased rather than diminished. A special thanks is extended to my supervisor, George Hall, who introduced me to the early Marx, and to William Weiblen of Wartburg Theological Seminary who procured the scholarship funds for my studies.

I am deeply indebted to a number of people for their generous and able assistance in revising and preparing the manuscript for publication. I offer my sincere thanks to: Joel Samuels, Peter Kjeseth, and Hemchand Gossai, who read the manuscript and made invaluable suggestions to improve the quality of the work; Pam and Kris Humbert, for advice and hours of typing; James Melvin, my student assistant; Earl Janssen; Marie Gossai; Dorothy Burt; Don Burt, who provided us with the computer equipment we needed; and, Joe Stradcutter, whose immense knowledge of computers made the final production of this work a reality. I would also like to thank Carl Braaten and Donald Bloesch for their encouragement and recommendation that I publish this work, and to Heidi Burns of Peter Lang Publishing, Inc., who invited me to submit my manuscript.

I thank our sons, Winston and Alexander, who endured the inevitable disruption of family life this project entailed. Finally, I owe an incalculable debt to my wife, May. Without her encouragement, tenacity, and hard work in all areas in the preparation of the revised manuscript, this publication would not have been possible.

INTRODUCTION

We are concerned with three interrelated areas of study: Marx's anthropology; the theology of the cross; and Christianity, Marxism and the Caribbean.[1] We will begin with an analysis of Marx's anthropology and continue with an argument for a theology of the cross. Then, we will conclude with a description of Caribbean man and woman and articulate a theological response to their situation.

The overriding motivation in undertaking this theological project is existential. It is an attempt to respond to the ongoing challenge for the church to articulate the Christian faith in a manner that is intelligible and relevant to the contemporary world. Implicit in this challenge is a recognition of the temporal and historical nature of the church's statements of the faith throughout the centuries in various societies, under diverse conditions, including times of persecution for the faith. It is also a tacit confession of the dynamic activity of the Spirit, who has called the church into being and who sustains and preserves it through the Word and sacraments.

Confessing the faith in a way that is intelligible to the contemporary world is an intrinsic demand of the gospel itself. The message of God's reconciling love through the suffering, death and resurrection of Jesus Christ is mediated through the Spirit in Word and sacrament. Thus, the scriptures, the creeds, and the traditions and teachings of the church, which have come down to us through the ages, are not the objects of faith but the essential means through which the message of the gospel is communicated and clarified. The mission of proclaiming the gospel today will not be effectively and evangelically done by simply articulating so-called modern creeds which are more suited to the spirit of the times (*Zeitgeist*) than are the old formulations. According to Wolfhart Pannenberg, that route would be "the cheap way out."[2] Christian identity is defined in relation to the scriptures, the creeds and traditions. This is not to deny that there has not been distorted and even dehumanising uses of them. But genuine evangelical confession requires us to take due account of them. Speaking about this dilemma in relation to the Apostles' and Nicene creeds, Pannenberg writes:

> The more or less obscure discomfort with certain formulations should not
> lead to the cheap way out—to the excluding of the creed from use in church
> and its replacement by other, supposedly more contemporary formulae,

which at best could never fulfil the function of the old creeds—that through them the individual Christian can enrol himself in the communion of all Christendom. But even as regards the content of faith, nothing is gained by a change of words. What is needed is an explanation and understanding of the things of the Christian faith, which have found their expression in the ancient credal formulations. To reject these formulations simply because we find them incomprehensible is uneducated …. We could only justify their rejection if they had to be discarded because they were simply wrong. But today's widespread lack of comprehension of the credal formulae is a call, not for their abolition, but for their explanation.[3]

This lack of comprehension of "the credal formulae" and of the scriptures as a whole, concerning the God of Abraham and Sarah, Isaac and Rebeccah, Jacob and Leah and Rachel, … and of Jesus the Christ, is acutely present in the Marxist challenge to evangelical theology. Both Marxists and Christians need to be reminded that the Triune God works on behalf of humanity for its total reconciliation. We will point the way to the cross of Christ, where we find God, through the death and resurrection of the Son, engaged in the most definitive and decisive activity on behalf of humanity and the whole creation. It is God's nature to love, a love which includes suffering. Thus, the event of the cross and resurrection is the unique expression of God's love for humankind. Through Word and sacrament, the Holy Spirit bears witness to God's reconciling love in the crucified and risen Jesus Christ. In short, our theological response will be Trinitarian.

The concern with the task of Christian confession, in word and deed, in the Caribbean is unique. It must be done within societies whose alienated identity is bound up with colonialism, slavery and indenture and in dialogue with Marxism. The identity of the Caribbean man and woman is rooted in the Judeo-Christian tradition in two significant ways. First, it emerged from the colonising impact and influence of western European civilisation upon peoples from Europe, Africa and Asia. (The arrival of the first Europeans resulted in the almost total decimation of the indigenous island populations.) Second, it also emerged from the salvific efficacy of the gospel among the oppressed who experienced the love of God in Christ in the midst of their enslavement and suffering, some of whom were inspired to express their freedom by working to undermine the oppressive system under which the masses lived. Unfortunately, the message of the gospel was often experienced as law, since the gospel was often used to domesticate slaves and members of the lower strata of society, making them docile and manipulable. This fact cannot be overlooked by the church in its attempt to carry out its mission of reconciliation through Jesus Christ. At the same time, however, the church must not be afraid to proclaim the scandal of the cross which gives it its peculiar identity as an eschatological community with historical relevance and concreteness.

In the face of the ambiguous experience of the Judeo-Christian tradition, it is not surprising that Marx's anthropocentric philosophy, with its emphasis upon humanity's salvation through its own liberating *praxis-theoria* , might be and actually is appealing to many in the Caribbean, not least among significant sectors of the intelligentsia, including the political leadership. Marx stands within the Judeo-Christian tradition. Whereas, on the one hand, the church must (and does) evaluate and judge its action in terms of the law, on the other hand, Marx's philosophy judges the church and society in terms of its "principle of ideology." At times the two will coincide, but this does not provide the basis for the church either to dispense with the use of the law in preference to Marx's "principle of ideology," or to turn a blind eye to the Marxian critique. In the freedom of the gospel, the church can find the courage to adopt a critical, not compromising, attitude towards Marx's philosophy, including his concept of ideology.

Our primary thesis on Marx is: Marx's anthropology and his theory of history are an anthropocentric theory of real, historical and ultimate way of salvation. Marx's philosophy is a *Weltanschauung*. In his early writings, Marx sketched out his world view, which was intrinsically atheistic and anthropocentric. This world view remained implicit throughout his life, even in his mature writings. In relation to alienated Caribbean man and woman who live in an explosive situation, Marx's *Weltanschauung* does not merely promise a way out of the economic morass in which they find themselves but a radically different self-understanding and conception of total reality which are in contradiction to a trinitarian-theocentric view of reality. Their new self-understanding, according to Marx, can only result from a radical transformation of the productive process from which all superstructures, including consciousness, are derived. Marx's world view is totally immanental. The only meaning given to transcendence is that of historical transcendence through human *praxis*. Humanity acts in harmony and in conjunction with the material forces of history, i.e., the mode of production. Humanity's future, its ethical standards, its whole society, are to be entirely the product of its own activity. Only humanity is capable of ultimately and completely liberating itself and the whole of society.

Marx's outlook stands in stark contrast to the Christian view of reality, in which transcendence is defined in terms of God and in which humanity's ultimate future is not its own creation but a gratuitous gift of God received in faith. Whereas Marx sees human alienation as historically produced, which, therefore, will be historically transformed through human revolutionary recreation of the productive process, Christian theology sees humankind as fundamentally alienated from God and reconciled only through the loving *praxis* of God in the suffering, death and resurrection of Jesus Christ. Yet, Christian theology does admit that human beings, and certainly Caribbean man and woman, suffer from socio-economic and political alienation which the church must both verbally denounce and visibly strive to minimise, if not totally eliminate. The church does so on behalf of the neighbour. In a curious and ambiguous way, the church's credibility in Caribbean society is bound up with its response to this challenge in the name of the gospel for the sake of the suffering in society.

In presenting Marx's anthropocentric, atheistic world view, we are suggesting that there is a continuity between the "early" and "mature" Marx. The continuity is rooted in Marx's use of the term alienation and his indebtedness to Hegel and Feuerbach. The concept of alienation is not peculiar to Marx, or Hegel, or Feuerbach, for both before and after their time, it has been used in varying and different senses. Moreover, Marx's preoccupation with humankind leads to a consideration of his critique of religion, atheism, and false consciousness as a whole, followed by an attempt to piece together Marx's definition of human nature, which Marx assumes cannot be defined *a priori*. We conclude Marx's description of humankind as alienated *species-being* with Marx's projection of unalienated human future which human beings alone will create.

Discussion of Marx's theory of history naturally follows the presentation of his anthropology. The two are inseparably bound together. Marx views history as universal history. He posits it as the de-alienating and ultimately free creative activity of human being-in-community. All alienating forces are historical. Here, we will note the dialectical interplay between the mode of production and human activity, i.e., between historical materialism and proletarian messianism. Finally, we conclude this section with a consideration of a Marxian ethics.

Pannenberg aptly summarises our focus on Marx's anthropology and theory of history:

> A critique that only zeros in on one or another of Marx's conclusions,
> whether it be the prophecy of the demise of capitalism or the utopia of the

communistic society of the future, would be a critique that would not do
him justice. His thought draws its power from its anthropological roots.[4]

In our account of Marx's anthropocentric world view, we will show the
interrelatedness of Marx's "prophecy of the demise of capitalism" and his prophecy
of "the utopia of the communist society of the future," which are derived from and
built upon his preoccupation with alienated humanity and its transcendence of
alienation.

Following the discussion of Marx's anthropology and his theory of history, we
will then turn to the theology of the cross as an evangelical response to the challenge
of Marx's anthropocentric *Weltanschauung*. Our response stems from the conviction
that God is neither absent from nor unmoved by human suffering. God's freedom
and sovereignty do not dehumanise humanity nor promote its alienation but effect its
salvation and reconciliation, *coram Deo* and *coram mundo*. It is precisely because the
Holy One is both the God of wrath and the God of love that the Triune One stands
above humanity as judge and suffers on behalf of and with humanity in history. To
speculate about who this God is leads to a theology of glory. This God of Abraham
and Sarah, Isaac and Rebeccah, Jacob, Leah and Rachel, and of Jesus Christ, reveals
godself in the cross and resurrection of the Son. On the cross God the Father suffers
the forsakenness of the Son and the Son experiences the forsakenness of the Father,
for he cries out: "My God, my God, why have you forsaken me?" Jesus Christ
suffers death and the grave because of God's love for humankind, and because of
the Son's love of the Father. Jesus' suffering and death on the cross are seen in the
context of this manifold nature of God's love. Jesus pays the price of human sin,
including alienation, and breaks the power of the forces of evil that have held
humankind and the whole creation in captivity. The triumph of God's activity,
through Christ, is in both cross and resurrection. The two are held together. Thus,
theology of the cross includes both the suffering and death of Jesus, as well as his
resurrection.

Because of the salutary event of Jesus Christ, Christian theology dares to speak
of God in the face of Marx's challenge to theology. In the midst of humankind's
historical experience of all forms of alienation, God is not absent, even when it
appears that God is. The Divine is present in hiddenness, in suffering and shame, in
weakness and humility, in love and freedom. The paradox of God's revelation is
that God reveals in the contrary. This is intrinsic to the scandal of the cross.

In arguing for a theology of the cross as an evangelical response to Marx's

Weltanschauung, we will look at Martin Luther's *theologia crucis*, followed by a discussion of Jürgen Moltmann's "Trinitarian political theology of the cross." Finally, we will turn to a critical consideration of the "Theology of human familyhood" in liberation theology in Latin America.

The geo-cultural sphere in which we are concerned to explicate the Christian faith is the area comprising the Commonwealth Caribbean. Following our discussion of the theology of the cross, we will focus our attention upon the meaning of alienation in this area. We will give special attention to colonial history and its legacy, alienation and pluralism, as well as to some of the specific characteristics of alienation in the region and among its peoples. The emerging picture will form part of the background against which we will sketch out the directions which Caribbean theology might pursue, as expressed in the tentative suggestions made by certain ecumenical voices in the Caribbean church. In tracing some of the implications for doing theology in the Caribbean arising from these tentative suggestions, we will look at the question of the theological understanding of alienation in the Caribbean. The task of maintaining the inherent unity between faith in God and love of neighbour, as well as the tension between the "already" and the "not yet" (i.e., between prolepsis and eschatological fulfilment) which the church has, leads us to a critical treatment of Luther's doctrine of the two kingdoms. We will conclude with a summary of the total picture that emerges from this work.

NOTES TO INTRODUCTION

[1] By Caribbean is meant those areas which today make up the (British) Commonwealth Caribbean. This means that the non-English-speaking islands, including Cuba, Puerto Rico, Haiti and the Dominican Republic, the French Islands, and the Dutch Islands are not included. Besides the English-speaking islands, including St. Lucia, we include Guyana and Belize (on the South and Central American mainlands, respectively), which have shared a common history with these islands.

[2] Wolfhart Pannenberg, *The Apostles' Creed*, trans. by Margaret Kohl (London: SCM Press Ltd., 1972), p. 13.

[3] *Ibid.*, pp. 13–14.

[4] Wolfhart Pannenberg, *What is Man?*, trans. by Duane A. Priebe (Philadelphia: Fortress Press, 1970), pp. 116–117.

CHAPTER I
MARX'S ANTHROPOLOGY

A.
The "Early" and the "Mature" Marx

In our attempt to uncover Marx's anthropology, we are confronted by the unavoidable problem of deciding where in the plethora of Marx's writings to look. This problem poses a crucial hermeneutical task for the student of Marx, since the primary and more significant works of his youth were not published until the 1930's. Among these were his primary philosophic writings, which have come to be known as the *Economic and Philosophic Manuscripts of 1844*.[1] The relative neglect of these early texts has meant that only Marx's later works, which have been labelled "mature" and "authentic" and which were already published and in use, have been regarded as authentic writings of official Marxism.[2] In the Soviet Union, for example, the *Communist Manifesto*, *German Ideology*, and, above all, *Das Kapital,* which were all published after 1844, are considered the literary corpus of authentic Marxism. Marx's thought has crystallised around these works,[3] and any attempt to deviate from them was not merely discountenanced by the authorities but radically suppressed by them.[4]

Despite a rather pervasive dismissal of the early texts by both the guardians of official, mature Marxism and the non-Marxist critics of official Marxism, the twentieth century saw the emergence of a growing and sustained interest in these so-called corrupt Marxian writings. Indeed their publication, in 1932, was both a symptom of this interest as well as an added stimulus to it. Adam Schaff explains that there was a growing realisation among scholars that "a fuller knowledge of the young Marx's intellectual evolution is necessary for the deeper understanding of the origins and development of Marxism ... [and that] false political considerations [had] militated against the discussion of early Marxian humanism." Schaff adds that a "second reason for the topicality and attraction of" the young Marx may be described as existential. He notes, for example, that in the ideological struggle in Poland, in the 1950's, there was a commonality of interest in humanity in the young Marx and in the concerns and struggles of young Poles. He tells us:

The young Marx, as is easily understandable against the background of his

> age and his personal development, wrestled with the problem of the human individual and his relationship to society and nature (the world) .... It is not surprising that in circumstances of psychological shock and ideological chaos, they began to interpret the 'newly discovered' Marx in their own way, although in fact, because of textual difficulties and complicated connections between Marx and the young Hegelians, unknown to our readers, they simply did not understand him.[5]

The rediscovery of the early humanistic Marx created an ideological and a methodological problem. To those who had gradually become disenchanted with the cold, scientific and impersonal mature Marx of official Marxism, the salutary concern of the early, philosophic Marx for the individual provided new impetus to the study of Marx's philosophy. The early Marx was seen as a necessary corrective to the excesses of official Marxism. The early Marx's philosophy was first and foremost concerned with humanity in its present predicament of alienation under the capitalist system. Marx argued for the relativity of "ideology," which meant that no programme for the transformation of society could be legitimately considered applicable for all time.[6] Naturally, such an understanding of this "unhistorical" and "subversive" Marx was a serious threat to the hitherto existing "historical" Marxism. For example, Iring Fetscher reports that Georg Lukács and Karl Korsch were reproached by those "from the side of the social democratic and Communist orthodox writers" for their undue interest in the young Marx.[7] The summary dismissal of the early writings by the guardians of the authentic Marx could not and did not avert the ideological crisis within the Marxist bloc. On the contrary, the protective action which was taken by the authorities to correct this heretical tendency merely intensified the crisis. Moreover, western interest in existentialist themes, especially alienation, contributed, albeit indirectly, to the crisis.

In the debate on how to appropriate rightly the early philosophic writings, two apparently antithetical halves of Marx's thought emerged.[8] This accentuated the crucial question of the relevance and accuracy of the existing general method of historical investigation.[9] Critical questions were raised: Of what value is the thought of the young Marx for an accurate understanding of the writings of the mature Marx, and vice versa? Are all the writings of Marx to be treated as a whole on the assumption that there is an implicit (and explicit) continuity of thought throughout Marx's works? Is there continuity within discontinuity?

B.
Continuity within Discontinuity in Marx's Thought

There is unanimity among scholars that in his early texts, Marx displays a youthful preoccupation with philosophical anthropology and a "corresponding critique of human culture."[10] However, there is no such unanimity that in his mature writings Marx is primarily concerned with "philosophical anthropology." Scholars argue, instead, that in those writings, Marx's primary concern is the enunciation of the inherent weaknesses within the capitalist system which, he is convinced, would eventually undermine it and lead to its ultimate collapse. The lack of unanimity stems from the dispute over the continuity in Marx's philosophic perspective, that is, the extent to which Marx is a philosopher even in his later works. There is general agreement among scholars that in his later writings Marx was more the economist, sociologist and political scientist than the philosopher. Raymond Aron notes that "it might be said that, from 1848 until the end of his life, Marx apparently ceased to be a philosopher and became a sociologist and, above all, an economist."[11] Furthermore, Aron points to the centrality of Marx's economic analysis:

> Marx's thought is an interpretation of the contradictory or antagonistic character of capitalist society. In a certain sense, Marx's whole canon is an attempt to show that this antagonistic character is inseparable from the fundamental structure of the capitalist system and is, at the same time, the mechanism of the historic movement.[12]

There is a contradiction between what Aron says here and his suggestion elsewhere that Marx "until the end of his life ... remained in a certain sense a philosopher." The contradiction may be corrected by noting that, for Aron, the distinction between the economist of the later writings and the philosopher of the early works hinges upon what is central to Marx at a particular time, in contrast to what may be nascent and secondary, or obsolete. For Aron, whereas Marx the economic theorist was in his nascent stage of development in the early Marx, Marx the philosopher was more obsolete than merely hidden in the later Marx.[13]

Daniel Bell, who argues that, "having found the answer to the 'mysteries' of Hegel in political economy, Marx promptly forgot all about philosophy," corroborates Aron's arguments.[14] For Bell, Marx ceased to be the abstract speculative philosopher when he realised that philosophy could be realised and, hence, transcended only in economics. But Marx did not cease being a practising philosopher. Indeed, Bell adds, Marx was never really interested in economics. Bell sums up Marx's excursus into economics thus:

> The question why men were propertyless turned Marx to economics. For a man whose name is so linked with the 'dismal science,' Marx was never really interested in economics. His correspondences with Engels, in later years, is studded with contemptuous references to the subject (which he at one time referred to as the 'economic filth'), and he resented the fact that his detailed explorations in the economic mechanisms of society prevented him from carrying on other studies. But he continued because, for him, economics was the practical side of philosophy—it would unveil the mystery of alienation—and because he had found in the categories of political economy the material expression of that alienation: the process of exploitation.[15]

Marx's pursuit of economic theory was the result of his more fundamental preoccupation with alienation. Beneath his elaborate and often vague and laborious discussion of political economy was the primary motivating consideration: the condition of human beings in capitalist society.

It would seem natural and useful for us to establish that the theme of human alienation is the primary and overriding concern of both the early and mature Marx. Bell's argument appears on the surface to support this conclusion. Yet, elsewhere Bell argues that the "historical Marx" rejected the concept of alienation. In the early Marx there was a double vision of alienation: economic and humanistic. However, "Marxist thought developed along one narrow road of economic conceptions of property and exploitation, while the other road, which might have led to new, humanistic concepts of works and labor, was left unexplored."[16] The implication here is that in the movement of the concept of alienation from the purely speculative, philosophic, and humanistic realms to the categories of economic analysis of property relations under capitalism, a split occurred between the early and mature Marx.[17] This implication is inconclusive. The unveiling of the mystery of alienation in order to reveal the concrete reality of economic exploitation did not mean that alienation ceased to be the primary motif in Marx's thought after 1844. Rather, it persisted throughout his writings. This recognition is crucial for a balanced treatment of the concept.

Despite the argument for continuity in Marx's thought, the debate concerning Marx's and Engels' attitudes after 1844 towards the early writings of Marx continues to be inconclusive. It is not clear whether Marx abandons his early writings, deeming them inaccurate in their description of his mature thinking. David McLellan comments:

> Certainly he did not care much about the fate of his early manuscripts. In the preface to his *Critique of Political Economy*, he said that he and Engels had abandoned the manuscript of *The German Ideology* (1846) 'to the gnawing criticisms of the mice all the more willingly as we had achieved our main purpose—self-clarification'.[18]

Even in the pre-1844 years, Marx understands that in his early writings he is aiming at self-clarification. He is attempting to provide the philosophic basis for his later economic discussions. In explaining the aims of the journal, *Deutsch-Franzosische Jahrbucher,* Marx declares:

> So we can summarize the tendency of our journal in one word: self-understanding (equals critical philosophy) by our age of its struggles and wishes. This is a task for the world and for us. It can only be the result of united forces. What is at stake is a confession, nothing more. To get its sins forgiven, humanity only needs to describe them as they are.[19]

Speaking about the "reform of consciousness," he further explains that the aim of seeking self-clarification "consists in putting religious and political questions in a self-conscious, human form." Thereby, "the world [would] perceive its own consciousness by [being awakened] from dreaming about itself."[20]

It would be stretching the point to suggest that, having achieved the objective of self-clarification in his early writings, Marx is able to move on to something totally new. Instead of claiming that there is such a radical break, it would seem more reasonable to argue that the explicit philosophy in Marx's early writings continues to provide the basic framework for his later, economic analysis of capitalism.

There is general agreement among scholars that the continuity in Marx's thought depends upon the fundamental and persistent influence of Hegel upon Marx. Though Marx rejects Hegel's primary thesis that reality is the self-positing of

Absolute Spirit, he, nevertheless, continues to use Hegelian categories in both his early and later works.[21] Admittedly, he is attempting to realise philosophy through revolutionary, historical *praxis*. But he seeks to do so precisely by attempting to place Hegel "right side up." Consequently, Marx's writings are an attempt to dispute Hegel's claims by replacing them with his own philosophical and, later, economic interpretations.

Commenting on the pervasiveness of Hegel's influence throughout Marx's writings, Robert Tucker observes that the "inversion of Hegel's dialectic of history was the constitutive act of the mature Marxian dialectic." The obvious conclusion to be drawn, Tucker notes, "is that he considered the manuscripts of 1844 the birthplace of *mature* Marxism, the founding documents of scientific socialism."[22] Tucker adds that the presence and influence of the Hegelian dialectic in its materialist form, in both the early and the later writings of Marx, clearly show that for both Marx and Engels "there were not two Marxisms but one." Tucker concedes, however, that there is some truth in the argument for two Marxisms, i.e., only "in the peculiar and limited sense in which the adult may be said to be a different person from the child." Tucker explains that according to Marx and Engels

> scientific socialism, embryonic already in Hegel's *Phenomenology*, was delivered into the world in Marx's manuscripts of 1844. The philosophical terminology of the latter was simply the umbilical cord binding the new-born child to its philosophical parent. And mature Marxism was the baby grown to adulthood. Consequently, it was perfectly proper to speak of the mature doctrine in terms applicable to original Marxism.[23]

Tucker's "developmental" view of the unity in the Marxian literary corpus appears somewhat similar to Bell's view discussed earlier. Both Tucker and Bell espouse the view that Marx's later writings arose out of his early philosophical thought. However, whereas Tucker sees no discontinuity between the philosophy of the early Marx and the political economic theory of the later Marx, Bell argues that Marx abandons the early philosophy. Bell's argument would lead one to conclude that the later Marx was only minimally a Hegelian, if at all. On the other hand, it is true, as McLellan points out, "that Marx always remained in some sense a Hegelian; and that the early writings are important since they document the formation of Marx's attitude to Hegel's philosophy."[24] The argument may be advanced even further (with Lenin): "It is impossible to fully grasp Marx's *Capital* and especially the first chapter, if you have not studied or understood the whole of Hegel's *Logic*. Consequently, none of the Marxists for the past half century has understood Marx!"[25]

The publication of the *Grundrisse der Kritik der Politischen Oekonomie* (*Elements of a Critique of Political Economy*) 1857/1858, for the first time in 1939, revealed the fundamental influence of Hegel upon the later Marx. Problems and concepts, such as alienation and objectification, which Marx had reflected upon, especially in his *1844 Manuscripts,* were also considered at great length in the *Grundrisse*.[26] Viewed as the *Preface* to *Capital*, it certainly bridges the apparent hiatus between the early philosophic writings and the mature writings of political economy. But to conceive of the *Grundrisse* as an intermediary link is to suggest that *Capital* is the centrepiece of Marx's writings, a suggestion disputed by McLellan. He argues that the *Grundrisse*, not *Capital*, "is the centrepiece of Marx's work" "which permitted the generalizations in the famous *Preface* of the *Critique of Political Economy*." The generalisations "are only partial elaborations" of the *Grundrisse* itself. For its part, *Capital* does not even match the *Preface*, which is its centre and source of inspiration. "Marx himself describes it in a letter to Lassalle as: 'the result of 15 years research, that is to say the best years of my life'."[27]

It is not our concern to enter into the debate about the correct location of the *Grundrisse* and *Capital* in the pyramid of Marx's writings. We are content to point out that, along with the *1844 Manuscripts*, there is a continuity in Marx's thought firmly bound up with Hegel's influence upon Marx.[28]

Earlier, we mentioned that Marx attempts to come to grips intellectually and philosophically with the Hegelian system by focusing on alienation and objectification. The problems of alienation and objectification occupy Marx's attention and energies in the *1844 Manuscripts*. This preoccupation amply displays Marx's anthropology and remains his concern throughout his mature works. Helmut Thielicke notes that the young Marx's "doctrine of man which is not only not concealed but is even set forth programmatically"[29] permeates the entire corpus of his writings. The early philosopher, who later becomes an economist, a sociologist, and a political scientist in the years following the writing of the *1844 Manuscripts*, does not abandon his humanistic concerns. He does not cease to be a philosopher, for he does not completely dispense with Hegel's influence. Indeed, combining the latter with Marx's analysis of alienation and objectification demonstrates the continuity within discontinuity in Marx's thought.

Like the *1844 Manuscripts,* the *Grundrisse* is fragmentary in nature. The Hegelian categories, in which Marx formulates his thought, are obvious to the reader. "Questions that were prominent in Marx's writings in 1844—such as the true nature of labour and the resolution of the conflict between individual and community—are taken up again and filled out with a wealth of detail."[30] The following quotation gives an indication of the tone of the *Grundrisse*:

> Thus the ancient conception, in which man always appears (in however narrowly national, religious or political a definition) as the aim of production, seems very much more exalted than the modern world, in which production is the aim of man and wealth the aim of production. In fact, however, when the narrow bourgeois form has been peeled away, what is wealth, if not the universality of needs, capacities, enjoyments, productive powers, etc., of individuals, produced in universal exchange? What, if not the the full development of human control over the forces of nature—those of his own nature as well as those of so called 'nature'? What, if not the absolute elaboration of his creative dispositions, without any preconditions other than antecedent historical evolution which makes the totality of this evolution—i.e. the evolution of all human powers as such, unmeasured by any *previously established* yardstick—an end in itself? What is this, if not a situation where man does not produce himself in any determined form, but produces his totality? Where he does not seek to remain something formed by the past, but is in the absolute movement of becoming? In bourgeois political economy—and in the epoch of production to which it corresponds—this complete elaboration of what lies within man, appears as the total alienation, and the destruction of all fixed, one-sided purposes as the sacrifice of the end in itself to a wholly external compulsion.[31]

Here, we are confronted with a number of themes which are prominent in the early Marx's description of human alienation. We note the emphasis on the human being as a creature of "needs, capacities, enjoyments, productive powers, etc." Humanity produces itself through its productive labour. It is described as being more fully itself when it gains control of the forces of nature. It produces, "objectifies," what lies within itself. Unfortunately, human beings in bourgeois society are alienated and manipulated by forces external to themselves.

In *Capital,* Marx's primary mature economic work, the concern with humanity and alienation still persists and, indeed, in spite of the cloudy mists of economic details and categories, remains a primary concern.[32] *Capital* is Marx's most elaborate and significant attempt to realise philosophy through political economy, based upon a philosophic anthropology that is spelled out in the *1844 Manuscripts* and partly reiterated and further developed in the *Grundrisse*. The term alienation and/or its meaning occur several times in *Capital*.[33] For example, Marx says that "the character of independence and estrangement which the capitalist modes of production as a whole gives to the instruments of labour and to the product, as against the workman, is developed by means of machinery into a thorough antagonism."[34]

McLellan adds that for Marx the anthropological resonances and continuities between the *Paris Manuscripts* and *Capital* "is not only a question of terminology." It is also a matter of "context." The "conception outlined in the *Paris Manuscripts*" "of man as a being who creates himself and the conditions of his life" is the basis for "the equation of work and value" on which rests "the main theme of Volume 1 of *Capital*, surplus-value." According to the *Paris Manuscripts*, human nature is constantly developing, through cooperation with others, self and the world around. In *Capital*, Marx describes how the fundamental role as "initiator and controller of the historical process" has been alienated. The new owner of humanity's essential role is "the inhuman power of capital." McLellan points out further that "the counterpart to alienated man, the unalienated or 'total' man of the *Manuscripts*, also appears in *Capital*. In the chapter of Volume 1 on 'Machinery and Modern Industry,' Marx makes the same contrast between the effects of alienated and unalienated modes of production on the development of human potentiality."[35]

Concluding his argument for continuity between the Marx of the *1844 Manuscripts* and the Marx of *Capital,* McLellan rightly draws attention to the fact that "the section of *Capital* that most recalls the early writings, is a final section of Chapter I, entitled 'Fetishism of commodities'."[36] In McLellan's estimation, "the whole section is reminiscent of the section on alienated labour in the *Paris Manuscripts* and of the notes on James Mill which Marx composed in 1844."[37] On the question of labour's objectification of itself in its products, Marx writes:

> A commodity is therefore a mysterious thing, simply because in it the social character of man's labour appears to them as objective character stamped upon that labour; because the relation of the producers to the sum total of their own labour, is presented to them as a social relation, existing not between themselves, but between the products of their labour.[38]

We began by acknowledging that the apparent existence of an early and a mature Marx presents a hermeneutical problem concerning the source of information related to Marx's anthropology. Whereas the early Marx was more the philosopher than the later Marx (who was ostensibly more the political economist than the speculative philosopher), an essential unity exists between the early and later Marx. The unity is centred around Hegel's influence on Marx, most clearly seen in the discusssion of the themes of alienation and objectification in both the early and mature Marx . There is no doubt that Marx, in his mature writings, came to speak of alienation in concrete terms, such as the "fetishism of commodities." But his attempt to ground alienation in the material base of the productive process is also to be found in his *1844 Manuscripts,* albeit in a nascent state.[39]

We, therefore, agree with those scholars who argue that there is a continuity within a discontinuity in Marx's thought. Continuity is found in the persistence of Marx's concern with alienation, which is described in philosophic terms in his early writings and in economic terms in his mature works. At the same time, we find that even in his early writings, Marx devotes some attention to the problem of grounding philosophy in the material process of production.

By the same token, we find that the philosophical anthropology of his early writings continues to provide the basic framework within which he analyses bourgeois capitalism. There is a break in Marx's movement from an explicit to an implicit philosophical anthropology. A shift in emphasis occurs in his mature work, especially *Capital.* There he is concerned with alienation in relation to the inherent "laws" of capitalism that would lead to its eventual demise and the end of all alienation.

Our primary concern in the preceding analysis is to show that, viewed as a whole, Marx's writings are primarily concerned with humanity as the creator of its own history. Despite the developmental changes that take place in Marx's anthropology,[40] the anthropology of the early Marx remains the presupposed functional anthropology of the mature Marx. Kostas Axelos succinctly states:

> The building of Marxian doctrine is a methodical development around the theme of man as endowed with a will capable of taking hold of the world by virtue of technique. ... Marx believes he has brought about the permanent collapse of a heaven now empty, its gods gone; and he can hardly allow that heaven continue to overshadow earth. Marx is determined that his anthropology and philosophy of history, as well as his program of salvation

and his, shall we say, eschatological vision, be altogether real and deeply, radically immanent.[41]

In his anthropology and philosophy of history, so rooted in socio-economic realities, Marx purports to ignore metaphysics. But he is unsuccessful. In asserting that human beings create themselves (and history, for history is the account of human creative activity) through their interaction with nature, Marx boldly declares that salvation—the transcendence of alienation—will be ushered in by human beings. Thus, whatever may be said about Marx as philosopher, economist, sociologist, and political scientist, his anthropology (and concomitantly his theory of history) is pivotal to his understanding of reality.

C.
Alienation in Popular Usage[42]

For Marx, the human being, whether worker (proletariat) or bourgeois capitalist (owner of the means of production), is alienated. Their alienation reached its apogee under the modern industrial capitalism of Marx's day. To define what constitutes being human, without arguing for a fixed human essence, entails the concept of alienation. Its centrality in Marx's anthropology leads us to an examination of the meaning(s) the term had for Marx.

Before we do so we must take note of the problem of definition that attends the concept alienation. We are bombarded by a widespread and variegated usage of the term, not only by contemporary writers, but also by writers, thinkers, and artists throughout the centuries. In fact, some argue that the popularity of the term today does not stem primarily from Marx's usage. It has come down to us via another route.[43] Be that as it may, no one would seriously dispute the impact of the publication of the *1844 Manuscripts* (in which the concept is central) upon the popularisation of the term. The availability of the *1844 Manuscripts* in 1932 (in English in the 1950's), coupled with a renewed interest in Hegel, served to popularise further the use of the term alienation.[44]

Popularisation of any concept, which is employed with relative ease and frequency by writers who represent many varied disciplines and different points of view, certainly does not allow for any systematic and precise meaning of the term. Not only do the phenomena described by the concept vary with each discipline, but, also, even within a particular discipline, the term may be applied to phenomena of a significantly varied kind. Needless to say, it is impossible to delineate any one precise meaning of the term. An analysis of the usage of alienation quickly reveals inconsistency and imprecision. Frank Johnson offers a useful summary of the problem:

> Most terms which possess scientific bite are characterized by a reasonable specificity of denotation, a clarity of meaning within particular disciplines, and an absence of serious internal paradox or ambiguity. None of them adhere to the word, alienation. Alienation is used to denote a great variety of often quite dissimilar phenomena. Moreover, its meanings within separate disciplines are confusingly interrelated, and the word, of course, is stricken with severe inconsistency and vagueness.[45]

Let us look at some illustrations of the variation and ambiguity in the meaning of the term alienation. We will follow Walter Kaufmann's discussion on the subject and, to a lesser extent, Richard Schacht's. The vagueness and inconsistency in the meaning of the term is evident when it is used as an ontological category in the conception of reality. In relation to this usage Kaufmann tells us that "alienation" and the German word *Entfremdung* are "a human state of being—the state of *being* alienated or estranged from something or somebody." He justifies the usage of the term as an ontological category by noting that similar to "its two German equivalents" "the verb 'alienate' is transitive," "and its literal meaning is 'to make strange, to make another's'." In contrast "the noun 'alienation,' like the German *Entfremdung* and unlike *Entäusserung,* does not usually bring to mind an activity, except in special contexts where it functions as a technical term." [46]

The active sense of separation which alienation connotes is illustrated in the different ways in which the young Marx and the early Sartre use the term. Kaufmann explains that "Sartre concentrates on the psychological processes that lead men to see themselves as objects, as things, as unfree." In contrast, "Marx concerns himself with the economic processes that lead to much the same result." While both thinkers focus on human beings' loss of freedom, they offer divergent explanations of this phenomenon: "Marx sees the unfree as victims while the early Sartre insists that we are our own victims, that we really are free, and that we are at fault for not realizing it."[47] The distinction between Sartre's and Marx's explanations (in psychological and economic terms, respectively) of human beings' loss of freedom is significant. As we will see, Marx views psychological alienation as derivative, for it emerges from the more basic, "infrastructural," socio-economic alienation of the mode of production.

In his conception of human being, Plato provides us with yet another meaning of alienation. He does not stop at his division of human being into body and soul, but, as Schacht observes, "He further divides the soul into three parts, and he argues for the existence of the three parts by calling attention to instances in which they are at odds with each other and pull us in different directions." The conclusion to be drawn is clear: "Plato also knew the experience of the divided self. He felt at home neither in his body nor with his appetites."[48] The human being's divided self, whose separate parts exist in antagonism to each other, seeks release from alienation through separation of body from soul. Whereas Marx speaks of alienation in historical and existential terms, Plato uses ontological categories to describe the conflict between body and soul. In contrast, Marx argues for a more dynamic concept of human nature vis-à-vis Plato's static concept.

A somewhat different use of the concept of alienation is found in the Judeo-Christian tradition. Walter Kaufmann correctly observes that in Judaism and Christianity, the individual is to be reminded constantly that he/she is a pilgrim, an alien in this world. Both religions

> agree in their original challenge to men to alienate themselves from nature, society, and themselves. The individual is not supposed to feel altogether at home in nature; Judaism lifted man out of nature and stressed the discontinuity between man and nature, the cardinal differences between man and animal. Moreover, it is one of the leitmotifs of the Hebrew Bible that the people are not supposed to be 'like all the nations' but a people apart. Theoretically, this could have meant that their sense of community compensated them entirely for their alienation from all other nations. ... we find a succession of imposing figures who not only tell their people that they should be different but who are themselves thoroughly alienated from their own society.[49]

In contrast to the negative connotation of the term in Marx and Sartre, alienation is used here in a positive sense. The believer is to pursue alienation or "separateness" in order to minimise, if not totally avoid, the corrupting influences of the outside environment. The communities of Judaism and Christianity are to be closed off from evil and corrupting influences and forces. Paradoxically, even within each community there have been some, such as the Jewish prophets, Moses, Elijah, Amos, Hosea, and Jeremiah, who have found that they were strangers among their own people.[50]

On the contemporary scene, there are several writers who argue that, in spite of the fact that alienation has been employed in many different contexts, nevertheless, certain common features may be discerned from its various uses.[51] Arnold Kaufman, for example, asserts: " 'to claim that a person is alienated is to claim that his relation to something else has certain features which result in avoidable discontent or loss of satisfaction'."[52] Lewis Feuer, to take another example, declares that "the word 'alienation' [is] used to describe the subjective tone of self-destructive experience." He adds, " 'Alienation' is used to convey the emotional tone which accompanies any behavior in which the person is compelled to act self-destructively."[53] Finally, Kenneth Kenniston argues that "most usages of 'alienation' share the assumption that some relationship or connection that once existed, that is 'natural,' desirable, or good, has been lost."[54] Schacht correctly concludes that "while each of these general analyses may be plausible, they are by no means identical."[55]

Our brief survey of the concept of alienation shows that the term is used in both an active and a passive sense. With the exception of its use in the Judeo-Christian tradition, it is used to describe an undesirable state which must either be transformed radically or accommodated creatively. In the active sense "the individual *experiences* something as 'other' or separated from him." Here the individual is conscious of the state of his/her existence. Both the individual's thoughts and feelings tell him/her that he/she is either a stranger or else something or someone is a stranger. In contrast to the active sense, the passive sense of the term alienation is seen in the situation "in which the individual is *alleged* to exist in a condition of separation from something, of which he may be unaware." Schacht provides a perceptive analysis of the difference between the two senses in which the term alienation is used and points to the problem of achieving a precise and unambiguous definition of the term. When used in its active sense *"feelings* of alienness are involved." The one who is described as alienated apprehends certain things as "separate, or strange, or different, or remote, or indifferent, or incomprehensible, or distasteful, etc." On the other hand, when used in its passive sense, such feelings "are not the issue. The alienness in question is rather the individual's purportedly factual separation from something, which is detected through an objective comparison of his actual state with a conception of what the relevant sort of unity or identity would be like." It is obvious that a real objectionable confusion would occur in the situation "in which the term is allowed to function in both ways." To use the same terminology in both cases would most likely mean that the "important distinction" between the two senses would be blurred.[56]

As we shall see later, Marx's use of the term alienation shares in this ambiguity, for he combines the two senses of the term in his analysis of "alienation in its totality," as he sees it in bourgeois capitalism.

From the differing usages of the term alienation to characterise a situation of separation and/or a loss of unity, we are led to ask whether there is an essential state of unity and harmony which is disrupted and/or whether it is possible to regain or attain that lost unity. The first question may, but does not necessarily, imply the second. In fact, writers who conceive, albeit vaguely, of a primaeval unity, do not necessarily envisage a return to such unity. Instead they seek to understand the separation in order to find ways and means of living creatively with the disharmony and lack of unity. On the other hand, writers who argue for a struggle for the attainment of unity and end of separation do not necessarily conceive of a lost state of non-alienation.

The question of alienation raises the issue of whether human beings are separated from their "essence." In other words, does alienation arise out of a disparity between human "essence" and "existence?" What is self-alienation? These are difficult questions which have not been adequately answered with any notable degree of consistency in the use of the term alienation. The popularisation of the term does not allow for its clarity and precision of meaning. The proliferation of different and conflicting meanings is a serious obstacle to any attempt to understand a particular writer's usage of the term. In our case, Marx's concept of alienation needs to be stripped of the un-Marxian overcoating in which it has been dressed due to the popularisation of the term. This is not to deny that in comparing and contrasting Marx's use of the concept with that of others we are not aided in understanding Marx. We now move on to Hegel's description of alienation for Hegel, more than anybody else, influenced Marx's use of the concept.

D.
Hegel's Usage of Alienation

Marx's philosophy of *praxis* is built upon the premise that Hegel's philosophy marked the culmination of the development of western philosophy.[57] Hegel was seen as the modern Aristotle.[58] Speculative philosophy had reached its zenith and, therefore, according to Marx, it must be transcended by realising it. The synthesis in thought which Hegel had pursued and achieved must be actualised in reality. For Marx, this actualisation and realisation of philosophy was to be achieved in the socio-economic realm. Let us look briefly at the dilemma which Hegel faced and what he tried to achieve.

Charles Taylor, in his monumental work on Hegel, attempts to give "an idea of the fundamental problems and aspirations which Hegel's philosophy was addressed to." He suggests

> that we can best see these in the light of the yearning of his time to find a way of life and thought which would unite two powerful aspirations, which were both connected yet opposed. One is that unity with nature, other men and himself which man demands as an expressive being; the other is to the radical word autonomy which reached paradigm expression in Kant and Fichte.[59]

Hegel's realisation, by the early 1800's, that "these two aspirations were opposed to each other" led to the further discovery "that freedom required the breaking up of the expressive unity, of the original undivided wholeness within man and communion with other men and nature, which he, like many contemporaries, attributed to an earlier age—principally that of ancient Greece."[60] This process of fragmentation was inevitable and necessary "for the full realization of man as rational and free agent."[61] Indeed, this "necessary division was to be healed in a higher reconciliation."[62]—a reconciliation already immanent in the one process of fragmentation.

Taylor is correct in his conclusion that "the major task of philosophy for Hegel can be expressed as that of over-coming opposition. The oppositions are those which arise from the breaking up of the original expressive unity."[63] In Hegel's view, philosophy was primarily concerned with *Entfremdung* and *Aufhebung*, "alienation" and "reconciliation." It was a philosophical basis that was certainly attractive to Marx, who was concerned with human beings as they were in the bourgeois capitalist society of his day.

Explaining Hegel's dialectic, Taylor points out that Hegel posits the universe "as the conditions of existence of God or *Geist*."[64] Absolute Idea or Spirit undergirds everything that exists. It is necessary for the existence of Spirit that it creates the conditions whereby it becomes manifest. Spirit does not exist apart from the vehicles or embodiments in which it becomes manifest. The primary embodiment of Spirit is human being. Through human being, Spirit is manifested as finite being though it remains infinite.[65] Finiteness, i.e., location in time and space, becomes necessary for Spirit's consciousness of itself as real. Spirit's existence therefore requires the relational consciousness of itself embodied and expressed in the finite human creature.[66]

The process of Spirit's self-expression is inextricably bound up with the rational expression of freedom. Spirit is free to realise itself through expressing itself in finite being. In the expressivist view, freedom "is the condition in which self is adequately expressed. Hence full self-awareness is impossible without freedom."[67]

In externalising itself in finite being, Spirit gradually comes to conceive of the finite as separate from itself. The Infinite (Spirit) stands opposed to the finite. Although the finite proceeded from and, thus, is a part of Absolute Idea, it finds itself in opposition to *Geist*. Externalisation leads to alienation. The necessity for Spirit's existence in the finite leads inevitably to separation and opposition. The consequent alienation and its projected unity are known through the activity of consciousness.

In his description of separation or alienation, Hegel has a twofold usage of the concept of alienation. In categorising the twofold usage, Schacht speaks of "alienation$_1$", where Hegel "uses it to refer to a separation or discordant relation, such as might obtain between the individual and the social substance, or (as 'self-alienation') between one's actual condition and essential nature." Further, "alienation$_2$" is where Hegel "uses it to refer to a surrender or sacrifice of particularity and willfulness, in connection with the overcoming of alienation$_1$ and the reattainment of unity."[68]

In the first sense of alienation ("alienation$_1$"), Hegel considers the situation in which separation occurs after a prior state of unity. Spirit, for instance, in coming from universality to particularity through human embodiment, is at first at one with itself—i.e., there is unity between universality and particularity. However, in the course of time the particular person, the individual, comes to conceive of himself/herself as distinct and separate from the social substance.[69] For Hegel, this is "a desirable development," since "it marks the emergence of a dimension of distinct individuality and independent existence." Schacht points out that the emergence of the latter "is necessary if man's essential nature is to be realized completely."[70] The process of "alienation$_1$" results in "self-alienation$_1$." According to Hegel, human being is essentially spiritual. Therefore, as Schacht notes, "loss of universality thus has the result that one 'thereby alienates himself from his inner nature and reaches the extremity of discord with himself'." When one (the individual) loses one's universality through a disunion with the social substance, one no longer possesses one's essence. In consequence, one alienates oneself from one's essence and thereby exists in the state of self-alienation$_1$.[71]

Hegel uses the term alienation in a sense different from that of alienation$_1$ when he attempts to describe how alienation$_1$ and self-alienation$_1$ will be transcended.[72] This usage, which Schacht labels alienation$_2$, is intended to connote an act of wilful surrender on the part of the alienated person. One—the alienated individual—can attain a higher unity with the social substance and one's essence only if one wilfully gives up one's assertion of individuality upon which one had hitherto insisted. The individual can no longer insist upon the supreme importance of his/her individuality at the expense of universality. Rather, one must surrender "the possession of an individual will which is not yet surrendered *qua* will."[73] Hegel summarises the relinquishment of individuality thus: "For the power of the individual consists in making himself conformable to that substance, i.e., *in relinquishing his self*, and thus establishing himself as the objectively existing substance.[74] For alienation$_2$ and its consequent unity with the social substance to occur, the individual must surrender his/her particular interests, desires and inclinations to the point where universality is not lost to or submerged in particularity but is thereby realised.[75]

E.
Marx's Criticism of Hegel

It should not come as a surprise that Marx, who wrote, "The philosophers have interpreted the world in various ways; the point, however, is to change it,"[76] considers Hegel's analysis of alienation and its transcendence to be too abstract and speculative. In his evaluation of Hegel's description of alienation, Marx argues that Hegel concentrated his thought on the abstract categories of consciousness and self-consciousness. He asserts that for Hegel,

> the alienation of self-consciousness is not regarded as the expression of the
> real alienation of man's essence reflected in knowledge and thought. The
> real alienation (or the one that appears to be real) in its inner concealed

essence that has first been brought to the light by philosophy, is nothing but the appearance of the alienation of the real human essence, self-consciousness.[77]

Hegel, Marx adds, conceives of alienation as an *awareness* of finite being, who, as consciousness embodied in human beings, comes to think of himself/herself as alienated. There is no grounding of alienation in the social conditions in society. Transcendence of alienation requires a mere change in self-awareness. All this, Marx says, is too abstract and more apparent than real. Speaking about transcendence here, he writes:

> On the one hand, this supersession is a supersession of something thought and thus private property as thought is superseded in the thought of morality. And because this thought imagines that it is directly the opposite of itself, sensuous reality, and thus also that its action is sensuous, real action, this supersession in thought that lets its object remain in reality believes it has really overcome it. On the other hand, since the object has now become for it a phase in its thought process, it is therefore regarded in its real existence as being a self-confirmation of thought, of self-consciousness and abstraction.[78]

In other words, conceiving of alienation in terms of consciousness is not real alienation. Conceiving of transcendence in terms of a change in consciousness is illusory. Throughout the process of supersession, it is only abstract self-consciousness that is confirmed in its existence.

Marx finds a circularity in Hegel's argument that reality is the self-positing of Spirit.[79] In noting that the process requires "an agent, a subject" which "only comes into being as the result ... [of] the subject knowing itself as absolute self-consciousness ... God, absolute spirit, the idea that knows and manifests itself," Marx concludes:

> Real man and real nature become mere predicates or symbols of this hidden, unreal man and unreal nature. The relationship of subject and predicate to each other is thus completely inverted: a mystical subject-object or subjectivity reaching beyond the object, absolute subject as a process (it externalizes itself returns to itself from its externalization and at the same

time reabsorbs its externalization); a pure and unceasing circular movement within itself.[80]

Richard Schacht and Richard Norman, among others, question the full validity of Marx's arguments that in Hegel, alienation and its transcendence are conceived in thought only.[81] Schacht draws attention to a contrary example in which Hegel describes alienation in terms of a separation between the social substance and the individual. In this situation, it is the "thought" that is the reality of alienation. Schacht writes:

> The individual regards the social substance as something alien as a result of *conceiving* of himself in a certain way. He ceases to do so when he comes to *see* himself and the substance in a different light. All of this takes place at the level of 'consciousness and self-consciousness,' and would be inconceivable in any other terms.[82]

Schacht concludes that it is "no objection to Hegel's discussion that is is cast in these terms, even if there should prove to be phenomena of a more 'concrete' nature which are also characterizable as instances of alienation.[83]

In his argument, Norman suggests "that Hegel sees the overcoming of alienation in thought as requiring the return of pure thought to the real world, and therefore as depending on the overcoming of social alienation." In contrast, Norman adds that at a deeper level Marx is correct in his criticism of Hegel. "The trouble with Hegel's account is that, having brought the alienation of pure thought back to its roots in social alienation, *he then treats social alienation as itself an alienation of consciousness.*"[84] The difference between Hegel's conception of alienation and Marx's is brightly limned in the contrast between the conception of the independence of the social substance from the individual as only an activity of consciousness, on the one hand, and as an actual separation in the worker's relation to the social product, on the other hand. Marx insists that, when the individual does in fact come to see the social product as alien to himself/herself, it is because it is foreign and belongs to another.

Finally, Marx understands Hegel's use of alienation to mean objectification equals separation, i.e., opposition. Spirit, in realising itself through externalising itself in finite being, inevitably finds itself alienated from finite being. Finite being, which shows Spirit to be real, at the same time posits Spirit in opposition to it. Marx writes:

> What is supposed to be the essence of alienation that needs to be transcended is not that man's being objectifies itself in an inhuman manner in oppositon to itself, but that it objectifies itself in distinction from, and in opposition to, abstract thought.[85]

F.
Marx's Use of the Term "Alienation"

Under the influence of Hegel's usage of alienation as "separation" and "wilful surrender," Marx combines the two images in a single general sense of "separation through surrender." The fusion of meaning was not a deliberate act. Instead it was the result of Marx's failure "to distinguish them in his discussion of Hegel." Underlying the "many different applications" to which Marx applies the term is the suggestion of "the existence of a separation of some sort," a separation which "is related in some way to a certain surrender: namely, the surrender of one's control over one's product and labor." Moreover, in contrast to Hegel's twofold sense of alienation, in which the separation (alienation$_1$) is transcended precisely "*through* the surrender (alienation$_2$)," Marx sees the separation as the consequence of the surrender.[86]

Marx took the liberty to apply the term alienation to numerous and different situations. Though its basic sense of "separation through surrender" remains fairly consistent, we must take care to distinguish the various contexts in which the term is applied in order to grasp some of the depth of meaning which the term possesses in Marx's thought.

As its name implies, the *1844 (Economic and Philosophic) Manuscripts* clearly shows that Marx was concerned with the interrelationship between philosophy and economics. Steeped in Hegelian philosophy and confronted by the exploitative character of modern industrial capitalism, Marx could not avoid the question of alienation. Indeed he attempts to face the socio-economic and political plight of the worker, albeit in philosophic categories, in his analysis of alienation.[87]

Marx argues that in relation to production—humankind's creative work—there are essentially four categories of alienation: from product, productive activity, *species-being*, and fellow human beings.

First, human beings are alienated from their product. In political economy, the more the workers produce, the more they suffer from poverty. The workers' product is in the hands of someone else, the capitalist, the owner of the means of production. As the workers produce, the capitalist is enriched, since the former's compensation for their labour is not commensurate to the value of the product produced. The capitalist engenders this disparity by exploiting the surplus value of the workers' labour. The owners of means acquires their wealth precisely because of the exploitative nature of production, which they are able to manipulate to their advantage and to the workers' detriment. The product which the workers expend their labour to produce is alienated from them because someone else usurps their right to its value.[88] Money, which denotes the demeaning value of the workers' labour objectified in their product, is the impersonal link between the workers and their labour. In the productive process the workers are preoccupied with the wages they receive. Their value is not in the beauty and quality of their product. Though the product is the physical substance of their labour, the workers are not free to use or dispose of it as they will.[89] To the capitalist, the workers' value rests in their capacity to produce. The capitalist views the workers as mere producers of commodities. The workers, for their part, internalise this estimate of their worth and come to see themselves valued at the level of their wages. Marx aptly pictures this degeneration:

> The worker becomes a commodity that is all the cheaper the more commodities he creates. The depreciation of the human world progresses in direct proportion to the increase in value of the world of things. Labour does not only produce commodities; it produces itself and the labourer as a commodity and that to the extent to which it produces commodities in general.[90]

In producing commodities, the labourers create themselves as a commodity as well. Thus, in actual fact, they are the architects of their own alienation.

Marx passionately illustrates the hostility which the workers experience between themselves and their product(s), which now stands over against them:

> The object that labour produces, its product, confronts it as an alien being, as a power independent of the producer. The product of labour is labour that has solidified itself into an object, made itself into a thing, the

objectification of labour. The realization of labour is its objectification. In political economy this realization of labour appears as a loss of reality for the worker, objectification as a loss of object or slavery to it, and appropriation as alienation, as externalization.[91]

The workers' creativity, objectified in production, is experienced by them as loss because they are producing not for the sake of the object but for the wages.[92] They themselves do not appropriate the use and value of the products. The capitalist, a non-worker, dominates the workers and their products. Under the exploitative capitalist system, the product is not an affirmation but a denial of the human value of the workers. Consequently, Marx concludes that "the externalization of the worker in his product implies not only that his labour becomes an object, an exterior existence but also that it exists outside him, independent and alien, and becomes a self-sufficient power opposite him, that the life that he has lent to the object affronts him, hostile and alien."[93]

Second, the workers are alienated from the activity of production.[94] The whole process is dominated by the capitalist, who is driven by egoistical greed. Production is geared to maximise profits and not to benefit the workers. Consideration of the workers' welfare is secondary to the amassing of wealth, the primary motive of production.[95] The owners of means occupies their dominant positions not because they themselves have expended their physical energies to produce. Rather, it is the result of their relegation of the workers to material production which involves the expenditure of physical energies, while they elevate themselves to the positions of authority and expend only mental energy.[96] The division of labour serves to perpetuate alienation.[97] Marx sums up this kind of alienation thus:

> Therefore he does not confirm himself in his work, he denies himself, feels miserable instead of happy, deploys no free physical and intellectual energy, but mortifies his body and ruins his mind. Thus the worker only feels at home outside his work and in his work he feels a stranger. He is at home when he is not working and when he works he is not at home. His labour is therefore not voluntary but compulsory, forced labour. It is therefore not the satisfaction of a need but only a means to satisfy needs outside itself.[98]

The workers' activity turns into passivity; their creative power becomes their weakness. It is no wonder then "that when there is no physical or other compulsion, labour is avoided like the plague."[99] This is the epitome of the workers' alienation from the productive process.

Third, the workers are alienated from their *species-being*.[100] Humankind's *species-life* is turned into a means toward its individual life. Like other animals, human beings have physical needs. Unlike other animals, human beings have *species-needs*, needs related to humans' expression of the being they are. The physical, animal functions of eating, drinking and procreating, which human beings share in common with other animals, are met by the former in such a way that they show themselves to be creative, self-conscious beings, unlike other animals. They can freely express their creativity as they satisfy their physical needs.[101] But satisfaction of mere egoistic, animal needs are not their primary concern. In production, human beings are primarily concerned with the expression of their essence, which is freedom.[102] Human beings, Marx declares, have a capactiy for culture and for the cultivation and appreciation of the aesthetic.[103] In Hegel's terminology, human beings are concerned with the spiritual, in addition to and above their concern with the physical.

Unfortunately, in their present state, human beings are primarily concerned with the satisfaction of physical needs. The spiritual has been subordinated to those selfish ends. Acknowledging that "eating, drinking, procreating, etc. are indeed truly human functions," Marx immediately points out that, even so, "in the abstraction that separates them from the other round of human activity and makes them into final and exclusive ends they become animal."[104] Marx concludes that, in its alienated state, labour "alienates species-life and individual life, and ... in its abstraction it makes the latter into the aim of the former which is also conceived of in its abstract and alien form."[105] Human beings' vital activity and productive life work are only the means to the satisfaction of physical needs in order that physical existence might continue. In contrast, unalienated productive life is *species-life*. It is life that produces life, instead of impersonal things which are devoid of human essence.

In order to heighten the contrast between human being as unalienated *species-being* and human being as alienated worker, Marx further differentiates between human being and animal. Unlike the animal, for whom there is no distinction between itself and its vital activity, "man makes his vital activity itself into an object of his will and consciousness. He has a conscious vital activity. He is not immediately identical to any of his characterizations." Only human beings are capable of perceiving themselves as the beings they are. Animals cannot do this.

Consciousness distinguishes the former from "animal vital activity" and makes them *species-beings*. Only human beings see their own lives as objects to themselves. Unalienated human beings are able to act according to their species and, in so doing, affirm their *species-nature*. Thus their activity is free activity. On the other hand, "alienated labour reverses the relationship so that, just because he is a conscious being, man makes his vital activity and essence a mere means to his existence."[106] Whereas unalienated human beings see their species, as well as other species, as objects, without thereby being estranged from either of them, alienated human beings' objectification of themselves leads to their perception of such objectification as separate from and alien to themselves. Likewise, the workers view their essence, i.e., their *species-being*, as alien and hostile to themselves. Marx argues that the human being no longer relates to "himself as to the present, living species," that is, "to himself as to a universal and therefore free being."[107] Instead, he/she relates to himself/herself as to an enslaved being.

Human beings are not only capable of perceiving their needs and assessing their resources to satisfy those needs, but they are also capable of deciding how those needs may be met. They are capable of "technique."[108] They can and do build "mediations" between themselves and nature. They interact with nature, the organic objective world, which they fashion and shape, and which, in turn, fashions and shapes them. It is a process of mutual interaction.[109] Nature is perceived by the human being who is both a physical and a *species-being* in two complementary ways. It is the source of the resources for his/her survival and it is a part of him/her.[110] Marx describes the creative nexus thus:

> Physically man lives solely from these products of nature, whether they appear as food, heating, clothing, habitation, etc. The universality of man appears in practice precisely in the universality that makes the whole of nature into his inorganic body in that it is both (i) his immediate means of subsistence and also (ii) the material object and tool of his vital activity. Nature is the inorganic body of man, that is, in as far as it is not itself a human body.[111]

For Marx, unalienated human beings will live in creative harmony with nature. Even now, in an alienated way, they organise the productvie process, whereby they fashion "things according to the laws of beauty." They fashion things not only according to the standards and needs of the species to which they belong, but also according to the measure of every species. They know "everywhere how to apply its inherent standard to the object."[112] Advanced technology and human ways of using such technology are integral to this complex process.

The sad commentary on the condition of human beings in capitalist society, Marx makes clear, is that advanced and advancing technology have witnessed the continued degradation of human beings. Alienation has torn human beings from their creation and from nature, and vice versa. In the image of the world they have created, alienated human beings do not see that they have duplicated themselves, both intellectually and actively, in reality. The worker is torn from the object of production, including his/her "mediations," and from his/her *species-life*, "the real objectivity of his species." Moreover, alienated labour has turned "the advantage he … [had] over animals into a disadvantage in that his inorganic body, nature , … [has been] torn from him."[113] This process continues ineluctably.

Finally, Marx speaks of the alienation of human beings from fellow human beings. "Every self-alienation," Marx declares, "of man from himself and nature appears in the relationship in which he places himself and nature to other men distinct from himself." It is only through the real interpersonal relationships among human beings that alienation can appear in the practical, real world. Organisation of the productive process entails organising social roles and distribution of workers. Noting the active role human being plays in the ensuing relationships, Marx claims: "Through alienated labour then man creates not only his relationship to the object and act of production as to alien and hostile men; he creates too the relationship in which other men stand to his production and his product and the relationship in which he stands to these other men."[114] In their alienated state, human beings continue to create further alienation. Their perception of reality is distorted, and their actions are selfish and hostile. This is certainly a strong case for the conclusion that human beings are the architects of their own destiny, albeit an alienated one. The workers also make possible the position occupied by the capitalist, a position diametrically opposed to and dominant over that of the workers.[115] There is no doubt in Marx's mind that the owners of the means of production are themselves alienated. Even as they proceed to exploit the workers for their advantage, they further both their own and the workers' alienation.[116] Marx sums up the foregoing thus:

> Just as he turns his production into his own loss of reality and punishment
> and his own product into a loss, a product that does not belong to him, so
> he creates the domination of the man who does not produce over the

production and the product. As he alienates his activity from himself, so he hands over to an alien person an activity that does not belong to him.[117]

Marx's fourth usage of alienation elucidates his concept of the human being as a social being.[118] Human beings know that they are the being they are, *species-being* (in contrast to mere animal). They also know that they are distinct from other *species-beings*. In their pursuit of the satisfaction of *species-needs*, both physical and spiritual, they act communally.[119] They affirm themselves within community, not apart from it. In the unalienated society, unalienated human beings will experience concord and harmony with their fellows. There will be mutual exchange of creative activities without the concomitant dehumanisation of the workers which characterises alienated, capitalist society. Marx gives a glimpse of the communal harmony which would characterise the future communist society when he says:

> Exchange, both of human activity within production itself and also of human products with each other, is equivalent to species-activity and species-enjoyment whose real, conscious and true being is social activity and social enjoyment. Since human nature is the true communal nature of man, men create and produce their communal nature by their natural action.[120]

Marx's sanguine apocalypse is in polar contrast to his description of the disharmonious, non-affirmative, interpersonal relationships which exist among workers, and especially between the capitalist class and the proletarian masses. Referring to the antagonism between the two classes, Marx writes:

> The first remark to make is that everything that appears in the case of the worker to be an activity of externalization, of alienation appears in the case of the non-worker to be a state of externalization, of alienation.
>
> Secondly, the real, practical behaviour of the worker in production and towards his product (as a state of mind) appears in the case of the non-worker opposed to him as theoretical behaviour. Thirdly, the non-worker does everything against the worker that the worker does against himself but he does not do against himself what he does against the worker.[121]

It appears here that true *praxis* is reserved for the workers, and that the state of the non-workers is more static than dynamic, hence the ontological description of their condition.

G.
Religion, Atheism and False Consciousness

The unwary reader of Marx may be easily misled to conclude that there is no significant place for theory in Marx's concept of reality. This misunderstanding is often the result of the dichotomy that exists in his thinking between *praxis* and *theoria*. Marx accuses Hegel of conceiving of reality in terms of theoretical consciousness, mere activity of the mind. Drawing on Feuerbach's reduction of Hegel's *Geist* to human being as a *species-being*, Marx realises that humanity, and not *Geist*, is the centre of the universe. Despite Feuerbach's positive influence on Marx, Marx himself later criticises Feuerbach for not having gone far enough in his anthropological reductionism. Feuerbach was not radical enough; he failed to conceive of real sensuous human being. Feuerbach was wrapped up in his idealism and could only limit human being to an object of contemplation. Marx sums up Feuerbach's deficient conception of reality:

> The chief defect of all previous materialism—that of Feuerbach included—is that things [*Gegenstand*], reality, sensuousness are conceived only in the form of the *object*, or of *contemplation*, but not as *human sensuous activity*, *practice*, not subjectively. Hence it happened that the *active* side, in contradistinction to materialism, was set forth by idealism—but only abstractly, since, of course, idealism does not know real, sensuous activity as such. Feuerbach wants sensuous objects, really distinct from conceptual objects, but he does not conceive human activity itself as *objective* activity. In *Das Wesen des Christenthums*, he therefore regards the theoretical attitude as the only genuinely human attitude, while practice is conceived and defined only in its dirty-Jewish form of appearance. Hence he does not grasp the significance of 'revolutionary', of practical-critical, activity.[122]

Marx's insistence on *praxis* as the basis of all forms of consciousness does not negate the importance of consciousness. Indeed, as he himself admits, *praxis* and theory are bound together. Consciousness is derived from *praxis*. *Praxis* in turn is shaped by consciousness. The two form an intrinsic dialectical unity.

Now, in his description of human being, Marx is preoccupied with human being as an alienated being who must be (and who will be ultimately) rescued from his/her dehumanised and depersonalised state. Human beings suffer from total alienation; their consciousness of themselves and the world is distorted and demeaning. The capacity to perceive their world, to know that they are the beings they are (both individual and species), distinguishes human beings as *species-beings* vis-à-vis other animals. Although human beings still retain the quality of knowing who they are, and that they live in society participating in activities of the species, they, nevertheless, suffer from illusions and distorted perceptions of reality. Their thinking mirrors their alienation and serves to perpetuate it. Both the capitalists and the workers suffer from false consciousness. The capitalists' attempts at micro-reform is doomed to failure from the very outset. They are not radical in their thinking, for they merely seek to reform society, having accepted it as it is. The legitimacy of their dominant and exploitative position in society is never questioned. They are unable to see that all their efforts at reform are only patchwork relief which are incapable of reducing, let alone ultimately ending, political and religious alienation. Despite the capitalists' efforts at reform, socio-economic alienation remains. Human emancipation is still a far cry from historical realisation. Marx is convinced that capitalists would not embark on a radical socio-economic transformation of society which would endanger their dominance over the workers. The workers, for their part, are still unaware that they are both the architect and victim of their own alienation. They are forced in their imagination to make real what is not. They suffer from ideology which is imposed upon their consciousness by the bourgeoisie.[123]

Thus alienated, the workers (and the non-workers) respond by creating various and sundry fetishes. "Imagination," Marx says, "born of desire gives to the fetish-worshipper the illusion that an 'inanimate object' is about to abandon its natural character and acquiesce in his lusts. Therefore, the crude desire of the fetish-worshipper smashes the fetish when it ceases to be its docile servitor."[124] This process recurs again and again and serves to reinforce and further human alienation. Because they are alienated, human beings' needs and desires do not accurately reflect the needs and desires of their *species-being*. Indeed, such needs and desires are distorted reflections of human essence. In the attempt to satisfy these needs and desires, human creativity is turned to alienating ends. Human beings constantly create fetishes. They impute to commodities and other objects of their own creation awe and power, and invest them with noble and highly esteemed qualities which rightfully belong to themselves. Their experience of their products, both practically and theoretically, is that of alienation. Sensing something higher and superior to what they presently experience, they continually fail to see and acknowledge that it is an integral part of themselves that has become separated from and dominant over them.

Marx has a healthy appreciation of the tenacious grip ideas can come to have over the mind. He argues that alienating ideas which distort reality must be radically rooted out. This is no simple task. In his initial reactions to French socialism, we gain an illuminating picture of Marx's understanding of the power of ideas.

> We are firmly convinced that the true danger does not lie in the practical attempt to carry out communist ideas but in their theoretical development; for practical attempts, even by the masses, can be answered with a cannon as soon as they become dangerous, but ideas that have overcome our intellect and conquered our conviction, ideas to which reason has riveted our conscience, are chains from which one cannot break loose without breaking one's heart; they are the demons that one can only overcome by submitting to them.[125]

Subsequently, Marx held the view that ideas are part of the superstructure which is built upon the socio-economic base of society. Then he realised that only transformation of the socio-economic base, especially the mode of production, will free the mind of enslaving and alienating ideas. Marx was convinced that, however much people are coerced into giving up their practices and ideas, such an attempt to end alienation would still be an abstraction and an ideological imposition.

Religion does not escape Marx's scathing denunciation. Like philosophy, religion is alienated consciousness. Marx is not as charitable as Hegel in his estimation of this abstract, speculative system of ideas. Whereas Hegel sees religion as expressing inadequately what philosophy expressed adequately, Marx regards religious consciousness as the nadir of false consciousness, the most extreme form of alienation. Before we present his treatment of religion, however, a word about Feuerbach's anthropological reductionism of religion would be in order, for it is via the latter that Marx attempts to turn Hegel right side up.

The two concepts in Feuerbach's philosophy which Marx finds most attractive and appealing are those of "projection" and "alienation."[126] According to Feuerbach, human being continually projects his/her noble self onto God, a creation of his/her consciousness. The question of the nature of God is really the question of the nature of humanity. Marx W.Wartofsky notes that "for Feuerbach, the question of proving God's existence becomes a meaningless question once it is revealed that the 'existence of God' is the unconscious religious metaphor for the existence of man's self-consciousness."[127] It is human self-consciousness that is real and not God.[128] The existence of God is, therefore, a derived and dependent existence functionally related to human self-consciousness.

Feuerbach continues to argue that the projection of a supreme Being superior to humanity is both necessary and inevitable. It is necessary for humankind to create God since human beings need one another. Human beings cannot know themselves to be the *species-being* they are apart from the other. As a being of consciousness, the human being requires objects, predicates, to know himself/herself in distinction from other beings. Wartofsky provides a useful summary of this argument:

> Man needs God because man needs man. Thus, the creation of God by the praxis of belief is an expression of the dependence of human beings on each other. According to Feuerbach, consciousness of an other as a being like myself, in the I-Thou relation, is the species nature. The very recognition of oneself as a species being is the very act of species being that constitutes the species itself as a species. But this is only the form of species being. Its content is the need for the other, the dependence upon the Thou as an existential condition. In this interpretation the essence of species being is not species consciousness as such, but the dependence of man on man, which expresses as species consciousness. The activity of species consciousness, its praxis, is its expression, or its objectification of this dependence.[129]

To be a *species-being* means that every human being has a need for other *species-beings*. However, because the existential conditions do not fully conduce to, but do in fact militate against, the experience and enjoyment of harmonious interpersonal relationships, human beings are faced with the critical question concerning the essence of their being: What is its true nature? Humanity suffers from alienated consciousness and consequently projects its noble qualities onto a being who gradually is regarded as superior to and independent of humankind. Humankind posits God. Projection is inevitable. Humankind has created its essence, albeit in an estranged form.

Feuerbach's aim is to give Hegel's concept of reality as the self-positing of *Geist* an anthropological centre. While Hegel argues that *Geist* is the most "real" and that human being is the "finite," transitory self-manifestation of Spirit, Feuerbach "stands Hegel upon his feet" by positing that humanity and its self-consciousness as *species-being* actually constitutes reality. The concept of self-positing *Geist* is illusory, for it is a mere projection of alienated human consciousness. Wartofsky notes that consciousness for Hegel "is the ontological ground of its manifestation." According to Hegel, consciousness is dynamic, not static. In relation to human essence, consciousness is ultimately the basis of human being. Feuerbach, on the other hand, argues that human essence is constituted by the process itself, that is, the dialectic. Noting this difference in Hegel's and Feuerbach's conception of consciousness, Wartofsky writes:

> The species concept is not the living nature in itself, but only as it is reflected upon as the object for consciousness. Hegel wants to find the ontological ground for the very possibility of such a species consciousness in the nature of consciousness itself. Thus, living nature is, for him, nothing but the external form, the projection, and thus, the objectification of the nature of consciousness itself. Feuerbach's move has a Kantian flavour: he finds his ontological ground for the possibility of species consciousness in limiting the 'living nature' that embodies this species to human nature. Moreover, the dialectical relation between consciousness and its object, in Feuerbach, rejects the notion of a prior essence either in the object, mankind as living nature, or in the subject, the consciousness of man.... In the dialectic as an evolutionary process, man creates himself as man, in the very process of coming to self-consciousness.[130]

There is no Absolute Spirit in Feuerbach which stands over and above humankind and to whom it owes the source and power of its being. Rather, the dynamic nature of human beings continues to change as new needs arise. Feuerbach argues that because those needs are alienated needs, then, inevitably, human nature manifests itself in the act of projection. Particularly in religion, humanity's predicates are projected onto God. Religion itself is transformed. Since God is ultimately humanity's own perception of itself, then, in order to understand and grasp the essence of human nature, one has to equate divine attributes with the higher and "ideal" attributes of humankind. With this anthropological reduction of religion before him, Marx proceeds to describe religion as a phenomenon arising out of the socio-economic base.[131]

Marx is concerned with human beings whose nature is ever-changing and inextricably related to the material base of reality. Like Feuerbach, Marx argues that it is self-consciousness which is real and which creates God, who is merely a figment of the imagination. God's existence is dependent upon the recognition of the world's imperfections. Human beings are faced with the perpetual need to cope with alienation, and in the process of doing so, they (as alienated consciousness) create gods who ostensibly make alienated life less burdensome, but, who, in actual fact, rob humanity of its being, making it despicable. Religion furthers, rather than halts, alienation. Humanity's consciousness is captive to the caprice of illusions about reality. Howard Parsons explains that, for Marx, religion deflects "man's attention from the conditions and problems of his real life, and rivets man to a 'fantastic' and 'illusory' happiness."[132] Humanity is deceived into believing that its condition is improved by positing God as the ultimate creator of all. The denigration of humankind, in consequence of God's increasing rise in stature, majesty and power, constitutes real idolatry. Parsons writes:

> For Marx, idolatry consists in man's production of a good on which he depends, which commands his devotion without his entirely knowing that it does, which man accepts with a certain degree of consciousness (and hence choice) as the center of his life, and which progressively destroys man because it stands in the way of man's free, unalienated labor, his fulfilment, and the creative transformation of the economic and social order.[133]

Here humanity is no longer the centre of its life and of the universe. Instead, God—humanity's own creation—is!

As the epitome of false consciousness, religion blinds human beings to their possibilities as creative beings. Their potentialities lie dormant, unrecognised by themselves, even as they rob themselves of their higher capacities by transferring them to the being of God. "In religion, man is still unconscious of himself, of the conditions of his enslavement, of his possibilities, of the need and possibility of his liberation, and of the way of his liberation."[134] Not only are the workers incapable of seeing the wretchedness of their alienation (because religion as ideology dulls their senses even as it legitimates their exploitation and dehumanisation), but they are also unaware that the possibility for liberation exists. Indeed, it exists with them.

Marx tells us that the workers, suffering as they do under alienation, find in religion an opiate which eases the burden of living under such depressing and depersonalising conditions. Human beings, whose nature is not only to have needs, but also to have the intellectual capacity to satisfy those needs creatively, wastefully lavish their creativity in furthering their alienation. Creative freedom is turned against them and intensifies their need of religion.[135] To take Marx's assertion that religion "is the opium of the people," by itself, apart from its context, as the definitive appraisal of the function of religion is blatantly to misconstrue Marx and deprive religion of the redeeming quality it has even in his estimation. In context the quotation reads:

> Religious suffering is at the same time an expression of real suffering and a protest against real suffering. Religion is the sigh of the oppressed creature, the feeling of a heartless world and the soul of soulless circumstances. It is the opium of the people.
>
> The abolition of religion as the illusory happiness of the people is the demand for their real happiness. The demand to give up the illusions about their condition is a demand to give up a condition that requires illusion. The criticism of religion is therefore the germ of the criticism of the valley of tears whose halo is religion.[136]

Here Marx's polemic on religion reaches its pinnacle. Having denounced religion as illusory, he states that it is an invaluable symptom of alienation. As long as it exists, alienation will continue to exist. Moreover, religion is not just an alienation of consciousness but a total alienation rooted in the distorted mode of production. In and through the human cry of despair and suffering, of protest and call to action, humanity's alienated religious consciousness expresses itself. Nevertheless, the cry is real and so are the protest and suffering. Religion, then, can and does both hide suffering and expose it. Once again, Marx repeats his central thesis concerning revolutionary *praxis*: If the cry is heard and radically understood, then the demand to relinquish and transform those materially based conditions through which illusions eventuate will prevail.

What is the function of a philosophy of atheism in counteracting and eventually eradicating the influence and existence of religion? Marx criticises Hegel for conceiving of alienation only within consciousness. He also criticises Feuerbach for not being fully radical in his reduction of God to human projection. Feuerbach is still too abstract, since he has not reduced religious self-alienation to its secular base. The secular base, Marx claims, "must itself, therefore, first be understood in its contradiction and then, by the removal of the contradiction, revolutionised in practice."[137] In Marx's estimation, Feuerbach fails to conclude his reductive process by not pointing to the necessity for such revolutionary *praxis*. Bearing in mind Marx's attitude to Hegel's and Feuerbach's conceptions of reality, we are not surprised to find that Marx does not advocate a philosophy of atheism to eradicate religion.[138]   However, he does not deny that theoretical and ideological atheism have no value in minimising the influence of religion. Atheism is a mediation which will disappear when alienation at the socio-economic base is transcended. Marx asserts:

> Once the essential reality of man in nature, man as the existence of nature for man, and nature for man as the existence of man, has become evident in practical life and sense experience, then the question of an alien being, of a being above nature and man—a question that implies an admission of the unreality of nature and man—has become impossible in practice. Atheism, as a denial of this unreality, has no longer any meaning, for atheism is a denial of God and tries to assert through this negation the existence of man; but socialism as such no longer needs this mediation; it starts from the theoretical and practical sense-perception of man and nature as the true reality.[139]

What was Marx's primary concern in his criticism of religion as false consciousness? The answer is unmistakably humanity—universal, social, and sensuous being. In his description of humanity's essence, he points out that freedom is a human characteristic which will come to full expression after alienation has been transcended. Religion denies human beings their autonomy, impinges upon their freedom and mars their dignity. Atheism, as a theoretical activity, is not an end in itself but a transitory stage in humanity's quest for de-alienation. Marx is not primarily concerned with religion. Such a concern would only lead to further alienation, since religion is part of the superstructure. Rather, Marx is concerned with human beings' historical "becoming" as they shape and influence, and are shaped and influenced by, the productive process in society. Since Marx denies the ultimate existence of anything which transcends humankind, he logically attacks religion. Marx's attack upon religion is a consequence of his anthropological concern, not the reverse. Russell B. Norris correctly notes that, for Marx, atheism "is grounded not in political or scientific negations of religion, but squarely in the affirmation of human autonomy."[140] Marx illumines alienated humanity's loss of autonomy in religion:

> A being only counts itself as independent when it stands on its own feet and it stands on its own feet as long as it owes its existence to itself. A man who lives by grace of another considers himself a dependent being. But I live completely by the grace of another when I owe him not only the maintenance of my life but when he also created my life, when he is the source of my life. And my life necessarily has such a ground outside itself if it is not my own creation.[141]

In summary, then, Marx does not attack consciousness *per se* but only religious and other ideological forms of consciousness. We now turn our focus to Marx's description of human nature. It is a crucial consideration, for it brings us to the central issue in our study which is Marx's concept of the human being. How does Marx define human being without reference to God?

H.
Marx's Concept of Human "Nature" ("Essence")

Marx fails to define in precise and unambiguous terms what he means by human "nature" ("essence"). He is convinced that humanity is not what it ought to be and certainly not what it will be in a future, unalienated society. Moreover, it is inconclusive to argue that Marx finds a satisfactory and comprehensive definition of human nature in what God, especially the "God-man" in Christianity, is. Although this is a guide, it is static and Marx refuses to accept it as binding for all time. This definition would be *a priori* and contrary to his principal thesis that consciousness— and this would include any definition of human nature—is socio-economically determined. To accept it as binding for all time would be anti-revolutionary and would contribute to the alienating autonomy of consciousness. Further, it would mean that certain forms of consciousness are absolute and will not, therefore, eventually become obsolete in another era when the socio-economic base of society had been transcended and a new matrix of material conditions emerged. Temporality and change are inherent in Marx's *Weltanschauung*; absolutes and immutability are anathema.

Marx perceives the world with humanity at its centre no longer subservient to God but in command of its own destiny. He espouses Feuerbach's doctrinal self-description:

> My doctrine in brief [says Feuerbach] is as follows: Theology is anthropology. I.e., that which reveals itself in the object of religion—in Greek, called *Theos*, in German, *Gott*—is nothing other than the essence of man. In other words, the God of man is nothing other than the divinized essence of man.[142]

However, Marx goes beyond Feuerbach in positing that human essence is socio-economically determined. In his estimate, Feuerbach has not been sufficiently radical in his anthropological reductionism. In his sixth thesis on Feuerbach, he writes:

> Feuerbach resolves the religious essence into the human. But the human essence is no abstraction inherent in each single individual. In its reality it is the *ensemble* of social relations.
> Feuerbach, who does not attempt the criticism of the real essence, is consequently compelled:
> 1. To abstract from the historical process and to fix the religious sentiment as something for itself and to presuppose an abstract—*isolated*—human individual.
> 2. The human essence, therefore, can with him be comprehended only as 'genus', as a dumb internal generality which merely naturally unites the many individuals.[143]

Marx insists that there is no fixed human essence or nature. What constitutes the human person is not to be abstracted from outside of humanity. There is no God or other power external to and separate from humankind that determines what constitutes human essence. Human essence is self-created, even as the worker participates in productive activity.

It is disputed whether Marx unambiguously argues that there is no fixed human essence. In Marx's system, labour is the worker's life which becomes objectified in the product produced. When both the labour and the product are alienated from him/her, then it is the worker's own "self" which is alienated from him/her. Marx explains that "life is but activity" and so what is alien to the worker is "the *personal* physical and mental energy of the worker, his personal life." Since another directs the worker's "*personal* physical and mental energy," the worker's very life is not his/her very own. The worker is self-alienated.[144]

Marx also speaks of self-alienation when he wishes to convey the idea of "a *total loss* of humanity."[145] Alienated labour produces spiritually and physically dehumanised human beings. Here self-alienation, according to Schacht, is "virtually synonymous with 'dehumanization' (*Entmenschung*)."[146]

The second understanding of self-alienation as a separation of essence and existence raises the crucial question of whether Marx was undecided about a fixed, constant human nature spanning all time.[147] Eugene Kamenka raises this question when he notes an "obvious distinction between Marx's conception of alienation in the *Paris Manuscripts* and his later conception."[148] He states:

> In the *Manuscripts*, he still sees man as alienated from a generic, social being which is at once the universal nature common to all men and the essential nature underlying man's empirical development. In the *Theses on Feuerbach,* the *German Ideology* and the *Communist Manifesto* he rejects this conception specifically. There is no eternal or essential human nature from which man has become alienated, no 'Man in general, who belongs to no class, has no reality, who exists only in the misty realm of philosophical fantasy.'[149]

Kamenka contrasts what Marx says in his sixth thesis on Feuerbach with Marx's description of human being as a *species-being*. Whether or not there is a fixed human essence does not preclude human beings from displaying what is uniquely their "species-nature" vis-à-vis "animal nature."[150] Only human beings have the capacity for culture. They alone are capable of recognising themselves to be the creatures they are. In so doing, they "become" the beings they are. Human beings can and do create "mediations" between their needs and the means whereby they may satisfy those needs.[151] Despite this summary of Marx's argument that the human being is a *species-being*, what human nature is still remains an enigma in Marx's writings.

John Plamenatz poignantly describes the dilemma of discerning whether Marx argues that human nature, which is self-created, is constant and fixed or is constantly being created:

> To hold that we cannot explain how living and working together with others of his species affects man in ways in which it does not affect other animals without attributing to him capacities which are peculiar to him and yet not products of social intercourse (though developed by it) is one thing; to hold that there are among his social activities some (namely, those that constitute 'material production') which determine in general the character of the others, is quite another.[152]

Plamenatz admits that "both of these assertions might be true" but also claims that the truth of the first assertion does not consequently imply the truth of the second. Marx, he points out, does not explicitly say this. "Marx does not even distinguish between the two questions. Rather, he seems at times to vacillate between the two, as if he thought them equivalent." In Plamenatz's view, Marx's disciples follow their master in maintaining this ambiguity.[153]

We may logically conclude that since Marx argues against a fixed human nature, then human nature is relative, i.e., it is both relative to and a function of the economic mode of production.[154] The workers become what they are through work, which is their creative activity. Their essence arises out of a constellation of variables, such as their relationship to the *species-being*, to their product, to the activity of production, and to other *species-beings*. They are motivated by needs, both physical and spiritual, and it is in satisfying these needs that their nature is formed. Culture, which reflects the state and level of their *nature*, influences their needs and their creative activity. In turn, culture is influenced and shaped by them. In each succeeding generation, new needs arise and old ones disappear. These needs reflect the nature and level of the productive process. Consequently, human essence is transformed and evolves to succeeding higher levels.[155] Many crucial questions still remain unanswered: What is universal essence, and what is particular essence? What is the relationship between the two? What are the specific criteria for delineating what is human nature?

The question of criteria raises a further significant question: From where does the criteria come? Marx believes that they are immanently present in the socio-economic base. His answer is far from satisfactory; it does not demonstrate that Marx was the thorough empirical materialist he assumed he was.[156] However, religion and other forms of false consciousness cannot provide the criteria. They are themselves alienated and alienating forms of consciousness.

This vagueness is illustrated in Marx's discussion of morality and law. In anticipation of the unalienated society, Marx gives the impression that there will be harmony in the essence of alienated beings. For example, Marx suggests that the laws of the future society will reflect the inner core of human essence—freedom. A "true" law indicates the existence of freedom, not the absence or suppression of it. Marx asserts that "only when his behaviour has actually shown that he has ceased to obey the natural law of freedom, does the state law compel him to be free. Similarly physical law only appears alien to me when my life has ceased to be the life of these laws, when it it sick. Thus a preventive law is a meaningless contradiction."[157] It is appropriate to ask: Would a true law be a preventative law when it is transferred from one age to another? Marx does not offer an answer.

It is futile to search for Marx's definitive answer to the critical question of what constitutes human nature. We may find answers which show what it is not. For example, it is not a metaphysical abstraction related to God. But it remains an enigma to us. Marx is as dogmatic as he is vague in his description of human nature. Axelos notes this dilemma:

> It is man who produces man, according to Marx. By producing his life, man produces himself. Man owes his (human) being, his essence, and his existence to his productive labor alone. Man is created neither by God nor by Nature. As man, he has created himself. Marx's humanism is altogether radical. He recognizes no court of determination higher than that of human productivity. Production is an absolutely *thetic* power; in it resides first positing action. Production is as well the motor force of negativity, and it develops *antithetic* powers. Finally it is in production, and by production, that the supreme *synthesis* is worked.[158]

The student of Marx is left to wonder what is precisely meant by the claim that human beings realise and create their own essence. Do they realise what they essentially are? Do they become what they already are? Or, do they become what they create? We return once more to the question of essence and existence and are without a definitive resolution of the issue.[159] We may tentatively summarise the foregoing discussion thus: the creative power of humanity is its essence. This essence is freedom—creative freedom to transform nature and to satisfy physical and spiritual needs.[160] In the process of satisfying needs, human nature, which is comprised of spiritual needs, becomes a new matrix of human needs. Thus, through his/her work the worker expresses the essence of being human.[161]

I.
Communism, the Future Society and the End of Alienation: Marx's Utopian Vision

Marx's picture of alienation reflects the state of the worker in nineteenth-century, bourgeois-capitalist society in western Europe. Inevitably, Marx's description reflects the visionary in him, even though he claims objectivity. In his speculations about unalienated society, communism, we see Marx's utopianism at its best. Convinced that alienation was historically produced, Marx dared to predict that it would likewise be historically eradicated.

Humanity's rightful place is at the centre of creation. While nature provides the raw materials for human beings' creative activity and acts upon and shapes them, human beings give the world its shape as they transform nature. History is the mutual interaction between human beings and nature which leads to the humanisation of nature.[162] This presupposition about the humanisation of nature undergirds Marx's postulation of the transcendence of human alienation, which is synonymous with the complete transcendence of alienation. Here we glimpse an optimism that befits the Jewish prophet, rather than the cold, calculating empiricist who refuses to project a future beyond that which can be verified by the objective data available.[163] Unfortunately, Marx neither describes in full the future society he envisages nor does he articulate in clearly defined terms the path to be trod and the means to be used in the achievement of the transcendence of alienation and the realisation of free, uninhibited, humanised, creative humanity.[164] Nevertheless, the glimpse that we are able to catch provides indispensible insight into his understanding of history. History will eventually become, and continue to be, the story of humanity's transcendence of alienation and its creation of the truly human essence.

Before we embark on our discussion of history and the transcendence of alienation, we must first piece together some of the fragmentary descriptions of the unalienated society that Marx gives us.[165] Marx describes a reality that has never been known in the history of the universe. He does not give a picture of a lost paradise which is about to be regained, since he does not believe that there once was a paradise—all history to date has been a history of alienation.[166] He is convinced that the future is ever open and yields the dynamically new. Static terms, therefore, are inappropriate to describe history.

Marx argues that in the future, free society, there no longer will be any state which acts as an "intermediary between man and his freedom."[167] The emergence of the future society will mean that the state has disappeared. As long as the state exists, even when it facilitates an increasing measure of freedom for its citizens, human beings are still alienated, for they recognise themselves by detour—i.e., through the state. Even in a state in which its citizens have gained political emancipation, the communist society is still a far cry. Since Marx saw religion as a phenomenon—part of the superstructure—whose presence in any so-called free state is a blatant reminder that alienation still plagues such a society and its people, his criticism of the situation in the North American states is noteworthy. He writes:

> The question is: what is the relationship of complete political emancipation to religion? The fact that even in the land of completed political emancipation we find not only the existence of religion but a living existence full of freshness and strength, furnishes us with the proof that the existence of religion does not contradict or impede the perfection of the state.[168]

Marx concludes that the future, unalienated society is nowhere in existence, not even where there has been political emancipation. Political emancipation is not human emancipation; hence, religious emancipation is still to be effected, even when political emancipation has been legislated into operation.[169]

Marx points out that in the perfected political state, dichotomies continue to exist; in fact, they are integral to the existence of such a state. For instance, there is the opposition between the "species-life of man" and the "material life." Egoism remains unchecked and is even fostered by civil society, which stands opposed to the state. Marx explains:

> The perfected political state is by its nature the species-life of man in opposition to his material life. All the presupposition of this egoistic life continue to exist in civil society outside the sphere of the state, but as proper to civil society. When the political state has achieved its true completion,

man leads a double life, a heavenly one and an earthly one, not only in thought and consciousness but in reality, in life. He has a life both in the political community, where he is valued as a communal being, and in civil society where he is active as a private individual, treats other men as means, degrades himself to a means and becomes the plaything of alien powers.[170]

Marx adds that the political state cannot extricate itself from the insiduous and perpetual domination of religion, which, even at its best, is profane and limits human beings' experience of freedom. He claims:

> The political state has just as spiritual an attitude to civil society as heaven has to earth. It stands in the same opposition to civil society and overcomes it in the same manner as religion overcomes the limitations of the profane world, that is, it must likewise recognize it, reinstate it and let itself once more be dominated by it. Man in the reality that is nearest to him, civil society, is a profane being. Here where he counts for himself and others as a real individual, he is an illusory phenomenon. In the state, on the other hand, where man counts as a species-being, he is an imaginary participant in an imaginary sovereignty, he is robbed of his real life and filled with an unreal universality.[171]

However, political emancipation is not without any positive value. It is a necessary step towards complete human emancipation. "Political emancipation is of course a great progress. Although it is not the final form of human emancipation in general, it is nevertheless the final form of human emancipation inside the present world order."[172] The problem with political emancipation is that it is mistaken for real human emancipation.

Marx's description of human emancipation and the future society forms part of the core of his argument that human beings are the measure of what is human. Human beings are rightfully the Subject and Centre of history. On the question of human emancipation, Marx argues:

> All emancipation is bringing back man's world and his relationships to man himself.
>
> Political emancipation is the reduction of man, on the one hand to a member of civil society, an egoistic and independent individual, on the other

hand to a citizen, a moral person.

> The actual individual man must take the abstract citizen back into himself and, as an individual man in his empirical life, in his individual work and individual relationships become a species-being; man must recognize his own forces as social forces, organize them and thus no longer separate social forces from himself in the form of political forces. Only when this has been achieved will human emancipation be completed.[173]

Here is yet another illustration of Marx's rhetoric concerning the need for human beings to assume control of the forces of history which are intrinsically theirs. What Marx makes clear is not how they will achieve this utopia; rather, he reiterates his thesis that as long as human beings are not in control of those forces, they remain alienated and unfree.

Noting that for Marx "the true communist revolution could not be political, as was the bourgeois revolution, but is human and social," Axelos comments:

> It is in ceasing to be the alienated worker and the abstract citizen that man can become what he is: species-being. It is in ceasing to be the egoistic individual that he can regain his community essence. The recovery by man of all his properties, the abolition of the worker and the citizen in favor of the real man, the regaining by species being of all activities: this is the meaning of human emancipation. Such was Marx's thinking when he tried to exorcise the ghost of political communism.[174]

The anticipated eruption of human emancipation will usher in freedom hitherto unexperienced in the world. Whereas under capitalism, the workers are reduced to mere wage-earners, enslaved by private property, which is their own crystallised labour estranged from them, under communism they will be free to choose whatever occupations they desire. Thereby, they will be able to develop themselves in a wholistic way and not be inhibited by restraints in either the mode of the production or the relations of production. This is a fairy-tale world. Marx and Engels provide a vivid contrast between the alienated work situation and the unalienated, free world of productive and creative human activity:

> And finally, the division of labour offers us the first example of the fact that, as long as man remains in naturally evolved society, that is, as long as

53

a cleavage exists between the particular and the common interest, as long, therefore, as activity is not voluntarily, but naturally, divided, man's own deed becomes an alien power opposed to him, which enslaves him instead of being controlled by him. For as soon as the division of labour comes into being, each man has a particular, exclusive sphere of activity, which is forced upon him and from which he cannot escape. He is a hunter, a fisherman, a shepherd, or a critical critic, and must remain so if he does not want to lose his means of livelihood; whereas in communist society, where nobody has one exclusive sphere of activity but each can become accomplished in any branch he wishes, society regulates the general production and thus makes it possible for me to do one thing today and another tomorrow, to hunt in the morning, fish in the afternoon, rear cattle in the evening, criticise after dinner, just as I have a mind, without ever becoming hunter, fisherman, shepherd or critic.[175]

Whereas in natural society (*naturwüchsigen Gessellschaft*),human activity is naturally not voluntarily divided, thereby making the workers' own labour an alien power that subjugates and depersonalises them, in the free society, they will exercise freely the will to choose among an innumerable variety of activities which will facilitate their humanisation. History—human creative activity with nature—will show human beings' humanisation of nature. No longer will the primitive natural order persist and dominate humanity. Axelos provides a useful summary of Marx's sanguine vision:

> In the world of planetary technique and the most powerful development of
> the totality of productive forces, in the world that will have completely
> transformed nature into history and stripped all that is of natural character,
> in the world that will no longer know the distinction of labor into
> mechanical work and spiritual work nor the opposition of city and country,
> the communist man will be able, following his will and good pleasure, to
> give himself to these primitive, ancient, and medieval activities; he will be
> able to *hunt, fish, raise livestock,* and *criticize.*[176]

Ironically, Marx's description of the future society arises from alienation itself. Thus, we may ask whether his claims that he is promoting the humanity of human beings are plausible. Is his perspective not inherently ideological, legitimating fundamental dehumanising tendencies in both human beings and society? Axelos grasps this dilemma, for he asks: "Is not this anticipatory vision of total man's activities in total society, such as is expressed by the fanatic opponent of all ideology and every utopia, itself ideological, touching as it may also be in its naïveté and its rural, idyllic tones?"[177] The implication that Marx is ideological is certainly to be noted, even when it is also appreciated that Marx was thinking in universalistic terms spanning all of humanity and human history and not only the industrial societies of his time.

Marx argues that with the abolition of the State and the transcendence through communism of private property, the division of labour, money—all that perpetuates human alienation—the triumvirate of the essence of reality—society, nature, and humanity—will be free to work cooperatively and harmoniously. Human nature will be restored and through mutual interaction with nature and with society, human beigns will continually develop their authentic nature. It cannot be otherwise. Axelos explains:

> The realization of man's naturalism along the axis of the humanism of nature can take place only by way of society and through the life and social activity of men. Nature must not be given a privileged position at the expense of man and society, nor man at the expense of nature and society, nor society at the expense of nature and man.[178]

In short, all hierarchical systems must and will be abolished in the future society. Marx assumes that the three—society, nature and humanity—are interrelated and form a "common being." Hence, they must not be separated from each other. "Properly speaking, one must not even distinguish here these three aspects of the same being, of common being, of the *being*-in-becoming of totality. Indivisibly naturalistic, humanistic, and socialistic, communism will reconcile what was in conflict."[179] Marx's concern draws its inspiration from his primary preoccupation with the human being as a social being. The future society is not postulated as an abstraction which will replace the present alienating and abstract society.

The society of the future will be naturalistic, humanistic and socialistic. Human beings will no longer be dominated by envy, greed, egoism, physical need that seek utilitarian gratification. Rather, they will ever pursue that which makes for human self-realisation. Under communism, their focus will be on the future. Axelos tells us:

When man will have overcome his fragmentation and the duality that arises between the sensuous and material aspect of beings and things and their meaningful, spirit-order (*spirituel*) aspect, thereby finding the unified expression of the unity proper to his essence, then will he be able to appropriate his being in a universal way by appropriating at the same time the universal essence of all that is.[180]

Everything—humanity, nature, society—will be in a state of perpetual change, impelled by the future, which will not be bogged down by the past, which is plagued by alienation. The future will bring new and harmonious mutations ever conducing to reconcilation.[181] The enigma in describing this future is well-illustrated by Axelos's criticism of Marx's failure to attend to the acute difficulty of achieving a reunification of what has become separated:

Marx pays scant attention to the difference that separates any *original unity* from an *enterprise of unification*, and he does not let himself be bothered by the extreme difficulty involved in any attempt to *reunite* what was *separated*, when he conceives active humanism as generating total man and total society, and the total activity of men as inserting organically into Totality.[182]

Disregarding the current alienated state of affairs, Marx envisages a future that will be free of *exclusiveness, acquisitiveness,* and *having.* He argues:

Similarly the positive supersession of private property, that is, the sensuous appropriation by and for man of human essence and human life, of objective man and his works, should not be conceived of only as direct and exclusive enjoyment, as possession and having. Man appropriates his universal being in a universal manner, as a whole man. Each of his human relationships to the world—seeing, hearing, smell, tasting, feeling, thinking, contemplating, feeling, willing, acting, loving—in short all the organs of his individuality, just as the organs whose form is a directly communal one, are in their objective action, or their relation to the object, the appropriation of this object. The appropriation of human reality, their relationship to the object, is the confirmation of human reality.[183]

Humankind, the centre of the universe and the architect of its own liberation, will in the future society rightly appropriate subject and object and thereby realise its human essence which is universal human essence.

Marx's description of communism as human emancipation is partial and incomplete. Our concern throughout has been with the picture Marx gives of society which he calls unalienated and which he envisages will supersede the present alienated one. Because the term communism may be construed to mean a static state to be achieved, he frequently substitutes the term future society instead. But future society is not without its ambiguity and like communism connotes a static future goal. However, when Marx uses the term communism, he is certainly thinking of a future not yet present, a future that is "naturalistic, humanistic, and socialistic."[184] It is a dynamic future. It "is the movement whose burden it is to accomplish the task of universal reconciliation and to allow the full satisfaction of the totality of human needs, needs that renew themselves endlessly as they are satisfied."[185]

Marx is convinced that alienation can and will be transcended through human activity. Not only is alienation created by human beings, it will be historically superseded by them. Marx bases this hypothesis on the premise that "communism is for us not a *state of affairs* which is to be established, an *ideal* to which reality [will] have to adjust itself. We call communism the *real* movement which abolishes the present state of things."[186] As might be expected from one who wished to realise philosophy in *praxis*, Marx insisted that communism is a practical movement, negating that which negates the human essence. It pursues the satisfaction of practical needs by practical means. It involves practical-critical activity and not one in isolation from the other. Axelos summarises:

> It is in movement and its 'essence' is mobile. It posits negation as negation in order to negate the world as it exists, the world that nevertheless provides it with its preconditions; and it comes to posit the negation of negation as a new and unprecedented position, as the point of departure for the movement that moves toward the total, practical appropriation of all that *really* exists.[187]

The future to which communism moves is open and is characterised by the ongoing process of the negation of the negation. It is a positive process which human beings know and understand fully, for they are (will be) simultaneously the creator and the created. Marx points out:

Communism represents the positive in the form of the negation of the negation and thus a phase in human emancipation and rehabilitation, both real and necessary at this juncture of human development. Communism is the necessary form and dynamic principle of the immediate future, but communism is not as such the goal of human development, the form of human society.[188]

The final goal, then, is not communism, necessary (and inevitable) though it may be for human emancipation. Communism is a phase in the process of human development which will be eventually transcended. It is therefore limited. Failure to recognise this will lead to distortion of the liberation process and will stultify human growth. Such a failure would be castigated by Marx as ideological. It would demean and disintegrate the community of humanity, nature and society. To avoid such a blatant retrogression, communism must be understood for what it is. Axelos concludes that "though it is the movement of victory over Totality and of the (re) conquest of the essence of human totality, it hardly escapes limitation. Communism will be in turn transcended, but not before it has been completely realized."[189]

Marx's optimistic, utopian vision is based upon his acceptance and transformation of the Hegelian dialectic. Although Marx applies the dialectic to socio-economic categories in order to realise philosophy, he, nevertheless, continues to view reality in dialectical terms, i.e., in terms of inherent contradictions which possess their own solutions as higher syntheses. Unlike Hegel, he envisages a historical transformation of alienation and the emergence of the emancipated society. However, he continues to base his theory of history upon the Hegelian dialectic. The ongoing process of future contradictions will lead not to further alienations but to ever-higher syntheses and the realisation of an ever-widening freedom.

NOTES TO CHAPTER I

[1] As their name implies, these writings are fragmentary in nature. Marx himself did not give them a collective title, but they have come to be popularly called the *Paris Manuscripts, 1844 Manuscripts* or *Economic and Philosophic Manuscripts*. From here on we shall, for the most part, refer to them as the *1844 Manuscripts*. See Karl Marx, *Early Texts,* trans. and ed. by David McLellan (Oxford: Basil Blackwell, 1971), pp. xxvii–xxix.

[2] Marx's writings after 1844 have come to be popularly known as his "later" works. They are also referred to as the "mature," "authentic," "historical," "official" Marxian writings. It should be noted that reference to the "young" or the "mature" Marx is another way of indicating that it is with the thought, theory, or philosophy contained in the early or later Marxian writings, respectively, that we are concerned. See Robert A. Nisbet, *The Sociological Tradition* (London: Heinemann, 1966), p. 285.

[3] Daniel Bell, *The End of Ideology* (New York: Collier Books, 1961), pp. 386–387.

[4] See Erich Fromm, *Marx's Concept of Man* (New York: Frederick Unger Publishing Co., 1961), pp. 70–71.

[5] Adam Schaff, "Studies of the Young Marx: A Rejoinder," in *Revisionism,* ed. by Leopold Labedz (London: George Allen and Unwin Ltd., 1962), pp.188–189.

[6] Marx denounces "ideology" as "false consciousness." Ideas, he argues, are derived from the socio-economic base of society. In their state of alienation, human beings are constantly creating illusions of reality which are relative to each historical epoch. In our use of the term, we are intending a more positive connotation than Marx did. It is taken to mean a programme for the transformation of society. Whether positive or negative, Marx spoke of such programmes as transitory.

[7] Iring Fetscher, "The young and the old Marx," in *Marx and the Western World,* ed. by Nicholas Lobkowicz (Notre Dame: University of Notre Dame Press, 1967), p. 20.

[8] See *Ibid.*, p. 22.

[9] *Ibid.*, p. 20.

[10] Donald Clark Hodges, "The Young Marx—A Reappraisal," *Philosophical and Phenomenological Research,* Vol. xxvii, No.2 (December 1966), 219.

[11] Raymond Aron, *Main Currents in Sociological Thought* (New York: Basic Books, Inc., Publishers, 1965), p. 111.

[12] *Ibid.*, p. 113.

[13] *Ibid.*, p. 139. See also, p. 111.

[14] Bell, *The End of Ideology*, p. 362.

[15] *Ibid.*, p. 361.

[16] Daniel Bell, "The 'Rediscovery' of Alienation," *The Journal of Philosophy,* Vol. lvi, No. 24 (November 19, 1959), 951.

[17] See *Ibid.*, 935.

[18] Marx, *Early Texts,* pp. xxxii–xxxiii; see also, Daniel Bell, "The 'Rediscovery' of Alienation," 945.

[19] Marx, *Early Texts,* p. 82.

[20] *Ibid.*

[21] More will be said about Hegel's influence on Marx when we discuss the concept of alienation. See Bertell Ollman, *Alienation* (London: Cambridge University Press, 1971), p. 35, where he

perceptively notes Marx's heavy reliance upon Hegel's vocabulary.

22 Robert C. Tucker, *Philosophy and Myth in Karl Marx*, 2nd rev. ed. (London and New York: Cambridge University Press, 1972), p. 170.

23 *Ibid.*, p. 172; see also Max Braunschweig, "The Philosophic Thought of the Young Marx," in *Alienation*, Vol. 8, ed. by Gerald Sykes (New York: Basic Books, Inc., Publishers, 1964), pp. 503, 508.

24 Marx, *Early Texts*, p. xxxv.

25 V. Lenin, *Aus dem philosophischen Nachlass*, trans. by David McLellan (Berlin: 1949), p. 99, quoted in Marx, *Early Texts*, p. xxxv. Of course, Lenin's interest in Hegel was not the same as Lukacs' or the other scholars who, after 1932, became involved in deciphering the early writings of Marx.

26 See Marx, *Early Texts*, p. xxxix.

27 *Ibid.*, p. xxxviii; see also, Eugene Kamenka, *The Ethical Foundations of Marxism* (London: Routledge and Kegan Paul Ltd., 1962), p. 146; E.J. Hobsbawm, "Introduction," in Karl Marx, *Pre-Capitalist Economic Formations,* trans. by Jack Cohen (London: Lawrence and Wishart, 1978), pp. 9-11.

28 See Fetscher, "The young and the old Marx," pp. 31–32.

29 Helmut Thielicke, *The Hidden Question of God,* trans. by Geoffrey W. Bromiley (Grand Rapids, Mich.: William. B. Eerdmans Publishing Co., 1977), p. 35.

30 Marx, *Early Texts*, pp. xxxviii–xxxix.

31 Hobsbawn, "Introduction," in Marx, *Pre-Capitalist Economic Formations*, pp. 84–85.

32 See Kamenka, *The Ethical Foundations of Marxism*, p. 144, and Bell, "The 'Rediscovery' of Alienation," p. 943.

33 See Gajo Petrovic, "Marx's Theory of Alienation," *Philosophical and Phenomenological Research*, Vol. xxiii (September 1962–June 1963), p. 419.

34 See Marx, *Capital*, Vol. 1 (Moscow: 1954), p. 432, quoted in Marx, *Early Texts,* p. xxxvi.

35 Marx, *Early Texts,* pp. xxxvi-xxxvii.

36 *Ibid.*, p. xxxvii; see also Gaylord C. Le Roy, "The Concept of Alienation: An attempt at a Definition," in *Marxism and Alienation,* ed. by Herbert Aptheker (New York: Humanities Press, 1965), p. 9. "Marx did not drop the concept of alienation but he did come to subordinate it, to make it a part of a larger and more complex system of ideas. It is retained in the theory of fetishism of commodities in Marx's mature theory, but whereas in the early manuscripts alienation has a central importance, the theory of fetishism functions in the later work as only a subordinate part of a bold, extensive, and complex apparatus of theory."

37 Marx, *Early Texts*, p. xxxvii. Fetscher, "The young and the old Marx," p. 35, points out: "In [Marx's] study of the commodity character of products, his analyses from his early writings are taken for granted."

38 Marx, *Capital,* p. 488, quoted in Marx, *Early Texts,* p. xxxvii.

39 Marx S. Wartofsky, "Comment," in *Marx and the Western World,* ed. by Nicholas Lobkowicz, p. 40, disputes the argument that the "young" Marx is "abstract" while the "mature" Marx is more "concrete." He finds that this is "a positivist myth" and suggests: "A profound view of the integrity of Marx's views from 'young' to 'old' is to see in Marx the fundamental continuity of certain root-concepts—in particular, the central ones of alienation and objectification."

40 It is debated whether in his early writings Marx conceives of a fixed human essence. Kamenka, *Ethical Foundations,* pp. 150–151, argues that there is a change in Marx's conception of human nature. Marx, he points out, rejects his earlier concept of a fixed nature. Despite this change, Kamenka insists that the fundamental continuity between the early and mature Marx's conception of humanity is not destroyed.

[41] Kostas Axelos, *Alienation, Praxis, and Techné in the Thought of Karl Marx,* trans. by Ronald Brunzina (Austin: University of Texas Press, 1976), p. 49.

[42] The amount of material available on this topic is exhaustive. Among the works significant for our discussion are: Frank Johnson, ed. *Alienation* (New York: Seminar Press, 1973); Walter Kaufmann, "The Inevitability of Alienation," in Richard Schacht, *Alienation* (London: George Allen and Unwin Ltd., 1971), pp. xiii–xvi; Richard Schacht, *Alienation*, pp. lix–lxv; István Mészáros, *Marx's Theory of Alienation* (London: The Merlin Press, Ltd., 1970), pp. 27–65.

[43] See Schacht, *Alienation*, p. lix; David Cairns, *The Image of God in Man* (London: Collins, 1973), p. 219.

[44] Kaufmann, "The Inevitability of Alienation," in Schacht, *Alienation*, p. xvii, points out that "the modern interest in Hegel's and Marx's discussion of alienation seems to date from" the publication of George Lukacs' book, *Der junge Hegel (The Young Hegel).*

[45] Johnson, *Alienation,* p. 3.

[46] Kaufmann, "The Inevitability of Alienation," in Schacht, *Alienation*, p. xxii.

[47] *Ibid.,* p. xxiii.

[48] *Ibid.,* p. xxviii.

[49] *Ibid.,* p. liii. I am grateful to Peter Kjeseth for the following reminder made in private conversation: "It needs to be pointed out, however, that neither the Old Testament nor the New Testament simplistically calls people to alienate themselves from nature, society and themselves. The Psalms are extremely 'nature friendly.' Paul sees the redemption of nature tied up with the revealing of the children of God. Certainly, God's Old Testament and New Testament people were to be different, but this difference was for the redemption of societies—all nations would one day stream to Zion; the small Christian communities were to tell principalities and powers about God's plan for the unity of all."

[50] *Ibid.*

[51] Schacht, *Alienation,* p. lxiii.

[52] Arnold Kaufman, "On Alienation," *Inquiry,* Vol. 8, No. 2 (Summer 1965), p. 143, as quoted in Schacht, *Alienation*, p. lxiii; see also, p. 238.

[53] Lewis Feuer, "What is Alienation? The Career of a Concept," *New Politics,* Vol. No. 3 (Spring 1962), 132, as quoted in Schacht, *Alienation,* p. lxiii.

[54] Kenneth Keniston, *The Uncommitted: Alienated Youth in American Society* (New York: Harcourt, Brace and World, 1965), p. 452, as quoted in Schacht, *Alienation,* pp. lxiii, 238.

[55] Schacht, *Alienation*, p. lxiii.

[56] *Ibid.,* pp. 251–252.

[57] The legacy of Hegel was taken up particularly by his disciples, including the Bauer brothers, Bruno and Edgar, D.F. Strauss, Ludwig Feuerbach and Karl Marx. For an informative discussion of the "Young Hegelian Movement of the Left," see David McLellan, *The Young Hegelians and Karl Marx* (London: Macmillan Publishers, Ltd., 1969), especially, pp. 1-20; and Leszek Kolakowski, *Main Currents of Marxism,* Vol. 1, *The Founders,* trans. by P.S. Falla (London: Oxford University Press, 1978), pp. 81–95.

[58] For an illuminating but brief discussion of the main difference between Aristotle's philosophy and Hegel's "expressivist" philosophy, see Charles Taylor, *Hegel* (Cambridge: Cambridge University Press, 1975), pp. 15–18.

[59] *Ibid.,* p. 76.

[60] *Ibid.* For a definition of "expressivism," see p. 540; Taylor, p. 548, argues that Marx belongs to this tradition or movement.

[61] *Ibid.*

61

62 *Ibid.*; see also Kolakowski, *The Founders,* pp. 56–70, for his informative description of "Hegel's understanding of the movement of consciousness towards the Absolute."
63 Taylor, *Hegel,* pp. 76–77.
64 *Ibid.,* p. 88.
65 See Karl Marx, "Critique of Hegel's Dialectic and General Philosophy," *Early Texts,* p. 174. The implicit circularity in Hegel's argument, as described by Marx, is noted by Kolakowski, *The Founders,* p. 61.
66 See Taylor, *Hegel,* p. 89.
67 *Ibid.*
68 Schacht, *Alienation,* p. 35. For the purpose of ease in following his discussion on alienation, Schacht's use of the subscripts "1" and "2" when he speaks of "Hegel's two-fold Use of 'Alienation'"—"Alienation₁" and "Alienation ₂"—are retained in the main body of the text of this work.
69 *Ibid.,* pp. 38–39.
70 *Ibid.,* p. 38; see also, Taylor, *Hegel,* pp. 68–75.
71 Schacht, *Alienation,* p. 41.
72 *Ibid.,* pp. 50–52.
73 G.W.F. Hegel, *Phenomenology of Mind,* trans. by J.B. Baillie, revised second ed. (New York: The Macmillan Publishing Co., Inc., 1949), p. 509, as quoted in Schacht, *Alienation,* p. 46.
74 *Ibid.,* p. 517, quoted in Schacht, *Alienation,* p. 51.
75 Schacht, *Alienation,* pp. 51–52.
76 Taylor, *Hegel,* p. 74.
77 Marx, *Early Texts,* p. 165.
78 *Ibid.,* p. 172.
79 See Marx, *Early Texts,* p. 174; Kolakowski, *The Founders,* p. 61.
80 Marx, *Early Texts,* p. 174.
81 See Schacht, *Alienation,* p. 70; Richard Norman, *Hegel's Phenomenology: A Philosophical Introduction* (London: Sussex University Press, 1976), p. 98; see also Taylor, *Hegel,* p. 551.
82 Schacht, *Alienation,* p. 70.
83 *Ibid.*
84 Norman, *Hegel's Pheomenology,* p. 98.
85 Marx, *Early Texts,* p. 162.
86 Schacht, *Alienation,* p. 83.
87 See Kolakowski, *The Founders,* pp. 132–134.
88 See Marx, *Early Texts,* pp. 140–143.
89 John Plamenatz, *Karl Marx's Philosophy of Man* (London: Oxford University Press, 1972), p. 125, refutes Marx's conclusion that the worker is powerless to determine the use to which his/her product is put. According to him, even if the workers did find the system of production "oppressive and restricting," that "is not a sufficient condition" for them not to "understand and control it."
90 Marx, *Early Texts,* p. 134. See also, Kolakowski, *The Founders,* p. 139; Ollman, *Alienation,* pp. 198–204.
91 Marx, *Early Texts,* pp. 134–135.
92 *Ibid.,* p. 143; see also, Marx's attack on money, pp. 112, 178–183, 188–203.
93 *Ibid.,* p. 135.

94 See Ollman, *Alienation*, pp. 137–147, for a more elaborate treatment of Marx's understanding of the worker's alienation from his/her own productive activity.

95 See Schacht, *Alienation*, p. 92, where he perceptively notes the ambiguity in Marx's use of alienation.

96 Plamenatz, *Karl Marx's Philosophy of Man*, p. 153, correctly points out that the separation of mental from manual labour, along with production, constitutes the characteristics of the division of labour which give rise to alienation. Furthermore, he disputes Marx's assumption that these are necessarily connected.

97 *Ibid.*, pp. 149–160, notes the difficulty in determining precisely what Marx means by the term "division of labour." See also, Ollman, *Alienation*, pp. 157–165, where he attempts "to lay bare the ties between man's alienation ... and the whole sphere of economics."

98 Marx, *Early Texts*, p. 137.

99 *Ibid.*

100 See *Ibid.*, p. 167, where McLellan points out in footnote 1 the meaning of the concept "species-being" which Marx took from Feuerbach. For a systematic treatment of "Man's relation to his species," see Ollman, *Alienation*, pp. 151–153.

101 See Plamenatz, *Karl Marx's Philosophy of Man*, pp. 69-78, and Ollman, *Alienation*, pp. 111–115, for two helpful discussions on how human beings express their "species" character.

102 Ollman, *Alienation*, pp. 116–120, attempts to place Marx's thesis on freedom as the essence of human being in the context of various human activities under communism.

103 See Axelos, *Alienation, Praxis, and Techné*, pp. 175–194, especially, p. 176, where he notes that Marx displays an "extremely ambiguous and ambivalent" attitude towards art. Plamenatz, *Karl Marx's Philosophy of Man*, p. 49, criticises Marx's distinction between physical (basic) needs and *species-needs* by claiming that the two are interrelated. Thus, "many of the wants satisfied by material production could just as properly be called moral or spiritual as material."

104 Marx, *Early Texts*, p. 138.

105 *Ibid.*, p. 139.

106 *Ibid.*

107 *Ibid.*, p. 138.

108 See Ronald Bruzina, "Translator's Introduction," in Axelos, *Alienation, Praxis, and Techné*, pp. x–xiv.

109 See Kolakowski, *The Founders*, pp. 155–159.

110 See Marx, *Early Texts*, pp. 140, 149–154.

111 *Ibid.*, pp. 138–139.

112 *Ibid.*, p. 140.

113 *Ibid.*

114 *Ibid.*, p. 142.

115 *Ibid.*, pp. 142–143.

116 See Ollman, *Alienation*, pp. 154–157.

117 Marx, *Early Texts*, p. 142.

118 See *Ibid.*, pp. 149–151; Plamenatz, *Karl Marx's Philosophy of Man*, pp. 153–155.

119 Plamenatz, *Karl Marx's Philosophy of Man*, p. 69, argues that "these three processes—becoming self-conscious, becoming aware of other selves, and coming to recognize oneself as a being of a certain kind—are inseparable but distinct parts of the same process."

120 Marx, *Early Texts*, pp. 193–194.

121 *Ibid.*, p. 145.

[122] Karl Marx, Thesis 1 of "Thesis on Feuerbach," in Karl Marx and Frederick Engels, *Collected Works*, Vol. 5 (London: Lawrence and Wishart, 1976), p. 6.

[123] Marx, *Early Texts*, p. 142.

[124] *Ibid.*, p. 37.

[125] *Ibid.*, p. 48.

[126] Russell B. Norris, *God, Marx, and the Future* (Philadelphia: Fortress Press, 1974), p. 18.

[127] Marx W. Wartofsky, *Feuerbach* (London: Cambridge University Press, 1977), p. 305.

[128] Marx, *Early Texts*, p. 18.

[129] Wartofsky, *Marx and the Western World*, p. 338.

[130] See *Ibid.*, p. 224.

[131] See Marx's "Fourth Thesis on Feuerbach," in *Collected Works*, p. 7.

[132] Howard L. Parsons, "The Prophetic Mission of Karl Marx," *The Journal of Theology*, Vol. xliv (1964), 57.

[133] *Ibid.*, p. 59.

[134] *Ibid.*

[135] Marx, *Early Texts*, p. 116.

[136] *Ibid.* See also, Herbert Aptheker, *The Urgency of Marxist-Christian Dialogue* (New York: Harper and Row Publishers, 1970), pp. 25–28.

[137] Marx's "Fourth Thesis on Feuerbach," in *Collected Works*, p. 7.

[138] Marx, *Early Texts*, p. 53.

[139] *Ibid.*, pp. 156–157.

[140] Norris, *God, Marx, and the Future*, p. 28.

[141] Marx, *Early Texts*, p. 155.

[142] Ludwig Feuerbach, *Vorlesungen über das Wesen der Religion*, ed. by Wilhelm Bolin (Stuttgart: Fr. Frommann, 1908), p. 21, quoted in Schacht, *Alienation*, p. 68. (Translation provided by Schacht.)

[143] Frederick Engels, *Ludwig Feuerbach and the Outcome of Classical Germany*, ed by C.P. Dutt (New York: International Publishers Company, Inc., 1941), pp. 83–84.

[144] Karl Marx, *Early Writings*, trans. and ed. by T.B. Bottomore, foreword by Erich Fromm (New York: McGraw-Hill Book Company, 1964), p. 126.

[145] *Ibid.*, p. 58.

[146] Schacht, *Alienation*, pp. 102.

[147] See Axelos, *Alienation, Praxis, and Techné*, pp. 131–142.

[148] Kamenka, *Ethical Foundations*, p. 146.

[149] *Ibid.*; see *The Communist Manifesto, Selected Works*, Vol. 1 (Moscow: Foreign Language Publishing House, n.d.), p. 55; Vol. II, p. 8; Vol. III, p. 12, quoted in Kamenka, *Ethical Foundations*, p. 146.

[150] See Leszek Kolakowski, *Marxism and Beyond*, trans. by Jane Zielonko Peel (London: Pall Mall Press, 1968), p. 76.

[151] See Mészáros, *Marx's Theory of Alienation*, p. 82, and Plamenatz, *Karl Marx's Philosophy of Man*, p. 77.

[152] Plamenatz, *Karl Marx's Philosophy of Man*, p. 48.

[153] *Ibid.*

[154] See Fromm, *Marx's Concept of Man*, p. 24.

[155] See Mészáros, *Marx's Theory of Alienation*, pp. 173–175.

[156] Taylor, *Hegel*, pp. 180–181, 551–556, points out that the absence of criteria in Marx concerning the constitution of human essence is directly related to Marx's failure to provide a material substitute for Hegel's *Geist*, which Marx rejects.

[157] Marx, *Early Texts*, p. 36.

[158] Axelos, *Alienation, Praxis, and Techné*, pp. 315-316; see also, p. 135; Plamenatz, *Karl Marx's Philosophy of Man*, p. 34.

[159] See Axelos, *Alienation, Praxis, and Techné*, pp. 41–44; Kamenka, *Ethical Foundations*, p.150; Kolakowski, *Marxism and Beyond*, p. 70.

[160] See Mészáros, *Marx's Theory of Alienation*, pp. 165–168, for his discussion on, "The Limits of Freedom," in Marx's thought.

[161] See Gajo Petrovic, "The Philosophical and Sociological Relevance of Marx's Concept of Alienation," in Lobkowicz, *Marx and the Western World*, p. 138.

[162] See Joseph J. O'Malley, "History and Man's 'Nature' in Marx," *The Review of Politics*, Vol. 28, No. 4 (October 1966), 508–527, especially, 513–517, for a helpful discussion of the process of the humanisation of human beings and nature through their mutual interaction with each other.

[163] See Plamenatz, *Karl Marx's Philosophy of Man*, pp. 176–180.

[164] Taylor, *Hegel*, p. 554.

[165] Marx's vision of the future de-alienated society can, at best, only be partial, transitory, and fragmentary, because of the very obscure and fragmentary nature of his early writings in which he attempted to sketch a programme of de-alienation. See Plamenatz, *Karl Marx's Philosophy of Man*, pp. 3–5.

[166] See Axelos, *Alienation, Praxis, and Techné*, pp. 240–241, 221.

[167] Marx, *Early Texts*, p. 92.

[168] *Ibid.*, p. 91.

[169] See Axelos, *Alienation, Praxis, and Techné*, p. 233.

[170] Marx, *Early Texts*, pp. 93–94.

[171] *Ibid.*, p. 94.

[172] *Ibid.*, p. 95.

[173] *Ibid.*, p. 108.

[174] Axelos, *Alienation, Praxis, and Techné*, p. 233.

[175] Marx and Engels, "German Ideology," in *Collected Works*, p. 47.

[176] Axelos, *Alienation, Praxis, and Techné*, p. 257.

[177] *Ibid.*

[178] *Ibid.*, p. 241.

[179] *Ibid.*

[180] *Ibid.*, p. 242.

[181] Taylor, *Hegel*, pp. 550–551, disputes this conclusion. He argues that in Marx the future is a present state which cannot be transcended. Thus, to speak of complete reconciliation in the future is mere wishful thinking. Marx's view that history is *open* is unfounded.

[182] Axelos, *Alienation, Praxis, and Techné*, p. 242.

[183] Marx, *Early Texts*, p. 151.

[184] Axelos, *Alienation, Praxis, and Techné*, p. 247; see also, p. 245.

[185] *Ibid.*, p. 247.

[186] Marx and Engels, "German Ideology," in *Collected Works*, p. 49.

[187] Axelos, *Alienation, Praxis, and Techné*, pp. 267–268.

[188] Marx, *Early Texts*, p. 157.

[189] Axelos, *Alienation, Praxis, and Techné*, p. 268.

CHAPTER II
MARX'S THEORY OF HISTORY

A.
Premises for Transcending Alienation:
History as Universal History

No reader of Marx's description of alienation, with its wretchedness and dehumanisation, juxtaposed to the unfinished, speculative picture of the future society to be ushered in by communism, can help but wonder at his optimism about the historical transcendence of alienation. His description of alienation, one-sidedly economically determined though it is, is a most perspicacious analysis of nineteenth-century society. Marx has captured the state of the human being-in-alienation in bourgeois capitalist society.

By the same token, it cannot be seriously disputed that his fragmentary description of communism takes us into realms hitherto unexperienced in human history. Nowhere have human beings been able to avoid completely alienation, not even in primitive societies. History, for Marx, has always been a history of human alienation.[1] His expectation, therefore, that alienation will be transcended by human activity, leaves us wondering: How will this be achieved? Indeed, our query is sharpened when we realise that Marx did not have a clearly defined plan of action whereby human beings will liberate themselves and the whole of human history.

In our attempt to piece together his fragmented projections of how de-alienation will be achieved, we are led to investigate Marx's theory of history. History is alienated humanity's creation, and it will eventually become authentic human history. Are there forces, both human and non-human, which will collaborate to abolish alienation? What are the premises upon which Marx bases his optimism? Is the solution to the human predicament inherent in the situation?

The premises upon which Marx bases his argument for the historical transcendence of alienation are not empirically derived. Marx's primary premise is metaphysical. Neither before, during, nor after Marx's time, has there been a group of historically and empirically verifiable premises to demonstrate conclusively that history follows patterns which are empirically calculable. This does not rule out the possibility of discerning certain tendencies of and within history. Admittedly, Marx is concerned with the concrete activity of real human beings and with the concrete, material forces of production. We note, for example, his theory of history as universal history of alienation, as well as his argument that the abolition of private property is a *crucial* step towards the transcendence of alienation. However, Marx does not provide a scientifically verifiable programme for de-alienation. John Plamenatz correctly concludes that Marx's optimism about humankind's transcendence of alienation and its creation of the free society is a significant reminder of a latent prophetic zeal characteristic of the prophets in the Judeo-Christian tradition.

Marx is convinced that speculative philosophy reached its culmination in Hegel. There is no way beyond that point that is not ideological, except through *praxis*. This is the thrust of his eleventh and final thesis on Feuerbach: "The philosophers have only interpreted the world in various ways; the point is to change it." The translators of the *Collected Works*, (Volume 5) note that "Marx himself separated this thesis from the preceding ten, as though underlining its summarising character. We must understand the world in order to change it, instead of interpreting it one way or another in order to reconcile ourselves with what exists. Such in substance is the true meaning of this thesis." Moreover, there is another thought organically bound up with the foregoing one:

> The world cannot be changed by merely changing our notions of it, by theoretically criticising what exists; it must be understood, and then, proceeding from this, transformed by effective action, material revolutionary practice. This thesis concisely formulates the fundamental difference of Marxist philosophy from all earlier philosophy, including pre-Marxian materialism. It concentrates into a single sentence the effective, transforming character of the revolutionary theory created by Marx and Engels, its inseparable connection with revolutionary practice.[2]

This revolutionary *praxis* which Marx has in mind is not confined to any particular sector of humankind—not even to Germany or to bourgeois capitalist society. It is universal in scope. Over the years, through successive epochs, the base has broadened until the whole of humanity is finally divided into two camps or two classes: the exploited and the exploiters.[3] Marx illustrates this argument in his discussion in *German Ideology* of the connection between "the ideas of the ruling class" and "the ruling class itself:"

> For each new class which puts itself in the place of one ruling before it is
> compelled, merely in order to carry through its aim, to present its interest as
> the common interest of all the members of society, that is, expressed in ideal
> form: it has to give its ideas the form of universality, and present them as
> the only rational, universally valid ones. The class making a revolution
> comes forward from the very start, if only because it is opposed to a *class*,
> not as a class, but as the representative of the whole of society, as the whole
> mass of society confronting the one ruling class.[4]

The pretense of universality is not without substance, since the non-ruling class
does, if it is successful, gain benefits, not only for itself, but also for a wider mass
of alienated humanity. "Its victory, therefore, benefits also many individuals of
other classes which are not winning a dominant position, but only insofar as it now
enables these individuals to raise themselves into the ruling class." Partial,
temporary victories are achieved, but the mass of humanity continues to suffer
alienation. The small elitist ruling class feeds parasitically off the energies and
creation of the masses. The growing intensity of this inhuman struggle continues
unabated. Marx and Engels comment:

> Every new class, therefore, achieves domination only on a broader basis
> than that of the class ruling previously; on the other hand the opposition of
> the non-ruling class to the new ruling class then develops all the more
> sharply and profoundly. Both these things determine the fact that the
> struggle to be waged against this new ruling class ... has as its aim a more
> decisive and more radical negation of the previous conditions of society than
> all previous classes which sought to rule could have.[5]

At the very heart of this class conflict is the basic socio-economic conflict out of
which all other conflicts in history arise. We should note *en passant* that Marx
argues that conflict which leads to change arises when changes in the mode of
production inevitably result in disharmony between the forces of production and the
relations of production. Marx's optimism for a resolution of alienation rests upon
the new possibilites contained within the womb of ever-advancing technology.
Every succeeding generation finds "itself in possession of the productive forces won
by the previous generation which serve it as the raw material for new production."
Thus, all history is inextricably linked together. History is the history of all

humankind. Moreover, this process occurs even when the mass of humanity is unconscious of its participation. Even during the decadence of alienation, the resolution of the conflict is occurring, albeit in a hidden and obscure way. Noting Marx's letter to Annenkov (Brussels, December 28, 1846), Jean Hyppolite explains that during (and because of) this inter-generational transmission of the productive forces

> a connection arises in human history, a history of humanity takes shape which has become all the more a history of humanity since the productive forces of man and therefore his social relations have been extended. Hence it necessarily follows: the social history of men is never anything but the history of their individual development, whether they are conscious of it or not.[6]

Ignorance of its role in history will not characterise the proletarian class at the moment of its messianic overthrow of the alienated productive process. Then it will be fully conscious of its salutary activity for the benefit of the whole of humanity. Of course, during these preparatory epochs, parochialism, rationalism, and other exclusivistic and separatist attitudes and tendencies will be the order of the day. In spite of this, Marx is able to perceive history in its intrinsically universal scope and to proceed optimistically to announce the coming of de-alienation and of human reconciliation.

Marx's concept of the universal history of human alienation and development is related to his concept of human essence as comprised of needs. Human beings, like other animals, have certain basic physical needs which they seek to satisfy through their encounter with nature. Unlike other animals, human beings are able to create culture which they transmit from generation to generation. Culture is a human deposit of human beings' creative use of nature to satisfy their needs. The process gives rise to new and higher needs which are peculiar to the human species and are directly related to the level of technology that obtains at each particular stage of socio-economic development.

Yet, Marx speaks of needs of the *species-being* as if he were thinking of universal *species-being*. The needs of these *species-beings* are the same everywhere (at least they will reach that point during communism, if not before). Alienated workers find that the essence of all their needs is in the universal desire for freedom and redemption. This concept of history, which highlights the cry of the *species-being* for the satisfaction of its pervasive need of reconciliation and de-alienation, is yet another indication of Marx's understanding of history as universal history.

The history of nature prior to human presence in it and their mutual interaction with each other is an abstract and speculative question. History has its origins in human encounter with nature. "When you enquire about the creation of the world and man," Marx suggests, "then you abstract from man and the world."[7] Emphasising history as human creation, Marx categorically denies the creation of human beings or nature by any grand designer, any heavenly or spirit-creator. Marx himself says, "Spontaneous generation is the only practical refutation of the theory of creation."[8] Later he concludes:

> But since for socialist man what is called world history is nothing but the creation of man by human labour and the development of nature for man, he has the observable and irrefutable proof of his self-creation and the process of his origin. Once the essential reality of man in nature, man as the existence of nature for man, has become evident in practical life and sense experience, then the question of an alien being, of a being above nature and man—a question that implies an admission of the unreality of nature and man—has become impossible in practice.[9]

Marx does not subscribe to any metaphysical idea or belief in a being existent prior to creation. That would be tantamount to a denial of human autonomy and would thereby further alienation. To posit creation as the act of some being or agency outside of human being-in-nature is to deny that history is generated and created by human impulse. Human beings' roots would then be outside of themselves, and their experience of de-alienation would be subject to the caprice of some paternal/maternal benefactor. This is mere abstract and speculative thinking. It has no grounding in the real and actual conditions of life. Further, it is not scientific, and Marx wants to be certain that his theory of history is fully empirical. Axelos appropriately sums up Marx's argument:

> The origin of man is nature, his nature is human; the Nature with which he is involved is always social, and its becoming is historical. (Cosmic) Nature and (human) nature, (social) technique and (historical) becoming are therefore inseparably bound and manifest themselves together from the very beginning. The visible beginning of all that is, the originating act of the

World, is human history, for 'history is the true natural history of man',
and 'only naturalism is capable of comprehending the act of world history'.
The originating act of all that is, the place from which it all can be grasped,
is this point of intersection of the 'humanism of nature' and the naturalism
of man.[10]

In his survey of nineteenth-century capitalist society, Marx discovers what he
takes to be the nemesis of human freedom: private property. Workers have created
their own alienation, tangibly and potently present in the form of estranged surplus
production owned by the non-working employer. All around them, workers feel
totally alienated. Marx is convinced that this phenomenon will become universal as
capitalism spreads. But the function of private property in society is ambiguous.
"Precisely in the fact that *division of labour* and *exchange* are embodiments of private
property lies the twofold proof, on the one hand that *human* life required *private
property* for its realization, and on the other hand that it now requires the suppression
of private property."[11]

We return to the problem of the circularity in Marx's argument concerning the
causes and effects of alienation. Marx insists that private property arose out of the
exploitation of workers by capitalists who invariably kept back a disproportionate
part of the workers' production for themselves. It arose out of an already existing
mode of production. This alienated mode contributed to the further development of
succeeding alienated modes of production throughout history until the emergence of
the capitalist mode, which Marx adamantly maintains is the most alienated of all
modes. Such an alienated pattern of development was historically necessary and
inevitable. Private property also grew and spread, becoming increasingly pervasive
in each succeeding society. Along with the development in the mode of production
and private property, the development of "technique" also occurred. However, the
satisfaction of human needs was only partial. Axelos explains:

> Technique served up till now to provide a partial, select, and fragmented
> satisfaction of human needs, but that all took place within the world of
> private property wherein subjects were separated from objects. The
> abolition of private property will permit man to regain his human, that is,
> social, existence in the satisfaction of the totality of his needs in a human
> way.[12]

Marx concludes that, when the usefulness of private property is ended, then workers, in universal solidarity with one another, will engage in a revolutionary transformation of the productive process in order to abolish the alienating existence of private property.

Once again we are confronted by Marx's engimatic description of the abolition of private property in actual human history. Fired by his sanguine vision of the historical transcendence of alienation and the creation of everything for full and authentic human use, Marx boldly asserts:

> The supersession of private property is therefore the complete emancipation of all human senses and qualities, but it is this emancipation precisely in that these senses and qualities have become human, both subjectively and objectively. The eye has become a human eye when its object has become a social, human object produced by man and destined for him. Thus in practice the senses have become direct theoreticians. They relate to the thing for its own sake but the thing itself is an objective human relationship to itself and to man and vice versa. (I can in practice only relate myself humanly to an object if the object relates itself humanly to man.) Need and enjoyment have thus lost their egoistic nature and nature has lost its mere utility in that its utility has become human utility.[13]

The abolition of private property will effect a total human self-transformation. However, this has never been achieved before. With the abolition of private property, human beings will no longer be enslaved by egoistic need and enjoyment and mere utilitarian satisfaction of such selfish desires. Everything, the human senses, relationships, human essence will be fully humanised.[14] However much we may criticise Marx's vision as utopian and naive,[15] we cannot escape noticing his persistence in firmly anchoring his de-alienated future in human beings whose creative power is necessary for both their own humanisation as well as the humanisation of need and property. Axelos notes that "this can all actually take place in historical time, because the subjective and objective nature of man, the human essence of all that is, both allows it and requires it."[16]

What is Marx's fundamental premise that allows for his optimistic anticipation of the historical transcendence of alienation? Axelos argues that the "fundamental premise" "is *metaphysical* in nature." It goes beyond experiential data which do not validate Marx's optimism. Indeed, "Marx has never been able to establish the empirical existence of this natural, social, human, species essence of man—an essence whose whole history is but the history of alienation and which will show itself for the first time in the kingdom of universal reconciliation."[17]

At first glance, the term metaphysical strikes us as odd and inaccurate, for Marx himself castigates the presupposition of an other-worldly creator standing over and above humanity, regulating human affairs. But the term is appropriately used, since there is no empirical evidence for the utopia that Marx envisages. It is an other-worldly picture of the future of this actual and real, sensuous material world. Surprisingly, Marx was unaware of "the metaphysical dimension of his thought."[18] In the *German Ideology*, under the caption, "Premises of the Materialist Conception of history," Marx writes:

> The premises from which we begin are not arbitrary ones, not dogmas, but real premises from which abstraction can only be made in the imagination. They are the real individuals, their acitivity and the material conditions of their life, both those which they find already existing and those produced by their activity. These premises can thus be verified in the pure empirical way.[19]

In his comments on this text, Axelos raises serious doubts about Marx's assumption that the premises are empirically verifiable. He asks:

> But can the species essence of man, natural, social, human being, which is its own foundation, an essence never yet realized but nevertheless the thing that makes possible and necessary the transcending of alienation—can this basic metaphysical presupposition be verified in a purely empirical way? Can the prospect of radical dealienation, faith in the possibility of the total transcending of all alienation, and hope in future universal reconciliation be sustained on the basis of the data of experience? Are all those things implied in the wondrous development of technique as liberated from all impediments?[20]

B.
The Evolutionary Development of the Mode of Production

Marx was not totally immune to non-empirical ideas, even when he was dealing with alienation under capitalism and the necessity and possibility of its transcendence through human initiative. The bourgeois capitalist societies of his day provided the primary data for his formulations about the actual human state. He directed every concern and focus towards understanding the alienating influence of capitalism. Nothing was considered in isolation from capitalism.[21] This peculiarly Marxian outlook is directly related to his thesis of history as universal social history. Pre-capitalist formations were in some way related to the emergence of nineteenth-century industrial capitalism. Moreover, the ambiguous historical development of human nature also took place prior to the birth of capitalism. History had always been the history of human alienation; hence, even as technology advanced and culture was transmitted from generation to generation (reflecting a real development of human nature), alienation gradually grew worse until it reached its nadir under capitalism.

Marx insists that the history of alienation begins not with capitalism but with "pre-capitalist economic formations."[22] However, as Eric J. Hobsbawn explains, "Marx concentrated his energies on the study of capitalism, and he dealt with the rest of history in varying degrees of detail, but mainly in so far as it bore on the origins and development of capitalism." Hobsbawm adds that "now it is generally agreed that Marx and Engels' observations on pre-capitalist epochs rest on far less thorough study than Marx's description and analysis of capitalism."[23] Marx assumed *a priori* that the movement of history prior to the emergence of modern bourgeois capitalism had a definite link with capitalism. In his view, his study of pre-capitalistic economic formations confirmed his assumption. However, he did not demonstrate conclusively how the connection might be empirically verified. The Hegelian influence on Marx might account for Marx's assumption that there is a real unity, which the title "Pre-Capitalist Economic Formations" connotes.

Hobsbawm provides a useful analysis and summary of the main ideas of the *Formen*. Noting that "the *Formen* are both more general and more specific than the Preface, though they too ... are not 'history' in the strict sense," Hobsbawm argues that Marx is concerned with establishing "the general mechanism of *all* social change." Hobsbawm explains that this mechanism is the formation of social relations of production which correspond to a definite stage of development of the material forces of production; the periodic development of conflicts between the forces and relations of production; the 'epochs of social revolution' in which the relations once again adjust themselves to the level of the forces. This general analysis does not imply any statement about specific historical periods, forces and relations of production whatever.[24]

Hobsbawn points out that Marx's inclusion of pre-capitalist formations in his view of history as universal history is premised "on a materialist and not an idealist basis."[25]

Second, Hobsbawm notes that in "the *Formen* [Marx] seek(s) to formulate the *content* of history in its most general form. This content is *progress*." By progress, Marx means "something objectively definable, and at the same time pointing to what is desirable." Taking Marx's general description of progress at its broadest, Hobsbawn interprets it to mean "the triumph of the free development of all men."[26] According to Hobsbawm, Marx takes it as axiomatic that the phenomenon of progress (or emancipation) will be objectively seen and recognised as such. "Progress of course is observable in the growing emancipation of man from nature and his growing control over nature."[27] That this triumph is not only desirable but inevitable is not a matter of abstract, ideological hope and longing. It is also a matter of the empirical accuracy of Marx's analysis. "The strength of the Marxist belief in the triumph of the free development of all men, depends not on the strength of Marx's hope for it, but on the assumed correctness of the analysis that this is indeed where historical development eventually leads mankind."[28]

Marx distinguishes four principal pre-capitalist historical periods directly related to the socio-economic progress of society: the "Asiatic, ancient, feudal and modern bourgeois."[29] These four periods have followed in a natural progression from one to the next. Marx himself admits that there have been periods in which different societies have been at different socio-economic stages. However, he is more convinced that the so-called "Germanic system"—a particular manifestation of feudalism—is "the direct ancestor of bourgeois society" than are other forms of society.[30] Admitting to the difficulty in ascertaining from Marx's notes an accurate schematisation of the historical stages, Hobsbawm suggests:

The oriental (and Slavonic) forms are historically closest to man's origins, since they conserve the functioning primitive (village) community in the midst of the more elaborate social superstructure, and have an insufficiently developed class system .... The ancient and Germanic systems, though also primary—i.e. not *derived* from the oriental—represent a somewhat more articulated form of evolution out of primitive communalism; but the 'Germanic system' as such does not form a special socio-economic formation. It forms the socio-economic formation of feudalism in conjunction with the medieval town (the locus of the emergence of the autonomous craft production). This combination then, which emerges during the Middle Ages, forms the third phase. Bourgeois society, emerging out of feudalism, forms the fourth.[31]

Hobsbawm's summary is ambiguous and gives the erroneous impression of a "unilinear view of history." He, therefore, immediately adds the corrective:

The statement that the Asiatic, ancient, feudal and bourgeois formations are 'progressive' does not therefore imply any simple unilinear view of history, not a simple view that all history is progress. It merely states that each of these systems is in crucial respects further removed from the primitive state of man.[32]

Hobsbawm concludes that for Marx the relevance of his (Marx's) analysis of "particular socio-economic formations" is in the light it sheds on the "long-term transformation." To speak in chronological terms is to embrace centuries and continents in a broad sweep of thought.[33]

What picture of human beings does Marx give us here? The progress which Marx argues occurs in history, the growing emancipation of human beings which Marx sees arising out of the changing productive forces, is one of "human individualization."[34] Beginning with human beings in their original natural conditions down through the centuries until the eruption of modern bourgeois society, human beings have suffered the paradoxical experience of increasing isolation and alienation while, at the same time, they have moved closer to "the ideal of free individual development." In bourgeois society that ideal is closer to its realisation "than it ever was in all previous phases of history."[35] Reflecting upon the error of imagining primeval subservience of human beings to one another as a *natural condition,* Marx tells us:

> It is of course easy to imagine a powerful, physically superior person, who
> first captures animals and then captures men in order to make them catch
> animals for him; in brief, one who uses man as a naturally occurring
> condition for his reproduction like any other living natural thing; his own
> labour being exhausted in the act of domination. But such a view is stupid,
> though it may be correct from the point of view of a given tribal or
> communal entity; for it takes the *isolated* man as its starting-point.[36]

In support of his argument that individualism is more characteristic of bourgeois
political economy than any other stage in history, Marx boldly asserts once again that
"man is only individualised through the process of history." The human being
"originally appears as a *generic being, a tribal being, a herd animal* —though by no
means as a 'political animal' in the political sense. Exchange itself is a major agent
of this individualisation. It makes the herd animal superfluous and dissolves it."[37]
Marx intends us to understand that the social relations in which human beings
originally functioned were transformed, for those communal relations eventually
gave way to individualism and separation.

Marx was convinced, Hobsbawn argues, that in this state of total alienation there
are "immense possibilities for humanity." Hobsbawm points us to a passage in
Marx "full of hope and splendour:"[38]

> Thus the ancient conception, in which man alway appears (in however
> narrowly national, religious or political a definition) as the aim of
> production, seems very much more exalted than the modern world, in
> which production is the aim of man and wealth the aim of production. ...
> In bourgeois political economy—and in the epoch of production to which it
> corresponds—this complete elaboration of what lies within man, appears as
> the total alienation, and the destruction of all fixed, one-sided purposes as
> the sacrifice of the end in itself to a wholly external compulsion.[39]

Here Marx argues that although human beings in bourgeois society experience
"the universality of needs, capacities, enjoyments, productive powers, etc.," as "total
alienation," nevertheless, these powers are latently hidden within bourgeois society.
This is the occasion for hope in the future transcendence of alienation—the future is

dialectically present.

C.
"Crude Communism" to "Final Communism:" De-alienation through History

Abolition of one or more forms of alienation—for example, economic, political, social, religious, or ideological alienation—still leaves alienation intact. However, to treat all forms of alienation as equal in relation to the source of alienation is misleading and ultimately unproductive for the total transcendence of alienation. Alienation is at its root socio-economically determined. This is the beginning point. Consequently, an attack on private property strikes at the very nucleus of capitalism. This is a historical process, just as the process of pre-capitalist economic formations was historical. The movement from capitalism to final communism begins with inauthentic or crude communism. In other words, the process does not occur overnight; it takes time. There is a gradual humanisation of humankind and society.[40] We now turn to the development of communism which Marx discussed at some length in the *1844 Manuscripts*. In describing this development, Marx refers to three stages or forms of communism.

To begin with, crude communism, in its attack on private property, appears "first of all as generalized property." It is "in its original form only a generalization and completion of private property." At this stage its appearance has

> a dual form: firstly, it is faced with such a great domination of material property that it wishes to destroy everything that cannot be possessed by everybody as private property; it wishes to abstract forcibly from talent, etc. It considers immediate physical ownership as the sole aim of life and being. The category of worker is not abolished but extended to all men. The relationship of the community to the world of things remains that of private property.[41]

In the stage of "crude communism," private property is taken to its logical conclusion: it is "only community property." The primary difference between this stage and the previous one which it has negated is not that alienation has ended, but "that the community continues to maintain a relationship of ownership with the world of things."[42]

In describing the nature of this form of communism, Marx considers the degeneration of women in marriage to a universal state of prostitution as analogous to the universalisation of private property. He writes:

> This process of opposing general private property to private property is expressed in the animal form of opposing to marriage (which is of course a form of exclusive private property) the community of women where the woman becomes the common property of the community. One might say that the idea of the community of women reveals the open secret of this completely crude and unthinking type of communism. Just as women pass from marriage to universal prostitution, so the whole world of wealth, that is the objective essence of man, passes from the relationship of exclusive marriage to the private property owner to the relationship of universal prostitution with the community.[43]

Private property is the crystallised essence of workers' labour in the hands of non-workers. By universalising this essence, the workers gain control over their property and thereby end alienation. Before this stage occurs, however, in the intermediate stage of crude communism, the phenomenon of private property in the hands of a few becomes widespread everywhere and is no longer confined to a few select societies. Marx's analogy of prostitution to explain this stage in the development of private property is not clear. Marx sees the parallel in terms of the relative increase in freedom: the woman in marriage, by becoming the property of the community, is freed from her husband who hitherto had exclusive rights over her. Marx infers that this change in the status of woman is parallel to community ownership of the means of production. The ambiguity of this freedom is that the woman is reduced to prostitution. Freedom from the single capitalist (husband) leads to enslavement to the whole community. Prostitution is therefore not a final stage. The woman must eventually be freed from the community. Interpreted this way, Marx's analogy of prostitution supports his argument that crude communism is only a transitional stage which must be overcome by final communism.

Under crude communism, the alienated human essence is universalised.

> Universal envy setting itself up as a power is the concealed form of greed which merely asserts itself and satisfies itself in another way. The thoughts

of every private property owner as such are at least turned against those richer than they as an envious desire to level down. This envious desire is precisely the essence of competition.[44]

The process of competition must run its course before it can be transcended. Thus Marx continues:

> Crude communism is only the completion of this envy and levelling down to a preconceived minimum. It has a particular and limited standard. How little this abolition of private property constitutes a real appropriation is proved by the abstract negation of the whole world of culture and civilization, a regression to the unnatural simplicity of the poor man without any needs who has not even arrived at the stage of private property, let alone got beyond it.[45]

Such a process may be rightly called "generalized capitalism," since its principal tendency is towards universalised private property. Everything that "cannot be possessed by all as private property" will be abolished.[46] Furthermore, since crude communism is characterised by a real degeneracy, it is limited in scope and should not be confused with final, positive communism which will usher in the age of de-alienation, of real and not "sham universality," where humankind "is the universality and power of society" and not capital, as is definitely the case in crude communism.[47] In summary, then, "the first positive abolition of private property, crude communism, is thus the only form in which appears the ignominy of private property that wishes to establish itself as the positive essence of the community."[48]

Should transcendence end with crude communism, alienation would still continue to plague humankind and society. This is a sober warning to those who optimistically argue that the fundamental problems of humanity would be solved if private property were abolished through a radical programme of state nationalisation. It is an un-Marxian optimism, which, however, is not unrelated to the ambiguity in Marx's thought concerning the relation between the abolition of private property and the transcendence of alienation. It is helpful to see nationalisation of all property and industry as a form of generalised capitalism under crude communism. True to Marx, we are able to maintain the dynamic of this process.

The second form of communism is political in nature, and it is either democratic or despotic. Marx claims that, though the state may be subsequently abolished, political communism still remains incomplete and is "still under the influence of private property, i.e. the alienation of man." In spite of these deficiencies, however, communism with or without the state "knows itself already to be the reintegration or return of man into himself, the abolition of man's self-alienation." There is certainly a most decisive difference between the first two forms of communism. Yet, Marx warns, optimism must not run so high that the transitory and limited nature of this second stage is forgotten or intentionally overlooked. The inveterate enemy is private property, whose alienating influence irrevocably persists. Marx explains that, since the second form of communism "has not yet grasped the positive essence of private property or the human nature of needs, it is still imprisoned and contaminated by private property. It has understood its concept, but not yet its essence."[49] At the stage of political communism, proletarian awareness of the situation has not yet matched the revolutionary *praxis* which is explicitly and implicitly demanded. *Theoria* and *praxis* do not as yet constitute that dialectical and revolutionary unity which is necessary for total human emancipation.

The third form of communism will finally achieve the unity of *theoria* and *praxis*. Final communism is the solution to the riddle of history and knows itself to be this solution. Private property will be abolished and alienation transcended.

D.
The Class Struggle and the Proletarian Sense of Messianic Mission

In his critique of Hegel's conception of reality as the self-positing of *Absolute Idea* and of the historical movement as a movement of consciousness, Marx argues that it is the socio-economic conditions that determine consciousness and not consciousness that determines the socio-economic conditions. To conceive of the transcendence of alienation simply as an act of consciousness not rooted in the real transformative movement of the mode of production leads to further alienation. However, Marx goes on to assert that consciousness, *theoria*, which arises out of and is inextricably bound up with *praxis,* is indispensable for the abolition of all forms of alienation. Liberating consciousness is the consciousness of real, living human beings. It is a safeguard (at least partially) against the accusation that Marx is a dialectical materialist who sees the productive process, with human beings as part of it and not its centre, as the centre of human existence.

Marx does not subscribe to the view of an independent Nature following its own inherent course of historical development.[50] Human beings, Nature, and Society are all bound together in a mutually interactive process.[51] History is the product of human activity. It is the history of human alienation. This is pre-history, as opposed to real history which begins with the eventual transcendence of alienation. When history is viewed only as the process of dialectical materialism, then the "conscious-shaping" influence of human beings upon history (that is, their conscious transcendence of alienation and creation of a dynamic, non-alienated future) is denied reality. Hence, instead of speaking of dialectical materialism, we prefer to speak of historical materialism to describe Marx's conception of history. The latter does not deny the dialectical nature of history; rather, it acknowledges the primacy of humankind's shaping influence, especially in the transcendence of alienation, in the very dialectical movement of history.

With this in mind, we may now freely explore Marx's description of the messianic mission of the proletariat in the overcoming of alienation. In our description of Marx's concept of alienation, we have already seen that both the capitalist and the worker are alienated, suffering from alienating consciousness. The capitalist is driven by egoistic, limited desires, unaware of the alienating influence of the productive process as the root of all alienation. Through ideology (false consciousness), capitalists safeguard their position even while they attempt to alleviate the burden of the workers; but their efforts are to no avail in ending alienation and effecting human emancipation which the capitalists cannot really grasp. The workers, for their part, are ignorant of their condition and are the unsuspecting victims of ideological oppression by the dominant class in society. The workers do not possess a liberating awareness of their condition as members of a wider socio-economic class. "Other worldly" liberation is projected because of the proletariat's ignorance of their real state, the origin of it and the possibility of its historical transcendence. Such degradation reaches its nadir under bourgeois capitalism.

Notwithstanding this depressing state of human existence, Marx boldly announces "good news:" capitalism is carrying within its womb the necessity and real possibility of a proletarian revolution which would overthrow capitalism and its alienating stranglehold on humankind and society.

In the *Manifesto of the Communist Party*, Marx and Engels waste no time in announcing the new dawn that is about to arise under the auspices of the proletarian class. History, they argue, has been a history of class struggles:

Freeman and slave, politician and plebian, lord and serf, guildmaster and
journeyman, in a word, oppressor and oppressed, stood in constant
opposition to one another, carried on an uninterrupted, now hidden, now
open fight, a fight that each time ended, either in a revolutionary
reconstitution of society at large, or in the common ruin of the contending
classes.[52]

History has been characterised by conflict, revolution, transformation and ruin.
Society has never been conflict-free. Conflict and contradiction have intensified over
the centuries until the class struggle has polarised the bourgeois (capitalist) and the
proletariat (working class). But, the good news is: "Our epoch, the epoch of the
bourgeois, possesses, however, this distinctive feature: It has simplified the class
antagonisms. Society as a whole is more and more splitting up into two great hostile
camps, into two great classes directly facing each other—bourgeois and
proletariat."[53]

Both classes are the products of the socio-economic development of society. In a
rapid and cursory description of the development of the bourgeoisie, Marx and
Engels assert that "the modern bourgeoisie is itself the product of a long course of
development, of a series of revolutions in the modes of production and of
exchange." They note that "each step in the development of the bourgeoisie was
accompanied by a corresponding political advance of the class."[54] an advance made
through revolutionary action on the part of the bourgeois class. The bourgeoisie's
role, then, is in marked contrast to its present reactionary and anti-revolutionary role.
Marx and Engels observe that, for instance, in the transition from feudalism to
capitalism, the bourgeois class has reduced every relationship to its base—money
relation and economic exploitation—even as it has facilitated the gradual destruction
of all forms of deference. Marx and Engels explain further:

The bourgeoisie, wherever it has got the upper hand, has put an end to all
feudal, patriarchal, idyllic relations. It has pitilessly torn asunder the motley
feudal ties that bound man to his 'natural superiors,' and has left no other
bond between man and man than naked self-interest, than callous 'cash
payment.' It has drowned the most heavenly ecstacies of religious fervour,
of chivalrous enthusiasm, of philistine sentimentalism, in the icy water of
egotistical calculation. It has resolved personal worth into exchange value,
and in place of the numberless indefeasible chartered freedoms, has set up

that single, unconscionable freedom—Free Trade. ... [F]or exploitation, veiled by religious and political illusions, it has substituted naked, shameless, direct, brutal exploitation. The bourgeoisie has stripped of its halo every occupation hitherto honoured and looked up to with reverent awe. It has converted the physician, the lawyer, the priest, the poet, ... into its paid wage-labourers.[55]

For the bourgeois class to continue to exist, it constantly has to revolutionise "the instruments of production, and thereby the relations of production, and with them the whole relations of society."[56] The bourgeois class is convinced that it must be in the driver's seat if it is to survive and its dominance in all areas of life is to be perpetuated. Its impregnable and dominant status was achieved because over the years it has rapidly expanded and exploited a world market, improved the productive process and the means of communication, in addition to having "created enormous cities, ... greatly increased the urban population as compared with the rural ...."[57] Its record during its relatively short rule of about one hundred years is most impressive. Summing up this record, Marx and Engels write:

The bourgeoisie ... has created more massive and more colossal productive forces than have all preceding generations together. Subjection of nature's forces to man, machinery application of chemistry to industry and agriculture, steam-navigation, railways, electric telegraphs, clearing of whole continents for cultivation, canalization of rivers, whole populations conjured out of the ground—what earlier century had even a presentiment that such productive forces slumbered in the lap of social labour?[58]

It is obviously an explosive situation and, as far as Marx and Engels are concerned, one in need of immediate radical redress.[59] The time is ripe, for the bourgeoisie is no longer able to maintain its ascendancy. "The weapons with which the bourgeoisie felled feudalism to the ground are now turned against the bourgeoisie itself."[60]

In theological language, Marx and Engels envisage that, under capitalism the "fulness of time" has come. Prior to this time, the contradiction between the forces and relations of production had not coincided with the emergence of the proletarian class which is so totally alienated. Only when this coincidence occurs in history will the messianic and salvific proletarian revolution occur. Returning to the *German Ideology*, we are reminded that this epocal moment in history is not like previous moments, in which revolution was conceived and hatched in the minds of the philosophers. Marx and Engels state:

> This sum of productive forces, capital funds and social forms of intercourse, which every individual and every generation finds in existence as something given, is the real basis of what the philosophers have conceived as 'substance' and 'essence of man', and what they have deified and attacked: a real basis which is not in the least disturbed, in its effect and influence on the development of men, by the fact that these philosophers revolt against it as 'self-consciousness' and the 'unique'.[61]

The bourgeoisie have disturbed the real basis of society but they are unable to effect the abolition of alienation. The moment has not arrived for this to be enacted. Only when the socio-economic conditions are fully ripe will the great leap forward occur.[62] Marx and Engels explain:

> These conditions of life, which different generations find in existence, determine also whether or not the revolutionary convulsion periodically recurring in history will be strong enough to overthrow the basis of everything that exists. And if these material elements of a complete revolution are not present—namely, on the one hand the existing productive forces, on the other the formation of a revolutionary mass, which revolts not only against separate conditions of the existing society, but against the existing 'production of life' itself, the 'total activity' on which it was based—then it is absolutely immaterial for practical development whether the *idea* of this revolution has been expressed a hundred times already, as the history of communism proves.[63]

Even in their own time, Marx and Engels made triumphalistic pronouncements concerning the dawning of—again, in theological language—precisely such a "kairos." They write: "But not only has the bourgeoisie forged the weapons that bring death to itself, it has also called into existence the men who are to wield those weapons—the modern working class—the proletarians."[64] We rightly wonder what it is that makes the proletariat so unique.[65] Marx explains that they are the most debased class and are therefore the only class which, in seeking to emancipate itself from its conditions, is capable of emancipating the whole of humanity and of ending all alienation. In Kantian terms, only the proletarian workers are capable of making the movement from a class "in-itself" to a class "for itself" into a movement of universal consequences. Axelos summarises Marx's argument:

> Deprived of all property and all satisfaction, the working masses, even though they activate productive forces and produce the wealth, take account of the fact that they have only to overturn those who hold the means of production and direct the relations of production in order to gain access to a human existence. Being reduced to a state of subhumanity and crushed by inhuman powers, the majority of mankind is the motor of the movement that leads to the appropriation of man by man and for man. The individuals that compose this class are no longer empirical, particular individuals. They are nothing and they have nothing in the present world.[66]

In the face of such utter alienation, Marx and Engels sound their clarion call: "The proletarians have nothing to lose but their chains. They have a world to win. Workingmen of all countries, unite!"[67]

But the proletarians can only emancipate themselves and the whole of humanity if their consciousness is transformed. Marx implies that he anticipates such a transformation.[68] In his peculiar "sketchy" style, Marx draws the following conclusion: unlike those who conceived of real movement in thought alone, the proletariat conceive of historic movement in terms of the real, sensuous, material conditions of life which are firmly rooted in the production process. Whereas their historical precursors never fully grasped the messianic mission to emancipate the whole of humanity, the proletariat are fired by the vision of the possibility and inevitability of an unalienated future.[69] It is a future which is only theirs to create through their liberating *praxis*. They are no longer the victims of a false consciousness which leads them docilely to accept their lot in silence. There is a feeling of solidarity and mutual independence among them.[70] The proletariat is the only class in human history that is capable of discerning the readiness of the objective conditions for the abolition of all alienation. Only the proletariat can take the necessary steps to turn the productive process towards a communist future which, in turn, will be transcended.[71] In seeking to establish a connection between the proletarian consciousness, which Marx envisages, and Hegel's notion of the awakening consciousness (which is so important in the dialectic of Hegel's *Phenomenology*), Jean Hyppolite clarifies the nature of the proletarian consciousness:

> The awakening of consciousness is not the passive reflection of some state
> of affairs. It is that which alone can embody the dialectical contradiction
> and at the same time demand its resolution. The act in which the proletariat
> becomes conscious of the alienation of man signifies a contradiction within
> man himself. This contradiction is a real one and demands a solution
> precisely for the reason that it is at once *objective and subjective.* It
> expresses an empirical situation—man posited, as it were, outside himself,
> like an *object*—and the negation of that situation—man as an inalienable
> subject for whom it is impossible to recognize himself as a mere object. For
> Marx the proletariat is the subject that experiences to the extreme the
> contradiction of the human condition and is thereby capable of resolving it
> forever.[72]

Only the proletariat is capable of active, revolutionary self-consciousness.

The transformation of proletarian consciousness—the subjective side of the
conditions preparatory for the revolutionary emancipation of alienation—has a
strong note of inevitability.[73] Marx speaks in terms that would suggest that the
revolution is a foregone conclusion. He anticipates that both the objective and
subjective conditions of the revolution will occur simultaneously under bourgeois
capitalism. In spite of this, Schlomo Avineri raises the crucial question of whether
the awakening of the revolutionary consciousness in the proletariat is indeed
inevitable, given the objective conditions. He argues that such a question takes us
back once again to the problem of "determinism versus voluntarism." In his view,
the dilemma is transcended by the dialectical nature of the revolutionary
consciousness of the proletariat. However, he insists that, instead of providing any
guarantee concerning the success of the revolution prior to its occurrence or simply
assuming *a priori* that the revolution will succeed, Marx "only indicates its
possibilities historically." That is, he indicates that the revolution will occur,
provided there is a unity of theory and *praxis,* of the subjective and objective
conditions in history. Avineri sums up his argument thus:

> If a revolutionary consciousness exists, then the revolution is bound to
> happen. The activist and practical elements of this consciousness imply that
> circumstances will change with the self-change of the proletariat. In other

words, under these conditions the revolution is already taking place. If, on the other hand, such a consciousness is lacking, then the revolution lacks its main impulse and is stillborn. If the proletariat has self-consciousness, it will sustain the revolution. Its self-consciousness is already a major component of the revolutionary situation. If, however, the proletariat is still unaware of its own historical position, if it does not possess an adequate world view, then the objective conditions by themselves will not create the revolution until and unless the proletariat grasps that by shaping its own view of the world it also changes it.[74]

The proletarian revolution is a contingent revolution. Marx is not primarily concerned with predicting the inevitability of the revolution without paying regard to the nature and state of the revolutionary forces in history.

This interpretation of Marx is of special significance for our analysis of Marx's teaching about the historical inevitability of the revolution. It raises the following questions: Will the proletariat really possess such a consciousness? If they do not, and, consequently, the revolution remains in the womb of history or is stillborn, do they still qualify for the title proletariat in the Marxian sense? Given that the capitalist class will not be able to go beyond a certain point in preventing the revolution, and that sin is nothing more or less than historical alienation which humankind will ultimately transcend, who will ultimately bear the blame and responsibility for the non-occurrence of the union of theory and *praxis*? Furthermore, what if men and women, such as Marx and Engels, from the bourgeois class or more accurately the bourgeois intelligentsia, are possessed of a messianic consciousness but obviously are not the most deprived and dehumanised people in the world, do they qualify for the description proletariat?

The proletarian revolution has not yet occurred; it remains eschatological. Consequently, the questions above remain rhetorical. However, they are critical, not only for a historical appraisal of Marx's predictions, but also for a realistic and honest appraisal of all revolutions which are in one way or another connected to Marx's philosophy. All too often revolutions which were ostensibly advocated and enacted on behalf of the proletariat have resulted in further and even more inhuman oppression. While in some instances failure leads to cynicism, disenchantment, and even despair, in others it stirs the utopian zeal to lead the "true proletarian revolution." In short, Marx's "proletarian soteriology" continues to entice both proletarian worker and bourgeois revolutionary, self-styled or real.

90

E.
Marx and Engels: Dialectical and Historical Materialism

So far, we have observed that, according to Marx, the "pre-capitalist economic formations" have led to the birth of bourgeois capitalism, and that the development of communism from crude communism to positive, emancipating communism has emerged from , and is leading to, the total abolition of capitalism. We have treated the two movements as "separate" historical phenomena. The separation is chronologically necessary, since they occur in two different time periods: pre- and post-capitalist. However, they are bound together in an inseparable unity, since they are dialectically connected to each other. The actual historical movement is of one mode emerging from out of the womb of the one immediately preceeding it. Of course, Marx understands these modes in terms of their socio-economic bases, from which all superstructures are dialectically derived. Dialectic also involves negation, for what comes out of it is something new and different from its immediate precursor.[75] Nevertheless, an essential unity exists between the two modes. For Marx the Hegelian, it is the negation of the negation: the negation of all that negates human beings as authentic beings, that which alienates human beings and makes them mere things.[76]

The dialectical conception of real, material, sensuous reality is the primary argument used in support of the view that Marx was no determinist, be it teleological, economic, materialist, technological or mechanical.[77] Avineri explains:

> Marx's approach to communism demonstrates his belief that the crystallization of socialist forms of society cannot be achieved through a deterministic teleology, but grows out of the causal analysis of existing social forces. If communism cannot be understood otherwise than by its emergence from capitalist society, then the study of capitalism provides the best means to comprehend the development that will ultimately bring communism about. Moreover the emergence of communism from the womb of capitalist society draws attention to the dialectical relationship between the two societies. The possibility for a development in the direction of communism thus depends on a prior development of capitalism.[78]

Marx views the dialectical relationship between capitalism and communism as characteristic of the emergence of capitalism from its "pre-capitalist economic formations." Avineri concludes that "communism is nothing else than the dialectical abolition ... of those hidden potentialities which could not have been historically realized under the limiting conditions of capitalism."[79] Avineri is cognisant of Marx's implicit assertion, in the *Communist Manifesto*, that "what the bourgeoisie produces is above all its own grave diggers. Its fall and the victory of the proletariat are equally inevitable."[80] Commenting on this passage, Avineri says, "Capitalism thus creates urges that it cannot itself satisfy and it is in this sense that Marx refers to its digging its own grave."[81]

It is instructive for our purpose to examine in some detail the attempts by scholars to interpret Marx's dialectic in light of the apparent controversy concerning the inevitability of communism. We shall concern ourselves with the works of two scholars: William H. Shaw and Bertell Ollman.

In his study on Marx's theory of history, Shaw declares his intention "to champion a technological-determinist interpretation" in his work.[82] He explains that his interpretation "credits the forces of production with the determining role in history." Finally, he attempts "to illuminate more precisely the primacy of the productive forces and their explanatory role within historical materialism."[83] At first glance, Shaw's exposition of the foregoing purpose would be better placed under the discussion of Marx's materialist conception of reality. This conclusion follows the obvious concern of the writer with the primacy of the productive forces over all other forces in the historical movement of humankind and society. According to Shaw, "Marx believes that the introduction of new relations of production is contingent on the development of the productive forces in a way in which those forces are not dependent on the relations." Shaw adds that Marx was convinced that "without a sufficient level of productivity, communal production relations would only result in stagnation and decline in the mode of production—from which class distinctions would re-emerge."[84] Anticipating criticism of his Marxian hypothesis, Shaw states:

> A critic, even if he accepted this, might argue that given an adequate high level of the productive forces, certain superstructural elements are still necessary for a change in production relations. In a sense Marx would agree with this, but he avers that the presence of those other factors stem from the existence of the new productive forces. The emergence of these

forces (and, one supposes, men's consciousness of this) both stimulates
and makes possible the introduction of new relations of production.[85]

But the conclusion that Shaw is concerned with Marx's materialist conception of history does not rule out his discussion of the dynamic change that Marx sees occurring in human beings, society and nature through their dialectical inter-relationship.[86]

Do these changes in the relations of production and all forms of superstructural activities simply arise out of changes in the mode of production in a simple and direct relationship of cause and effect? Shaw replies in the negative, arguing that Marx did not propound an economic determinism.[87] To conceive of the relationship in direct and not dialectical terms would invariably lead to the postulation of "laws of development," which would mean that society simply follows an evolutionary process governed by pre-determined, inexorable laws. This would rule out the efficacy of human decision-making and creativity in determining and shaping society. Human beings would be simply mechanistically-determined and continually characterised by alienation, with no hope of real and total liberation. In short, human beings would not be the centre and in control of human history. On the question of economic determinism, Shaw writes:

> Just as for Marx there are no substantive general laws of economic life, though each period has its own, so with the connections between the economic structure and superstructural relations. It is a law for Marx that the superstructure is derived from the base, but this is a law about laws: in each social formation, more specific laws govern the precise nature of this general derivation. Engels seems to have appreciated this: 'All history must be studied afresh, the conditions of existence of the different formations of society must be examined individually before the attempt is made to deduce from them the political, civil-law, aesthetic, philosophic, religious, etc. views corresponding to them.'[88]

According to Shaw's analysis, the connection between the "economic structure and the superstructural relations" is not governed by inexorable laws which stand objectively outside of the particular historical epoch. Rather, these laws are integral and unique to the particular epoch in which they operate. Therefore, in using the term laws, Shaw points to Marx's conception of historical processes as dynamic rather than static *relations*. Moreover, when Shaw refers to Marx's thesis that "the superstructure is derived from the base" as "a law for Marx," it is not a law in the natural sciences. It cannot be tested by the empirical framework of the natural sciences. Indeed, to speak of presupposition, premise or assumption rather than law would be more appropriate.[89] Throughout Marx's works, the thesis that *base* is prior to and also gives rise to *superstructure* is central to his presuppositional framework.

Marx argues that the fundamental relationship between base and superstructure is dialectical. Not only does the base influence the superstructure, but the reverse also occurs. This process is characterised by progress, which arises out of the conflict between base and superstructure or, more precisely, between the mode and the relations of production which are in perpetual conflict. According to Shaw, Marx assumes that this conflict did not contain its own resolution. "Marx held that any specific capitalist society would in fact be racked by the contradictions which his theory delineates." However Marx "would not have maintained that it would proceed acquiescently to the end point of those contradictions in order to be redeemed by the negation of the negation." This conclusion conflicts with Marx's explicit and implicit statements about the historical transcendence of alienation through communism.

In his explanation of his interpretation of Marx, Shaw states:

> The point is not just that capitalism is prevented by the intervention of the proletariat from proceeding to its final collapse, but there is no final contradiction followed by disintegration. Capitalism begets contradictory tendencies, which increase in strength, but it neither contains within itself the possibility of their reconciliation nor permits the final triumph of one over the other: each violent disruption only restores the disturbed equilibrium. The increasingly antagonistic propensities of capitalism render it historically untenable: they do not imply that the system must 'self-destruct'—that is, that its continued existence becomes logically impossible.[90]

The problem with Shaw's argument is that, in refuting the deterministic exponents of Marx's theory of history, he minimises the use Marx made of Hegel's dialectic.[91] The minimisation of the influence of Hegel's dialectic upon Marx's conception of historical reality inevitably distorts Marx's conception. Shaw's distortion of Marx naturally follows from the notable omission of Marx's philosophic perspective from

Shaw's analysis.[92] Shaw's conclusion should therefore be viewed in light of the historical distance between Marx's time and the present, and, especially, in light of the fact that the proletarian revolution has not occurred in that interim period and that it seems unlikely to occur as Marx had predicted. Where the accuracy of Marx's analysis and prediction are brought into question, Shaw's argument provides plausible grounds for changing Marx's imminent eschatology to a less imminent one.

Contradictions in contemporary capitalism are certainly more varied and complex than those of the capitalism of Marx's day. These contradictions have accompanied the unprecedented technological development that has occurred since then. To be guided by Shaw's perspective does not allow for an accurate assessment of Marx's projection of historical de-alienation arising out of the contradictions in capitalism. This is a form of revisionism. Moreover, despite Shaw's decision to avoid the philosophical Marx, his analysis has a noticeable Hegelian influence.[93] Hegel conceives of reality as the self-positing of Absolute Spirit which externalises itself in order to realise itself in the process of objectification, which alienates and is then subsequently transcended. This process continues *ad infinitum* with each succeeding transcendence, attaining a level higher than the one previously attained. But in Hegel, alienation is an ineradicable reality. Marx, on the contrary, conceives of both alienation and its transcendence as historical phenomena. Alienation can be abolished completely. Despite the deficiency in Shaw's treatment of Marx's conviction that the dialectical transcendence of alienation is inevitable, Shaw opens up for us the crucial question of whether transcendence is dependent not only on the forces of production and the proletariat working harmoniously, but also on some force "outside" of the material conditions of life. Shaw points out that capitalism itself does not contain the possibility of the reconciliation of its inherent antagonistic propensities. At the same time, the antagonistic propensities "do not imply that the system must 'self-destruct'."[94] Contradiction is inherent in dialectic and, for Marx, reality is dialectical. Hence, there is no final, inevitable resolution of contradiction— that would be the end of the dialectic!

Ollman provides a provocative analysis of Marx's theory of history based on a "relational" concept of reality. He recognises that Marx openly acknowledges that a conceptual framework is indispensable to humankind's revolutionary transformation of history. Marx sees that concepts are absolutely essential for human beings to have a comprehensive grasp of the whole of historical reality.[95] Marx himself demonstrates the need for concepts in his own analysis of the historical human condition. Ollman does not find that Marx's approach, properly understood, contradicts Marx's materialist conception of reality. With this presuppositioin in mind, Ollman proceeds to elaborate a "relational" view of reality which, he argues, is central to Marx's thought.

"In his unfinished Introduction to the *Critique of Political Economy,*" Marx draws attention to the "distinction between subject and categories." Ollman points out the indispensable function of concepts as mediators of reality. "This distinction between subject and categories is simple recognition of the fact that our knowledge of the real world is mediated through the construction of concepts in which to think about it; our contact with reality, in so far as we become aware of it, is contact with a conceptualized reality."[96]

Ollman's interpretation of Marx's understanding of concepts reminds us of the definition of symbol. A symbol participates in the reality it describes.[97] For example, having pointed out that Marx declares the categories he is describing "to be 'forms,' 'manifestations' and 'aspects' of their own subject matter," and that "the categories of bourgeois society 'serve as the expression of its conditions and the comprehension of its own organization',"[98] Ollman concludes that the categories "express the real conditions necesary for their application, but as meaningful, systematized and understood conditions. This is not merely a matter of categories being limited in what they can be used to describe; the story itself is thought to be somehow part of the very concepts with which it is told."[99] Ollman offers another summary:

> Marx grasped each political-economic concept as a component of society itself, in his words as an 'abstract one-sided relation of an already given concrete and living aggregate'; that it is intimately linked with other social components to form a particular structure; and that this whole, or at least its more significant parts, is expressed in the concept itself.[100]

Ollman assumes that Marx's presupposition that concepts are derived from the socio-economic base of society is a sound one. In fact, according to Ollman, the intrinsic unity between the socio-economic base and the concepts used to describe it is clearly conveyed by the concepts themselves. Ollman therefore concludes that the unity must not be broken and the two components divorced from each other.[101]

He asserts further that the distinctiveness "in Marx's conception of social reality [indeed all reality] is best approached through the cluster of qualities he ascribes to particular social factors."[102] He illustrates his argument by referring to Marx's conception of capital. He points out that "where capital 'is something purely material, a mere element in the labor process',"[103] Marx portrays it as " 'that kind of property which exploits wage-labor, and which cannot increase except on condition of getting a new supply of wage-labor for fresh exploitation'."[104] In contrast to the view expressed here, where the inherent relational unity of the social factors is absent, Ollman makes the following suggestion:

> What requires emphasis is that the relation between capital and labor is treated as a function of capital itself, and part of the meaning of 'capital'. This tie is extended to cover the worker as well, where Marx refers to him as 'variable capital.'[105] The capitalist is incorporated into the same whole: 'capital is necessarily at the same time the capitalist ... the capitalist is contained in the concept of capital.'[106]

Ollman attempts to demonstrate, through these references to the varied conceptions of capital, that there is "a conception of capital," which Marx offers "in which the factors we generally think of as externally related to it are viewed as co-elements in a single structure." In summary, Ollman's thesis is: *"Every factor which enters into Marx's study of capitalism is a 'definite social relationship'."*[107]

Ollman applies the relational model of reality to Marx's analysis of the world which is in a state of perpetual change. In his application, he assumes that each social factor is "internally related to it own past and future forms, as well as the past and future forms of surrounding factors."[108] Marx sees the world as a "Totality" comprised of social factors that are constantly changing, thereby producing new and different matrices of social relations. Consequently, the "Totality" is not static but is dynamic, always acting and being acted upon by its constituent factors. A useful analogy of the dynamic state of both the "Totality" and its constituent factors is that of the image of the earth spinning on its axis while it rotates around the sun (the former movement is a smaller movement within a wider movement). Present, past, and future are all related and exist as a unity. Ollman sums up his explication:

> The present, according to this relational model, becomes part of a continuum stretching from a definable past to a knowable (if not always predictable) future. Tomorrow is today extended. To speak of such a relation between the present and the future within the context of formal logic would indicate belief in a vitalistic principle, divine will or some other

metaphysical device. But, here, all social change is conceived of as a coming to be of what potentially is, as the further unfolding of an already existing process, and hence, discoverable by a study of this process taken as a spatial-temporal Relation.[109]

The fluidity in this relational model facilitates a deeper and more functionally fruitful conception of Marx's vision of the underlying unity in history—of human beings, nature, and society. It is a constant critique of any attempt to render static Marx's open view of reality. In fact, we are better able to understand his world view as a process which is open to dynamic change. In this view, Marx's conviction of a historical transcendence of alienation is more realistic, for it posits the Marxian dialectic of progress arising out of the contradictions inherent in capitalism.

However, there are some significant shortcomings which are centred primarily around the interpretative accuracy of Ollman's exposition of Marx's conception of historical reality. Marx himself claims that all societal phenomena are socio-economically determined, i.e., they arise from the changes in the mode of production. The crucial priority of the socio-economic base is impaired in Ollman's relational model. In arguing that Marx did in fact conceive of reality in relational terms, Ollman obfuscates the causal connection that exists between the socio-economic base and the factors that are derived from it. The thrust of his argument allows for the levelling down of both groups of factors in the process of the historical transcendence of alienation. Shaw provides a perceptive summary of the foregoing critique of Ollman's interpretation of Marx:

> Ollman, for example, takes the line that Marx views the capitalist system in all its economies, social, political, and ideological aspects, as an organic whole without assigning causal primacy to any single realm. This absence of causality seems to be dictated in Ollman's mind by the very organicism of Marx's outlook. Not only do Ollman and others of similar persuasion appear to operate with a billiard ball model of cause and effect, but they make the mistake of supposing that the conceptual interrelatedness of events or social relations forbids their causal connection. Marx did have a very 'organic' conception of society, yet causal notions are integral to his social and historical views and to the scientific work which he believed himself to be carrying out.[110]

Marx's historical materialism implies that the forces of change and development are immanent within the very contradictions in society. Transformation is inherent in the process of history of bourgeois capitalism. It is self-evident that the new socio-economic conditions that will emerge out of the conflict have latent if not manifest de-alienating forces, which will eventually eradicate all alienation. But we are not told why the process operates in this way. The answer to that question would lead to metaphysical speculations: a *divine mover*, the force or power that undergirds everything. For Marx, to take that route would be to return to the enslavement of human consciousness, of the human being as a material, sensuous being. Marx prefers to have Hegel's dialectic of the negation of the negation as a *law* of human existence without the reality of Absolute Spirit. Despite Marx's preference, the question of God remains valid. For Christian theology, this question arises both in response to the challenge presented by Marx, as well as prior to Marx's challenge, that is, as a response of faith in the crucified and risen Lord, Jesus Christ. There is a distinction here which must not be forgotten. But there is also a unity in the two-faceted Christian response which must be preserved, for *gift* and *response* are the very character of the Christian faith. We will turn to the question of God shortly. First, let us look at the question of a Marxian ethics, which again points to the interplay between the metaphysical and philosophic thought of Marx, on the one hand, and his economic and materialist thought, on the other hand.

F.
Marx and Ethics

Throughout our discussion of Marx's philosophy that spanned both the early and the mature Marx, we have focused on Marx's anthropology. This task led us to the concept of alienation, which is central in both early and mature Marx, though later the concept is more implicitly present than explicity discussed, for it is replaced by other terms such as "exploitation" and "fetishism."[111] These terms certainly reflect the shift in interest in Marx's thought from philosophy to political economy. We have also seen that the crux of Marx's *Weltanschauung* was elaborated as early as1844, and with the exception of a few changes, this world view persisted throughout his entire career.

The explication of Marx's anthropology and of his theory of history has led us to a consideration of alienation and its transcendence through the abolition of private property under communism. Marx's analysis contains antithetical terms and ideas which demonstrate, on the one hand, that there is a state of human existence that is to be condemned, particularly that which obtains under capitalism. On the other hand, there is a state of human existence that is to be commended, namely, that under communism. The notes of condemnation and of commendation raise the unavoidable question of whether Marx is an ethicist. Does he have a system of ethics which is peculiarly his? What are the criteria upon which he makes his obvious evaluations? These and other related questions of ethics are critical for a balanced perspective of Marx's world view. Moreover, they gain added significance when they are raised in light of (and even because of) Marx's claims to a scientific analysis of human beings-in-society.

Marx is convinced that, when he criticises philosophy and religion as ideological, his premise is historical and scientific rather than moral or ethical.[112] When he argues that the workers must overthrow the existing mode of production, his assumption is that the very forces of history make the revolution possible. He sees a diametric difference between his philosophy of revolutionary *praxis* and a philosophy of ethics on how to behave in this world under the present order of things—all that he condemns as alienating human beings from their *species-being*. By the same token, we wonder on what grounds Marx justifies his critique of bourgeois political economy that prevents it from being labelled ideology as well. For Marx, the crucial difference between *praxis-theoria* and bourgeois ethics is that the former advocates a revolutionary transformation of the very base of society, while the latter merely attempts to preserve the *status quo*. The latter is the product of alienated, false consciousness. Even when it sees the acute need for change in society to alleviate human suffering, it merely appeals to human conscience. It is ideology. Despite these differences, it is difficult not to speak of Marx's philosophy as an ethical system. This difficulty may be formulated thus: On what basis does Marx make and justify his critique of bourgeois political economy that preserves his critique from being criticised as false consciousness and ideology? How can one criticise, condemn or advocate a particular form of human behaviour, as Marx does, without using some ethical or moral standards?

We now turn to a discussion of Marx and ethics. Our concern is the ethical teachings in Marx's works that pertain to his anthropology. We shall therefore not attempt a detailed and critical study of the subject, which has been so well done by Eugene Kamenka in his two well-known studies. In fact, we shall draw a great deal upon the resources Kamenka makes available.

Marx claims that the root of alienation lies in the alienated productive process which has been alienated since the very beginning of humankind's interaction with nature. The productive process did not exist in a static but in a dynamic state. The arrival of the capitalist mode of production brought with it total and complete human alienation. Marx spares no invectives against the system and its perpetrators. Karl Popper is convinced that Marx's "is fundamentally a moral condemnation."[113] Popper's conclusion is particularly significant when we observe with Kamenka that Popper was "a critic not at all interested in alienation."[114] Popper argues:

> The *system is condemned,* for the cruel injustice inherent in it which is combined with full 'formal' justice and righteousness. The system is condemned, because by forcing the exploiter to enslave the exploited it robs both of their freedom. Marx did not combat wealth, nor did he praise poverty. He hated capitalism, not for its accumulation of wealth, but for its oligarchical character; he hated it because in this system wealth means political power in the sense of power over other men. Labour power is made a commodity; that means that men must sell themselves on the market. Marx hated the system because it resembled slavery.[115]

While accepting Popper's argument that Marx's critique of capitalism is moral in nature, Kamenka is quick to point out that this is not a confrontation on the basis of "a moral *principl*e established independently of his inquiries." Furthermore, capitalism is not condemned "for not being 'what it ought to be'." Kamenka argues that, on the contrary, "the distinction between dependence and freedom ... rests ... on an empirical basis." Explaining his conclusion, he writes:

> If Marx and his readers are drawn toward freedom and repelled by dependence and alienation, this is not because he has striven to show what they 'ought to be'. It is rather because some goods, at least, operate in Marx and in many of his readers, so that the morality of freedom, the sympathies and antipathies of goods themselves, are something he and they can also feel.[116]

Kamenka's suggestion is that feelings of antipathy and sympathy naturally effuse from human beings. This is consistent with Marx's thesis that human beings are the measure of what is human. What neither Marx nor Kamenka tell us is how to determine whose feelings are correct. It is certainly not self-evident that the capitalist and the proletariat cannot and do not share the same feelings about many significant things, while simultaneously they have different and conflicting reactions to other significant phenomena.[117]

Capitalism is judged and condemned for being primarily geared to protect the interests of the ruling class. Marx argues that the whole socio-economic base of society must be revolutionised. Capitalism must be overthrown and totally abolished. The premise of his argument is not external to the actual conditions of life, but is intrinsic to them. Marx and Engels claim that they have discovered the laws of history which show that history is moving towards the proletarian revolution. Consequently, "in his mature work as much as in his earlier work, [Marx] wants to go somewhat further than" stating *natural feelings of antipathy and sympathy*. Kamenka explains:

> [Marx] wants to show that history is inevitably working toward freedom, toward the Communist society where men's production will no longer enslave them, but will become part of them, where tools will cease to be men's masters and become their servants. But however unfounded this view may be, it, too, is not—in Marx's sense—a moral view. It neither presupposes nor establishes a new moral *obligation* in place of those which Marx exposed.[118]

Despite Marx's assumption to the contrary, his condemnation of the bourgeois capitalist class and his advocacy of the cause of the proletarian class are based on a peculiarly *Marxian ethics*. Marx's ethics are unique for they attempt "to put the thought of science at the service of the proletariat."[119] It is a proletarian ethic.

The question of a Marxian proletarian ethic takes us back to the thorny problem of determinism and freedom, i.e., the question of the inevitability of the revolution and the place of proletarian initiative in ensuring the successful occurrence of the revolution. As a result of this dilemma, interpreters of the *ethical* content of his thought have become polarised into two schools: the *ethical* and *a-ethical*.[120] One notable student of Marx who shares the view that there are two such schools is Svetozar Stojanovic. Stojanovic himself "represents the view that Marx's thought contains ethical values which can serve as a point of departure for a Marxist ethics." He explains further that "Marx also gave occasion for the contrary—a-ethical— interpretation." The ambiguity in Marx's writings inevitably creates problems in the interpretation of his thought. It "creates difficulties for any Marxist-orientated philosophy of morals. In addition, however, there is one more, significantly larger obstacle, i.e., Marx's understanding of historical determinism."[121]

It is instructive to look at some of the evidence in Marx's works that support the argument that he was *a-ethical* in his philosophy. Marx himself points out that a change in his earlier outlook took place in the mature years of his life. He describes the change as a movement from the realm of speculative philosophy into the region of "real, positive science."[122] Stojanovic points out that Marx's later development was the latter's attempt "to establish a scientific socialism, as opposed to the moralizing-utopian socialism which had existed previously."[123] He adds that the proponents of the "a-ethical interpretation of Marx's thought" base their argument upon passages such as:

> Communists cannot preach any kind of *morality* at all, something that Stirner does altogether too much. They cannot pose any kind of moral demands at all to people: love one another, do not be egoists, etc. On the contrary, they know very well that egoism, just as well as self-sacrifice, *is* in specific conditions a necessary form of individual self-affirmation.[124]
>
> Communism is for us not a stable state which is to be established, an *ideal* to which reality will have to adjust itself. We call communism the *real* movement which abolishes the present state of things.[125]
>
> Law, morality, religion, are to him (the proletarian) so many bourgeois prejudices, behind which lurk in ambush just as many bourgeois interests.[126]

In the first passage, Marx reiterates his conviction that "egoism" and "self-sacrifice" are firmly tied to the "specific conditions" from which they arise, as superstructure is tied to base. To call upon people to be loving and altruistic would be to demand of them something that may be desirable but not realistic in view of the alienated socio-economic base of society. The second passage reminds us that Marx does not conceive of communism as an ideal, fixed state of human existence. He thinks of communism in terms of movement or process, a dynamic and not a static condition. Thus, morality, which posits fixed, eternal standards, is anathema to Marx. Finally, the third passage illustrates the point made earlier that "law, morality, religion" are tied to particular classes, and so they lack universality. They have the character of representing and appealing to particular vested interests.

In contrast to those who advocate the view of Marx's thought as "a-ethical," there are those who use passages such as the following to illustrate the ethical content of Marx's philosophy.[127]

> The criticism of religion ends with the doctrine that man is the highest being for man, that is, with the categorical imperative to overthrow all circumstances in which man is humiliated, enslaved, abandoned and despised, circumstances best described by the exclamation of a Frenchman on hearing of an intended tax on dogs: Poor dogs! They want to treat you like men![128]
>
> The social principles of Christianity preach cowardice, self-contempt, abasement, submission, humility, in short, all the qualities of the *canaille*, while the proletariat, not wanting to be treated as canaille, needs its courage, pride, and sense of independence much more than its daily bread.[129]
>
> The standpoint of the old materialism is civil society; the standpoint of the new is human society, or social humanity.[130]

In the first passage, Marx uses the "categorical imperative," which is a highly moral exhortation. The clarion call to the proletariat to usher in the revolution is sounded. The second passage deals with the contrast between the qualities, such as "cowardice, self-contempt, abasement, submission, humility," which vulgarise human beings, and those, such as "courage, pride, and sense of independence"—in short, freedom and dignity—which characterise authentic, unalienated humanity. The second passage indicates that Marx believes that the ethics of Christianity promotes human alienation and debasement. It endorses and sanctions "all the qualities of the canaille." In contrast, Marx asserts that the proletariat are motivated by a revolutionary zeal which leads them to reject the condition of the *canaille*, even if their physical needs are not met. In the ethics of freedom, "courage, pride, and sense of freedom" are valued above "daily bread."[131] It is not surprising that Marx does have a *system of ethics* nor that the ethics he articulates are peculiarly humanistic in intention. Stojanovic notes that "from his earliest through his latest works, Marx wrote as an heir of the great European humanistic-ethical tradition"[132]— a fact conceded by "many non-Marxist thinkers."

The discussion of these passages which illustrate the ambiguity in his thought— that is, the conflict between scientific, a-ethical statements and his ethical injunctions and evaluations—suggest that Marx did not construe the terms scientific and moral to mean "value-less" and "value-laden," respectively. The distinction he makes between these two concepts is based on his materialist conception of history. In this conception, scientific refers to the material conditions of life, while moral refers to whatever is abstracted from the real situation. This distinction does not refute the argument that Marx's outlook is ethical as well as scientific. In Marx's thought, *Sollen* and *Sein* form a dialectical unity. Stojanovic writes:

> From Marx's belief in the scientific character of his own teaching, of course, it does not at all follow that this teaching was not ethically colored. The point is that Marx did not take 'science' to mean 'value-free' intellectual activity, which is what certain Marxologists have in mind when they speak of 'science'. Marx never drew the kind of distinction between cognitive and value statements which would place the latter outside of the realm of science. We can never overlook the fact that Marx was a student of Hegel, and that Hegel had rejected Kant's dualism because he was convinced of the unity of the Is and the Ought, of *Sein* and *Sollen*.[133]

We conclude, therefore, that only by maintaining the dialectical unity between *ethical* and *scientific* can a truly accurate Marxian interpretation of Marx's writings be made. Such an interpretation argues for an interrelational dynamic in the functioning of the two concepts. While Marx's ethics takes seriously the material conditions of life that obtain under capitalism, by exposing and condemning its intrinsic evil in moralistic terms, his ethics also serves the interests of the scientific analysis of capitalism. Furthermore, it is intended to aid the proletariat in awakening a radical consciousness in them. At the same time, Marx's scientific analysis will promote the ethics of revolutinary *praxis*. Marx is convinced that the socio-economic dissolution of the capitalist mode and relations of production would lead to a moral revolution. Moreover, complete and total human emancipation cannot and will not occur if appeal is made only to the moral consciousness of human beings without the concomitant attempt to understand and change both the mode of production.

Marx's conviction that moral exhortations are impotent to effect the proletarian revolution best explains why he did not formulate a systematic ethical theory.[134] Stojanovic explains:

> In contrast to moralists, Marx held no illusions about the efficacy of moral judgements which do not coincide with real interests, and although he

evaluated capitalism from a humanistic standpoint, he did not feel the need
to formulate and explicate the principles upon which he had based these
judgements. Marx was a critic, and an ethical critic at that, but he was not a
systematic ethical theorist.[135]

There is great merit in recognising the ethical content in Marx's thought. This
recognition is crucial for a more accurate appraisal of Marx's emphasis upon human
creativity and responsibility for the abolition and the transcendence of all forms of
alienation. It is important that the centrality of human activity is not obscured,
neither partially nor totally. When this occurs, the struggle of human beings for their
redemption is left to the caprice of accidents in the historical forces. We return once
more to the argument that Marx conceives of human creativity and the material forces
of production as existing in a dynamic and dialectic unity. The following passages
illustrate the argument:

> Men make their own history, but they do not make it just as they please;
> they do not make it under circumstances chosen by themselves, but under
> circumstances directly encountered, given and transmitted from the past.[136]
>
> World history would indeed be very easy to make if the struggle were
> taken up only on condition of infallibly favourable chances. It would on the
> other hand be of a very mystical nature, if 'accidents' played no part. These
> accidents naturally form part of the general course of development and are
> compensated by other accidents. But acceleration and delay are very much
> dependent upon such 'accidents', including the 'accidents' of the characters
> of the people who first head the movement.[137]

Marx's preoccupation with human beingss as the subject of history who will be
self-determined when freed from alienation naturally leads to his rejection of any
utilitarian concept of human being. Utilitarianism lacks the ethics of human freedom
to create the new instead of merely seeking to live in harmony with its environment
by adapting to and being accommodated by the given situation. Kamenka writes:

> For utilitarianism takes the desires and expectations of man at any given
> moment as an ultimate; Marx's morality seeks to transform and 'enrich' his
> wants, to increase his expectations, to prevent him from finding 'happiness'
> by tailoring his demands to his satisfactions, by learning to like what he

gets. Utilitarianism works within a given social and political system and criticises it only where it fails to satisfy demands expressed within the system; Marxian humanism is prepared to transcend the system, to criticise the system itself for the wants and demands it creates.[138]

Despite the greater possibilities for human realisation and fulfillment in the ethics of "Marxian humanism" vis-à-vis the ethics of utilitarianism, (and of Christianity as Marx conceives it to be), Marxian ethics must have checks placed upon it. These checks are necessary in order to prevent the Promethean tendency in human beings from displaying the demonic side of their nature.[139] Our argument here takes us beyond Marx's ethics and, indeed, beyond his anthropology. It takes us to the fundamental shortcomings in Marx's anthropology. "The horrifying excesses of Hitler and Stalin,"[140] to take two modern illustrations, are stark reminders that any Promethean ethics, whether Marxian or not, which is allowed to operate freely without realistic restrictions, will degenerate into a demonic power that threatens the very existence of humankind and the creation. It is this fear which has led many scholars from various fields to advocate an anti-Promethean ethic as a check against the destructive potentialities within human beings.[141] Kamenka writes:

Man's potentialities are for good or for great evil; it is best if he does not become drunk with his own power, but proceeds little by little, respecting the actual, empirical desires of others and keeping within rules meant to restrain his passions and his experiments. This is the—anti-Promethean—message of a great deal of contemporary moral and political writing. It appeals greatly to the increasing number of (middle-class non-'coloured') men who are reasonably comfortable in their own existing society and believe in the capacity of a system that has institutionalised change and technological progress to deal with strains and injustices without major dislocation or revolutionary outbursts.[142]

Unfortunately, the anti-Promethean ethic promotes the interests and welfare of a small, privileged and influential minority whose institutionalisation of change is experienced today, by a growing majority, as alienating, oppressive and dehumanising. It is an explosive situation which, Marx would agree, calls for a radical proletarian ethics. Indeed, it is not surprising that various versions and brands of Marx's ethics are currently propagated in many areas of the world where alienation is felt to the very hilt. Precisely within this turmoil, the question of God seems ludicrous, anachronistic or presumptuous, but also the only way of hope, both within and beyond historical existence. This attempt to point the way to God, before whom humanity lives, is intrinsic to an evangelical theology of the cross.

NOTES TO CHAPTER II

[1] See Kostas Axelos, *Alienation, Praxis, and Techné in the Thought of Karl Marx,* trans. by Ronald Bruzina (Austin: University of Texas Press, 1976), p. 227.

[2] "Preface," in Karl Marx and Frederick Engels, *Collected Works,* Vol. 5 (London: Lawrence and Wishart, 1976), p. xv.

[3] See Karl Marx and Frederick Engels, *The Communist Manifesto* (New York: International Publishers Company, Inc., 1948), p. 9.

[4] Marx and Engels, *Collected Works,* p. 60.

[5] *Ibid.,* p. 61.

[6] Marx to Annenkov, Brussels, December 28, 1846, *Selected Correspondence, 1846–1895,* trans. by Dora Torr (London: Lawrence and Wishart Ltd., 1934), p. 7 as quoted in Jean Hyppolite, *Studies on Marx and Hegel,* trans. by John O'Neill (London: Heinemann Educational Books Ltd., 1969), p. xix.

[7] Karl Marx, *Early Texts,* trans. and ed. by David McLellan (Oxford: Basil Blackwell, 1971), p. 156.

[8] *Ibid.,* p. 155.

[9] *Ibid.,* pp. 156–157.

[10] Axelos, *Alienation, Praxis, and Techné,* p. 219.

[11] Karl Marx, *Economie politique et philosophie,* trans. by J. Molitor, Oeuvres philosophiques (Paris: Costes, 1927–1938), p. 163, quoted in Axelos, *Alienation, Praxis, and Techné,* p. 222.

[12] Axelos, *Alienation, Praxis, and Techné,* p. 222.

[13] Marx, *Early Texts,* p. 152.

[14] See Axelos, *Alienation, Praxis, and Techné,* pp. 222–223.

[15] Charles Taylor, *Hegel* (Cambridge: Cambridge University Press, 1975), p. 554.

[16] Axelos, *Alienation, Praxis, and Techné,* p. 223.

[17] *Ibid.,* p. 225.

[18] *Ibid.*

[19] Marx and Engels, *Collected Works,* p. 31; see also, Axelos, *Alienation, Praxis, and Techné,* p. 225.

[20] Axelos, *Alienation, Praxis, and Techné,* pp. 225–226.

[21] See Eric J. Hobsbawm, "Introduction," in Karl Marx, *Pre-Capitalist Economic Formations,* trans. by Jack Cohen (London: Lawrence and Wishart, 1978), p. 20.

[22] See Marx, *Pre-Capitalist Economic Formations,* pp. 68–120, where he sketches out this development.

[23] *Ibid.,* p. 20.

[24] *Ibid.,* p. 11. *Formen* is the beginning of the German title of Marx's work which has been translated into English under the title, *Pre-Capitalist Economic Formations. Preface* is of Karl Marx, *Critique of Political Economy.*

[25] *Ibid.*

[26] *Ibid.,* p. 12.

[27] *Ibid.,* p. 13.

[28] *Ibid.,* p. 12.

[29] *Ibid.,* pp. 11, 43–44.

30 *Ibid.*, p. 44.

31 *Ibid.*, pp. 37–38.

32 *Ibid.*, p. 38.

33 *Ibid.*, p. 14.

34 *Ibid.*, pp. 14, 96.

35 *Ibid.*, pp. 15–16.

36 *Ibid.*, p. 96.

37 *Ibid.*

38 *Ibid.*, p. 15.

39 *Ibid.*, pp. 84–85.

40 As we shall see, despite Marx's optimism about the arrival of the future free society, it is, nevertheless, inconclusive whether the humanisation of human beings will be gradual or cataclysmic. The word *gradual* is therefore used with caution in the text. It is to be noted that Marx encapsulates the whole of human history in his discussion of pre-capitalist economic formations.

41 Marx, *Early Texts*, p. 146.

42 Axelos, *Alienation, Praxis, and Techné*, p. 231.

43 Marx, *Early Texts*, p. 146.

44 *Ibid.*, pp. 146–147.

45 *Ibid.*, p. 147.

46 Axelos, *Alienation, Praxis, and Techné*, p. 231.

47 Marx, *Early Texts,* p. 147.

48 *Ibid.*, pp. 147–148.

49 *Ibid.*, p. 148.

50 Schlomo Avineri, *The Social and Political Thought of Karl Marx* (Cambridge: Cambridge University Press, 1968), p. 70.

51 *Ibid.*, pp. 72–77.

52 Marx and Engels, *The Communist Manifesto*, p. 9.

53 *Ibid.*

54 *Ibid.*, p. 10.

55 *Ibid.*, p. 11.

56 *Ibid.*, p. 12.

57 *Ibid.*, p. 13.

58 *Ibid.*, pp. 13–14.

59 See Marx-Engels, *Gesamtausgabe,* ed. Marx-Engels Institute, Moscow; Frankfurt a.M., 1973f., Section 1, Vol. 6, pp. 516–519, quoted in Eugene Kamenka, *The Ethical Foundations of Marxism* (London: Routledge and Kegan Paul, Ltd., 1962), pp. 153–155.

60 Marx and Engels, *The Communist Manifesto*, p. 15.

61 Marx and Engels, "The German Ideology," in *Collected Works*, p. 54.

62 See Axelos, *Alienation, Praxis, and Techné,* pp. 157–158.

63 Marx and Engels, "German Ideology," p. 54; see Avineri, *The Social and Political Thought of Karl Marx,* pp. 142–144.

64 Marx and Engels, *The Commuhist Manifesto*, p. 15.

65 See William H. Shaw, *Marx's Theory of History* (Stanford, Calif.: Stanford University Press, 1978), p. 113, for a useful discussion of the crucial difference between the rebellions of

earlier classes, such as slaves and serfs, and the proletarian revolution.

[66] Axelos, *Alienation, Praxis, and Techné*, p. 248; see also, Hyppolite, *Studies on Marx and Hegel*, pp. 122–125.

[67] Marx and Engels, *The Communist Manifesto*, p. 44.

[68] Karl Marx, *Capital*, "Afterword to the Second German Edition," p. 18, quoted in Hyppolite, *Studies on Marx and Hegel*, p. 147.

[69] Kamenka, *Ethical Foundations*, pp. 157–158, notes Marx's optimism about the future society as well as his uncertainty about the disappearance of alienation through the abolition of private property.

[70] See Avineri, *The Social and Political Thought of Karl Marx*, p. 92.

[71] This conclusion, which is a primary presupposition in Marx's anthropology and theory of history, shows an evolutionary development in his thinking. See Kamenka, *Ethical Foundations*, pp. 17–25.

[72] Hyppolite, *Studies on Marx and Hegel*, p. 124 (emphasis added). See also, Taylor, *Hegel*, p. 419, where he explains that the difference between Marx's concept of human freedom and Hegel's concept of the absolute freedom of *Geist* lies precisely in the fact that Marx sees freedom as a conscious act, whereas Hegel sees it as the fulfilment of *Geist*.

[73] See Avineri, *The Social and Political Thought of Karl Marx*, pp. 144–149.

[74] *Ibid.*, p. 144.

[75] See Marx and Engels, "German Ideology," p. 82.

[76] E.A. Olssen, "Marx and the Resurrection," *Journal of the History of Ideas*, Vol. xxix, No. 1 (January-March 1968), 135.

[77] See Hyppolite, *Studies on Marx and Hegel*, pp. viii-ix, 95–98.

[78] Avineri, *The Social and Political Thought of Karl Marx*, p. 150.

[79] *Ibid.*

[80] Marx and Engels, *The Communist Manifesto*, p. 21.

[81] Avineri, *The Social and Political Thought of Karl Marx*, p. 151. See also, Hyppolite, *Studies on Marx and Hegel*, pp. 147–148; T.A. Jackson, *Dialectics* (New York: Burt Franklin, Lennox Hill Publ. and Distrib. Co., 1936), p. 193.

[82] Shaw, *Marx's Theory of History*, p. 5. Avineri, *The Social and Political Thought of Karl Marx*, p. 153, holds a contrasting position to that held by Shaw. According to him, a technological, determinist position is more reflective of Engels' thought than of Marx's.

[83] Shaw, *Marx's Theory of History*, p. 5.

[84] *Ibid.*, p. 62.

[85] *Ibid.*, p. 63.

[86] *Ibid.*, p. 65.

[87] See Bertell Ollman, *Alienation* (London: Cambridge University Press, 1971), p. 17; also, Shaw, *Marx's Theory of History*, pp. 103–104.

[88] Shaw, *Marx's Theory of History*, pp. 69, 72. See also, "'Engels to Schmidt,' August 5, 1890," as quoted in Shaw, *Marx's Theory of History*, p. 69. P. M. John, *Marx on Alienation* (Columbia, Missouri: South Asia Books, 1976), p. 212, perceptively points out: "When the spontaneous possibilities of creative interaction between men and nature are replaced by mechanistic laws determined from the outside, man is moulded by circumstances instead of man moulding his own circumstances. When the fact that circumstances are changed by men is forgotten, it is an indication that man is alienated not only from nature but also from himself." Jackson, *Dialectics*, p. 190.

[89] See Ollman, *Alienation*, p. 18. Kenneth Neil Cameron, *Marx and Engels Today: A Modern*

Dialogue on Philosophy and History (New York: Exposition Press, Inc., 1976), pp. 28–31, indicates a preference for the word process vis-à-vis law to describe the phenomenon above. On the question of the relation between Marx's philosophy and science, see Taylor, *Hegel*, pp. 551–552, and Ollman, *Alienation*, p. 25.

90 Shaw, *Marx's Theory of History*, p. 101.

91 *Ibid.*, p. 81.

92 *Ibid.*, pp. 1–8.

93 *Ibid.*, pp. 109–110.

94 *Ibid.*, p. 101.

95 The term historical reality is used here to include both socio-economic, political, and philosophical factors or constituents of reality. This means that both infrastructure and superstructure are included.

96 Ollman, *Alienation*, p. 12.

97 See Paul Tillich, *Systematic Theology*, Vol. 1 (Chicago: University of Chicago Press, 1973), p. 239.

98 Ollman, *Alienation*, p. 12. See also, Avineri, *The Social and Political Thought of Karl Marx*, p. 68.

99 Ollman, *Alienation*, p. 12.

100 *Ibid.*, p. 13.

101 *Ibid.*, pp. 14, 25–26.

102 *Ibid.*, pp. 13.

103 Karl Marx, *Theories of Surplus-Value*, trans. by G.A. Bonner and Emile Burns (London: 1951), p. 302, quoted in Ollman, *Alienation*, p. 14.

104 Marx and Engels, *The Communist Manifesto*, trans. by Samuel Moore (Chicago: 1945), p. 33, quoted in Ollman, *Alienation*, p. 13. Here, Ollman also points out the contrast between capital as a "definite social relationship" and Ricardo's conception "where capital 'is only distinguishable as *accumulated labor* from *immediate labor*'."

105 See Karl Marx, *Capital*, Vol. 1, trans. by Samuel Moore and Edward Aveling (Moscow: 1958), p. 209, quoted in Ollman, *Alienation*, p. 13–14.

106 See Karl Marx, *Grundrisse der Kritik des Politischen Ökonomie*, (Berlin: 1953), p. 412, quoted in Ollman, *Alienation*, p. 14.

107 Ollman, *Alienation*, p. 14.

108 *Ibid.*, p. 17–18.

109 *Ibid.*, p. 18; see also, pp. 27–42, where Ollman discusses the philosophy underlying the internal relations between social factors of historical reality.

110 Shaw, *Marx's Theory of History*, pp. 70–71.

111 See Kamenka, *Ethical Foundations*, p. 144.

112 See Marx's "Fourth Thesis on Feuerbach," in Marx and Engels, *Collected Works*, p. 4.

113 K.R. Popper, *The Open Society and its Enemies*, Vol. II (London: George Routledge and Sons, Ltd., 1945), p. 199.

114 Kamenka, *Ethical Foundations*, p. 145.

115 Popper, *The Open Society and its Enemies*, p. 199.

116 Kamenka, *Ethical Foundations*, p. 145.

117 John Plamenatz, *Karl Marx's Philosophy of Man* (London: Oxford University Press, 1975), pp. 177–178, observes: "But why should the theories that appeal to the revolutionary workers be any nearer being true, any more free of illusion, than the theories of other revolutionary groups?

This is the question that Marx, so it seems to me, never answers. He is merely dogmatic, and resorts to forms or words whose persuasive power comes largely of their being echoes of Holy Scripture. The most alienated, the most dehumanized of men, in redeeming themselves will redeem mankind. What is this but another way of saying that the last will be first, that the humble will be raised up?"

118 Kamenka, *Ethical Foundations*, p. 145.

119 Antonio Labriola, *Essays on the Materialistic Conception of History* (Chicago: 1908), p. 75, quoted in Svetozar Stojanovic, *Between Ideals and Reality; a Critique of Socialism and its Future*, trans. by Gerson S. Sher (New York: Oxford University Press, 1973), p. 137.

120 Stojanovic, *Between Ideals and Reality*, p. 140, mentions the following scholars who argue that Marx's philosophy "has ethical content:" Eduard Bernstein, Maximilien Rubel, Karl Popper, John Lewis, Eugene Kamenka. In contrast to these, the following argue that Marx's thought is a-ethical: Werner Sombart, Benedetto Croce, Karl Kautsky, Max Adler, Rudolf Hilferding, Lucien Goldmann. Stojanovic also states: "Some of them hold that the absence of an ethical position is a shortcoming of Marx's thought and, therefore, seek to supplement Marx through Darwin (Kautsky), Darwin and Kant (Ludwig Woltmann), or Kant (the neo-Kantians)."

121 *Ibid.*, p. 138.

122 Marx and Engels, "The German Ideology," Part I, p. 15, quoted in Stojanovic, *Between Ideals and Reality*, p. 139.

123 Stojanovic, *Between Ideals and Reality*, p. 139.

124 Karl Marx and Frederick Engels, "Die Deutsche Ideologie," Part III, *Werke*, Vol. 3, p. 229, quoted in Stojanovic, *Between Ideals and Reality*, p. 139.

125 Marx and Engels, "The German Ideology," Part I, p. 26, quoted in Stojanovic, *Between Ideals and Reality*, p. 139.

126 Marx and Engels, *The Communist Manifesto*, p. 21. See also, Stojanovic, *Between Ideals and Reality*, pp. 142–143.

127 See Stojanovic, *Between Ideals and Reality*, pp. 140–141.

128 Marx, *Early Texts*, p. 123.

129 Stojanovic, *Between Ideals and Reality*, p. 141.

130 Karl Marx, "Theses on Feuerbach," Thesis 10, in Marx and Engels, *Collected Works*, p. 5.

131 See Marx, *Early Texts*, pp. 139–142.

132 Stojanovic, *Between Ideals and Reality*, p. 142; see also, Axelos, *Alienation, Praxis, and Techné*, p. 246.

133 Stojanovic, *Between Ideals and Reality*, p. 142.

134 *Ibid.*, p. 143.

135 *Ibid.*, p. 144.

136 "The Eighteenth Brumaire of Louis Bonaparte," in Marx and Engels, *Selected Works*, p. 97, quoted in Stojanovic, *Between Ideals and Reality*, p. 145.

137 "Marx's Letter to L. Kugelmann of April 17, 1871," in Marx and Engels, *Selected Correspondence*, p. 320, quoted in Stojanovic, *Between Ideals and Reality*, pp. 145–146.

138 Eugene Kamenka, *Marxism and Ethics*, second edition (London: Macmillan Publishers, Ltd., 1970), p. 22.

139 *Ibid.*, pp. 22–23.

140 *Ibid.*, p. 22.

141 *Ibid.*, pp. 22–23.

142 *Ibid.*, p. 23.

CHAPTER III
MARX'S *WELTANSCHAUUNG* AND THE GOD WHO IS *PRO-HUMAN*: TOWARDS A THEOLOGY OF THE CROSS

A.
The *Praxis* of God and the Salvation of Humankind

Marx's dismissal of religion as the epitome of false consciousness, and his concomitant emphasis upon the transcendence of alienation through human *praxis* naturally bring his philosophy into conflict with theology. His explicit atheism, in the form of his anthropocentric world view, is a critical challenge to the future of theology. To replace God with human being, and the *praxis* of God with human *praxis*, certainly raises the crucial question: How might theology continue to talk about God? If human beings can do the work hitherto associated with God, what is left for God to do? If they change the conditions that give rise to talk about God, then God is not only obsolete or irrelevant, God is dead, for God's historical usefulness has ended.

Talk about God has not died as Marx predicted. On the contrary, it has continued for almost a century and a half until today. Moreover, it has shown great awareness of various challenges, including the Marxian challenge, to Christian faith. In the encounter between Christian faith and Marx's world view, for example, some theologians have sought ways and means of making "talk about God" "come of age," even as humanity has "come of age."[1] Does this mean that theological maturation occurs when talk about God merely reflects the "spirit of the times?" Does theology necessarily lose its evangelical soundness in this process of reinterpretation and rejuvenation? How might we speak about God in response to the Marxian challenge?

These are crucial questions which are not confined to the challenge of Marx's *Weltanschauung* to theology. However, in the face of the Marxian challenge, they cannot be avoided. They are of central significance to our discussion since our response to Marx will not be in terms of an exhaustive Christian apologetic or an analytical appraisal of the accuracy or inaccuracy of Marx's claims. Rather, our response, which is mainly theological and doctrinal in nature, will be a formulation of the central features of a theology of the cross, which provides a solid basis for any apologetic undertaking. Such an undertaking is, however, beyond the scope of this work.

Human liberation in history and beyond history is inextricably bound up with the God whose divine self-disclosure is through the cross of Christ. Instead of enslaving humanity further as a "Zeus-like" god would, the God of, and who is also, Jesus Christ always acts on behalf of humanity. Such a God is not threatened by humanity's humanisation, nor does God wish to threaten human beings and prevent them from realising their authentic humanity. God is totally *pro-human.*

In meeting the Marxian challenge, theologians cannot simply resort to arguing the case of theism versus atheism. It would be speculative and abstract if the argument were characterised by the antitheses: "God exists" and "God does not exist." In spite of Marx's materialistic conception of reality, there is no way of empirically verifying that religion is a mere projection of alienated humanity. Indeed, the very nature of Marx's conception, which is not devoid of metaphysical elements, rules out empirical verification as an impossibility. But, by the same token, Christian theology cannot demonstrate that God exists. The implication of this dilemma for evangelical theology is that it must go beyond confessing that God is to an elaboration of the confession of faith concerning *who* God is and *where* God is. Christian faith is apostolic faith. It proclaims that God is Father, Son, and Holy Spirit. God is the Triune God who creates, redeems and sanctifies life.

We have looked at Marx's struggle on behalf of humanity. We must now show that Christian faith is not less concerned about humankind. Indeed, as disclosed by both the God of the cross of Christ and the transcendent salvation of humanity, Christian faith goes beyond Marx in seeking the historical as well as the transcendent salvation of humanity.

When we look at the sporadic and, consequently, ambiguous criticisms of religion in Marx's writings, it is clear that his protest against God is made in order that human beings might be human.[2] Marx's atheism is a form of "protest" atheism. "The essence of Marx's atheism," Ano J. van der Bent notes, "was not the theoretical denial of God. Instead, it resulted from the necessity of fighting against the church and political clericalism."[3] When Marx argues that God does not exist, it is his way of protesting against the God whose existence dehumanises humanity. God exists at the expense of humanity. Thus, in Marx's view, to deny the reality of God is a negative way of affirming human beings as the measure and end of what is human.

This point raises the question of whether Marx's atheism is methodological by nature and, hence, derivative. José Míguez Bonino, on the one hand, has noted that Father Giulio Girardi supports such a reading of Marx. According to Girardi, atheism is a secondary and not a primary thesis in Marx. Marx's atheism is a negative way of asserting "the absolute value of man over against a diminution of man which would be implicit in the acceptance of God. If the disjunctive God/man should prove false, atheism would cease to be necessary for Marxism."[4] Czech Marxist Milan Machovec, noting the transitory nature of Marx's atheism, adds weight to Girardi's argument:

> Atheism has meaning only as a critique, limited in place and in time, of certain dominant models used in contemporary religious faith. Marx developed his 'atheism' as a critique of the conventional nineteenth-century representations of God, and should these change, then the genuine Marxist would have to revise his critique.[5]

Henry J. Koren, on the other hand, claims that Marx's atheism is *a priori*, for it precedes the development of his anthropology and theory of history. He rejects the conclusion that Marx is a methodological atheist. In support of his argument, Koren writes:

> In one of his earlier works he even called the negative critique of religion 'a presupposition of all other critique'. In later life, however, he no longer ascribed such a fundamental role to the critique of religion, but was satisfied with incorporating it into his general theory of estrangement as an 'opium for the people' and an instrument of power in the hands of oppressors.[6]

In the light of Marx's assertion of the primacy of the socio-economic infrastructure in his conception of reality, it seems more logical to accept the argument that Marx is a methodological atheist. However, this does not necessarily invalidate the contrary argument that Marx *a priori* assumes atheism as a guiding hypothesis. It is not an either/or question: Is Marx a methodological atheist or is he an *a priori* atheist? There is a relational dynamic connecting these two opposing views of Marx's atheistic position. His overriding anthropocentric concern is premised upon Feuerbach's argument that the truth of God is humanity. He assumes an atheistic position which, in his view, he methodologically demonstrates to be true by placing humankind at the centre of human existence.

Marx's atheism does have a place in the "talk about God," for it raises the question of which God, Zeus or some other, is wholly *for* and not *against* humanity. If God is like Zeus, or some other being, who, though possessing all power, is incapable of "pathos," then humanity would be better off without God. Then, Marx's Promethean human being's defiance of the gods would be appropriate. Jürgen Moltmann explains:

> A man who experiences helplessness, a man who suffers because he loves, a man who can die, is therefore a richer being than an omnipotent God who cannot suffer, cannot love and cannot die. Therefore for a man who is aware of the riches of his own nature in his love, his suffering, his protest and his freedom, such a God is not a necessary and supreme being, but a highly dispensable and superfluous being.[7]

We recall that Marx is convinced that religion, in spite of its real protest against real suffering, is a potent means of furthering humanity's alienation. God is removed from and oblivious to human suffering.

In his writings, Marx's "protest" atheism is not designed to remind theology of its evangelical roots in the God of the Bible. Marx does not attempt to explicate the Christian confession that God suffers with and for God's people. Rather, in his protest atheism, he wished to point human beings to the need to liberate themselves from all forms of alienation. Marx regards protest atheism as only the temporary phase in the historical movement from alienation to de-alienation and the emergence of free, unalienated human beings in the free, unalienated society. However, despite its transient nature, protest atheism is still considered by Marx to be thorough-going atheism. It is intended to lead to a radical doctrine of "human being *for* human being" and not to a pure doctrine of "God *for* human being." Moltmann argues that the anthropocentric reductionism, which Marx derived in part from Feuerbach, leads to human deification. He concludes that this is *de facto* a reverse form of theism. Thus, while acknowledging the value and necessity of such an atheism that opposes a conception of God apart from the cross of Christ, Moltmann soberly reminds us that

> atheism in rebellion against this kind of political, moral and philosophical theism has long been nothing more than a reversed form of theism, especially in modern times. It has not been able to break free from its

opponent. It thinks of man at God's expense as a powerful, perfect, infinite and creative being.[8]

The obvious antithesis and polarity between human being and God, in Marx's atheism, is bound up with his materialist conception of reality. Machovec supports this argument:

> The materialism of Marx means unambiguously the supremacy of man and of the human principle in the cosmos. It is not that Marx and his followers turn lifeless matter into a 'counter-ideal' to God, but rather that *man* with all his intellectual and spiritual gifts and values fulfils this role.[9]

Marx assumes that religion is epiphenomenal and therefore transitory. He is convinced that, with the transcendence of the alienated socio-economic base in society, human beings will no longer be religious. There will be no need for God. Christian faith, on the other hand, declares that humankind is not the centre of the cosmos. God is. To posit human beings as the measure of themselves and the ultimate source of their being and the meaning of their existence is not only idolatrous, but enslaving. Christian faith claims that the anthropological question contains the hidden question of God. Moltmann therefore asserts that "only a revolution in the concept of God" could make this fact clear and could "free" both God and humankind for liberating fellowship with each other.

> Without a revolution in the concept of God, however, there will be no revolutionary faith. Without God's liberation from idolatrous images produced by anxiety and *hubris*, there will be no liberating theology. Man always unfolds his humanity in relation to the divinity of his God, and he experiences himself in relationship to what appears to him as the highest being. He directs his life toward a highest value. He decides who he is by his ultimate concerns. As Martin Luther said: 'Where you put the trust of your heart, that in fact is your God.' That holds true for the Christian faith just as for every secular faith.[10]

Whereas Marx claims that only the consciousness of God is real (for God is humanity's consolatory projection), Christian faith argues that not only is the "consciousness of God" real, but God is real. Human consciousness of God results from God's self-disclosure. God exists prior to the emergence of human consciousness of God. Thus, Christian theology is based upon the presupposition that human beings ask the question of God because it is intrinsic to being human to do so. Therefore, according to Christian theology, to speak of God as being *only* a projection of human consciousness, as both Feuerbach and Marx do, is to distort the truth about humankind and God.

However, there is a sense in which talk about God is *human talk*. For example, all talk about God is done by human beings. What they say about God is always expressed in human language. Thus theological statements suffer from inadequacies inherent in all discourse, but this fact does not imply that talk of God is an empty projection, as Feuerbach suggests. God is a necessary idea for humankind. Russell B. Norris correctly points out that "it is a necessary idea because it is inherent in human nature to look for meaning and fundamental reality outside and beyond the phenomenal world. This reality, beyond all that we can measure, predict, and control, meets man and transcends everything sensible."[11] Human beings continue to be human only as long as they continue to perceive their essence as rooted in God. We must immediately add, however, that Marx's atheism confronts Christian faith with the crucial questions: Which God? Who is this God?

The challenge to theology which Marx's atheistic world view poses cannot be effectively met by merely advocating a theistic world view. Through Feuerbach's influence, when Marx speaks about human nature, he paints a picture of humankind in possession of the attributes hitherto associated with God alone. "Anthropocentric" faith has replaced the theistic faith of Marx's day.[12] In its attempt to refute such a pervasive tendency and to affirm the truth of its confession of faith in the Triune God who suffers for and with the people, Christian theology cannot simply resort to a speculative philosophy or point to the moral conscience or to mystical contemplation as the means of knowing who this God is. That would only lead (and has in fact led) to the "death of God." Míguez Bonino explains:

> Liberal theology, whether idealistic, Kantian or existentialist, has carried this purification (of Yahweh's essence) to its logical conclusion. The fundamental presupposition is always the same: there is an essence of God which we can know through philosophical speculation, moral conscience or mystical contemplation, before meeting the specific manifestations and concrete demands in which God comes—and has come to us. It is only natural that, when these philosophies prove untenable, and the 'essence' of

God vanishes, we shall have a theology 'of the death of God', the Christian
faith will be reduced to some form of philanthropic activity and Jesus left
hanging in the air as an example.[13]

Míguez Bonino is convinced that knowledge of God arises out of the *praxis* of
God. Any knowledge that speaks about God in static terms is not knowledge of the
God of the Bible. Such knowledge, Míguez Bonino claims, is unrelated to human
beings, and it degrades them. In contrast to this knowledge of God, he points to the
true knowledge of God who is known through God's *praxis* on humanity's behalf:

> It is precisely the characteristic of the Lord that he manifests his identity by
> announcing an action which involves man in an active relationship with his
> neighbour and with the world. There is no manifestation of God in
> Scripture in which a specific form of action is not included. God does not
> speak merely to inform or to notify: he speaks in order to invite, to
> command, to forbid a certain course of action. And this action is always
> related to a particular historical content—to men, nations, things, events.[14]

God makes godself known to human beings through the Divine *praxis*. When God
does so, God always takes human welfare with utmost seriousness.

Girardi argues that when we speak of God who seeks human welfare and shows
the Divine essence through *praxis*, we posit a Divine-human relationship which is
characterised by a "dialectic of love," and not by a "dialectic of master-slave." In the
"dialectic of love," human freedom, though subordinate to Divine freedom, does not
reduce human beings but upholds and upbuilds them. Girardi suggests that even
from the Marxian point of view, not all subordination to ends, *per se*, is excluded,
but only those forms which further alienate human beings by reducing them to
means. Marx's radical concern for humanity does not transcend Christian faith's
concern for humanity. Indeed, the latter surpasses the former, as is evident when the
"master-slave dialectic" is transformed into a "dialectic of friendship" by Christian
faith, which sees the "dialectic of friendship" as the interpretative key for
understanding humanity's total dependence on God. Accordingly, transcendence of
the alienation between humanity and God does not mean the destruction of one by
the other, for it results from a transformation of the relationship between humanity
and God. The situation is analogous to the transformation of inter-human alienation
through human activity.

120

The affirmation of God would, in fact, be alienating if our relationship with him were exhausted in the master-slave dialectic, e.g., in a voluntarism that would expose man and his destiny to the divine free will; but it ceases to be so if the relationship is understood in terms of a dialectic of love, as an encounter between two liberties. Finally, religious alienation, like every other form of alienation, must be fought in the name of religion.[15]

Girardi's argument raises the question of the congruency of the freedom of God with human freedom. Instead of accepting Marx's thesis that human beings realise their humanity through their own initiative alone, Christian faith points to God who is *pro-human* and through whom human beings become truly human. "But in order to satisfy man's expectations God must be God. In other words, God must be the totality of being and of value, and must, for this very reason, be infinitely superior to man, totally other than he and his complete master." The transformation of the "dialectic of master-slave" into the "dialectic of love" does not negate humankind's subordination to God. To make human beings equal with God would thrust upon them demands which would transcend their creaturely limitations. In spite of humankind's exaltation, alienation still persists. At the same time, elevation of humankind would mean that God would no longer be God. It follows that God must be God if humanity is to be truly human. The awesomeness of God's greatness and majesty are not aimed at human annihilation. "In reality, God's greatness does not destroy that of man, but forms the basis of it. Man cannot be great unless there is someone infinitely greater. His destiny must be in the hands of infinite love."[16] This is a rejection of Marx's thesis that all of reality is ultimately socio-economically determined and that humanity's need of God is not a genuine human need, but a dehumanising and transitory need that arises out of alienation. Marx's thesis is rejected because it is one-dimensional in scope.

Koren recognises that Marx's limiting of human existence to the immanent, socio-economic base of society denies human beings their authentic humanity. "We must ask ourselves whether Marx's *a priori* limitation of man's humanity to earthly existence does not violate man's integral humanity, for Marx simply dismisses the possibility that man can have a fundamental orientation to a supreaworldly God."[17] Authentic humanity is only possible under the aegis of the transcendent God confessed by evangelical Christian theology.

The question of God raises the question of human nature *coram Deo*. Such a conception is far more complex than and transcends Marx's materialist conception of human nature. In the light of this, it is not God's existence but God's absence that would mean humankind's alienation and diminution. Without God, human beings would not fulfil themselves but would ultimately destroy themselves. "Having killed God, man would not succeed in outliving him."[18]

It is well to recall that in Marx's theory of history there is a tension between human autonomy in shaping human destiny, in transcending alienation and in creating free, human essence, on the one hand, and the dialectical understanding of historical materialism, on the other hand. Marx's thesis is: human beings create in relation to the possibilities inherent in the level of the economic mode and relations of production. Human beings are both the subjects of the historical process as well as the prime agents for historical change. Koren reminds us of Marx's dilemma in deciding between historical necessity and human freedom, i.e., whether the laws of historical development or human initiative and creativity take precedence, in the historical transformation of nature, society and humankind:

> Marx's key statement in this matter is that man's production of his life is of necessity determined by the development of the material means of production. Is this development of production a physical process governed by laws that can be determined 'with the precision of natural science'? Or is it a development in which man's freedom plays a role, a history that implies the exercise of contingent human activities? Marx disagrees with Marx in this matter. When he states his fundamental perspective, he opts for the former, but when he concretely describes the development of the means of production, he specifically introduces the human subject with his ideas, will, purposes and intentions.[19]

According to Marx, humankind does not need to seek recourse to any higher agent or power than itself in order to fulfil its messianic role. To do so would be tantamount to further enslavement. But, as we have already pointed out, dependence upon and subordination to God ("Infinite Love") is liberating and not a curb on human initiative. Nevertheless, there are forms of dependence which Christian theology must reject. For example, Christian theology must reject that form of dependence upon God which has no place for human creativity in shaping the world and life in it. Dependence upon God does not mean that humankind is reduced to an instrument or thing. Ironically, in rejecting such a dependence, Christian theology is engaging in a form of protest atheism.

The following conclusion suggests itself. In response to Marx's world view, Christian theology must exercise a twofold critical function. On the one hand, it must denounce the limited one-dimensional conception of humankind. On the other hand, it must reject any conception of the Divine-human relationship which is contrary to the dialectic of love.

The concept of God advocated here is one in which God is seen as *pro-human*. God is the God of Abraham and Sarah, of Isaac and Rebeccah, of Jacob, Leah and Rachel, ... and of Jesus the Christ who is always acting on humanity's behalf and with whom human beings can enjoy a relationship characterised by the dialectic of love. With this concept of God in mind, it would seem reasonable to ask whether Marx would have still propounded an atheistic world view. This question gains significance for a theological response to Marx's world view if we accept Koren's argument that "Marx tacitly assumes Zeus is the typical image of God." Koren adds: "Zeus, however, is a primitive, intraworldly god, a god who is jealous of man's aspirations for independence and self-sufficiency, a god who wishes to keep man in slavery. In the eyes of an authentic believer such a god is merely a pseudo-god, not the God who transcends the world."[20] Christians should not hesitate in joining Marxists in their appreciation of Prometheus, who promotes human self-realisation, and in their rejection of Zeus, who enslaves humanity. However, in doing so, Christians need to remember that their stance is a response to the transcendent God who has called them to subdue and care for the earth (Genesis 1:28). Marx might have evaluated religion more positively if he had not conceived of God in terms of Zeus but in terms of the free, liberating God who acts on humanity's behalf, i.e., the God who is transcendent and immanent, who has called humanity to subdue and care for the earth. But we have no conclusive evidence to suggest that Marx would have been less an atheist and a materialist, that his view of the world would have been other than radically anthropocentric. Even if we were to speculate and to suggest that Marx could have held a theistic world view, in which God were seen as the God of the Bible, we must inevitably conclude that his theistic world view would have been ultimately transcended by an atheistic world view (perhaps similar to the one he did in fact formulate). In his theistic world view, God would have become human beings' agent for humanisation and would have eventually rendered godself obsolete when human beings would have attained to their "full stature." We need constantly to remember that Marx's atheism is inextricably tied to his fundamental assumption that historical materialism and anthropocentric reductionism constitute the dialectic of historical reality.

Let us return to Marx's one-dimensional conception of human being. Human beings are reduced to workers and producers. Koren provides a perceptive critique of Marx's anthropological reductionism:

> If man's self-realization is considered to be attained solely through productive work, man's existence is viewed as encompassed by being-a-worker. Work, then, is not merely a means of life but *the* way of life. ... Marx, however, through his neglect of the other dimensions of a meaningful existence, practically reduces man to nothing but a worker. Thus the relative value of work is absolutized, which results in a distortion of man's being.[21]

In spite of this limitation, Christian theology is confronted with a radical concept of work—the dynamic of *praxis*. It is with the view to change and transformation that human beings undertake to understand history *qua* universal history. In this understanding, which is always a dialectical process, human beings are constrained to act, to lead history to the realisation of human liberation. Human beings are involved as both subjects and objects of the creative and shaping dialectical process of history. It is humanity, Marx seems convinced, who will be able ultimately to take the reins of history and lead it to a liberating *telos*. Human capacity to perceive, to understand, and to act are a unity. The concern with liberation and transformation of the historical process is succinctly expressed by Donald MacKinnon:

> The Marxist is concerned less to understand than to change; his concern with understanding is the concern of a servant of change, a servant who seeks to grasp the interior dialectical movement of historical events, in order that he may work upon the opportunity which they provide to the effective mastery of their deepest tragedy.[22]

It is Marx's emphasis upon human *praxis* that prompts Jan M. Lochman to argue that "there is a place for Prometheus in our *teaching about God*," "in our *doctrine of evil*" and "in the Christian message of *grace and justification*."[23] Lochman contends that when it is placed in the right perspective, human *praxis* is not in conflict with the will of God for humanity and the world. *Praxis* for liberation is congruent with "the God of biblical faith [for God] does not intend to keep a man in his place in ontocratic chains; the God of the exodus and resurrection opens up the way out of all the human captivity, also out of the captivity of death. God is the God of freedom, the liberating God."[24] Consequently, there is a place for Prometheus in Christian theology, i.e., in terms of human beings' creative *response* to God's command to subdue and care for the earth. Grace calls to faith active in love. However, when the human creature's response is separated from the gift of God and is raised to an absolute position so that God is displaced (and human beings now become the centre of their existence and the sole architects of their own destiny), then, there is no place for Prometheus in a theology of grace. Grace and human endeavour are not in congruence with each other but in opposition to each other. The dialectic of love is destroyed. This is precisely what happens in Marx's *Weltanschauung,* where we find human *praxis* is removed from the ethical realm—response to God—and made the central means towards human liberation and fulfilment.

This foists an "unnatural" burden upon humanity. Consequently, humanity's work ultimately becomes enslaving rather than liberating. Peter C. Hodgson reminds us of Gerhard Ebeling's sober reflection on the legacy of the Reformation: "To be free *from* God would be the deepest bondage, for then we should have to judge and save ourselves, which is an impossibility."[25] In a similar vein, Ulrich E. Simon sombrely reflects on the message of Auschwitz concerning humankind. Human beings are made in the Divine image and, hence, to define human freedom in totally anthropocentric and atheistic terms is a denial of real human freedom. To be made *to be like God,* though never God, places human beings in "a unique place in the divine economy."[26] However, to argue for human beings' attainment of their authentic humanity outside of and apart from God and, thereby, to make of them "superhumans" is futile and dehumanising.

> The doctrine of the divine superman died at Auschwitz, and with it anthropology as a disguise for theology. The self-exaltation of man and the definition of reality in exclusively human terms lead to the denial of freedom which obliterates the human image.[27]

The Promethean mission of humankind, which Marx expounds, is premised upon a one-dimensional anthropology. Humanity's future is found entirely within history. According to Christian theology, however, humankind's humanity transcends history, for it has a uniquely eschatological dimension that transcends human history. It is a history that is inseparable from the grace of God in the cross and resurrection of Jesus Christ. God's grace has an indispensable eschatological dimension. Lochman writes:

> In Christian perspective, the hope of salvation is inseparably connected with the one name of Jesus Christ and with what his name stands for, that is, with the liberating involvement of the God of Abraham, Isaac, and Jacob. He is the God of the exodus, and the Father of Jesus Christ. His hope of salvation means history; it is, however, not the outcome of history. It mobilizes human energy and work; it is, however, not the sum total of that energy and work. It inaugurates an eschatological *revolution*; it is, however, an *eschatological* revolution: the possibilities of the Ultimate are not our ultimate possibilities. In one sentence: The hope of our salvation is in the liberating transcendence of God's grace.[28]

There is a diametric difference between Marx's emphasis upon the "absolute" transcendence of human *praxis* and Christian theology's confession of the transcendent grace of God. "The emphasis on the transcendence of grace as the final dimension of human life is the essential point in which Christianity and Marxism part their ways in the interpretation of the biblical heritage."[29]

Marx radically disagrees that humanity's search for meaning beyond the phenomenal world raises the question of God. While he does conceive of an open future, which is characterised by an anticipation of the dialectically new and surprising, he, nevertheless, limits his vision to that future which will arise from the liberating possibilities that will obtain when human *praxis-theoria* and the forces of history harmoniously combine. That is the Marxian historical *telos* towards which the dialectic of history is moving. Those "liberating possibilities," which Marx considers to be infinite in number, are in fact finite possibilities. They do not transcend the possibilities which are borne in the womb of history. Marx's future is not as open as we are led to believe. Christian faith, on the other hand, argues that the future of humankind is infinitely greater than that which is historically possible through human *praxis*. The future which Christian faith articulates is the future of the transcendent God who brings it in and who is the Absolute Future.[30] God as Absolute Future transforms the possibilities of human liberation latent in history so that the newness that is promised is ultimately not humanity's achievement. It is the gift of God. There is a disjunction between future in history and the future beyond history.

We have been developing a case for a particular form of discourse about God. Marx's atheistic and anthropocentric *Weltanschauung* raises the question of God: Who is God? We noted that to talk about the God of the Bible is to talk about a deeper and more comprehensive understanding of human nature than that presented by Marx in his materialist conception of reality. God is not an obstacle to human freedom. On the contrary, God is the only One through whom human beings are able to experience total liberation and authenticity. Humanity's future *coram Deo* is far more open than the future projected by Marx which human beings achieve totally through their own efforts without Divine assistance. God transcends history and comes as Absolute Future into history from outside of it. To speak of the transcendent God, who is immanent in history for humankind's sake, is to posit hope for humankind and the creation. Only the transcendent God of the resurrection, who is also the immanent God of the cross, can provide hope in the midst of the ambiguities of human existence.

In theological terms, Marx's anthropology and philosophy of history might be considered a form of a "theology of glory," for there is an explicit and integral triumphalistic note in Marx's world view. The "process of negation" in his concept of the dialectic of historical materialism contains a pervasive optimism about the successful transcendence of alienation.[31] His "philosophy of success" has no satisfactory means of dealing with existential realities, such as evil, suffering, defeat, and death. It does not tell us how such negating experiences will be destroyed. We are therefore left to speculate that they will somehow be abolished with the transcendence of the basic socio-economic forms of alienation. In the absence of God "the penultimate becomes ultimate for man. His total destiny then depends on his accomplishments. He lives with the possibilities of happiness and euphoria in the moments of his success. But he also lives under the law of frustration and despair in the face of defeat and guilt."[32]

In contrast to a "theology or philosophy of glory," in which human progress can be unambiguously identified and acclaimed, theologians such as Paul, Luther and Moltmann speak of a "theology of the cross," in which healing and wholeness are paradoxically present even when healing and wholeness are seemingly hidden from human sight. This perception is an act of faith. It is bound up with a theology of grace, of divine *praxis* for the sake of humankind. Lochman explains that in this theology "our salvation does not depend on the success or on the failures of our efforts. What is ultimate is not our accomplishment. The ultimate is not our failure and not even our death. The only ultimate, the proper future of man, is grace."[33]

Freedom and salvation of humankind are real, for they are rooted in God's grace in Christ.

Now, to speak of a theology of the cross vis-à-vis a theology or philosophy of glory means that there is an understanding of God and, consequently, of humanity in the theology of the cross which contradicts the understanding of God and humanity in a theology or philosophy of glory. Only a radical concept of God can meet the Marxian challenge to talk about God. Despite its failures to take seriously the ambiguity of suffering, evil, and death, the Marxian analysis of alienation challenges Christian theology to return to a theology of suffering and healing, i.e., a theology of the cross. In the theology of the cross, the resurrection is not absent but present in the *praxis* of the crucified Jesus Christ whose presence in the world, with broken, sinful, alienated humanity, *is* the presence of God. We are talking about the God who is both present with and is, simultaneously, the crucified Christ. God is the One who suffers for the healing of humanity and the whole creation.

We cannot escape the fact that the theology of the cross is essentially paradoxical. In this theology, contrary to natural appearances, where God appears to be absent, God is most present. Where God appears to be weak (as in the cross of Christ), God is most strong. This kind of talk about the strong and powerful God who is most present when God seems to be absent from the world and from the lives of people, especially of believers, is foolish and absurd. It is not without contradictions, which, in the eyes of Marx, might well be described as "opium for the people." Mystery and hiddenness are inherent in the peculiar talk about the God of the cross of Christ.

Further, in the light of Marx's critique of ideology as "false consciousness," it would seem appropriate to dismiss the theology of the cross as simply another theological manifestation of "false consciousness." Accordingly, the theology of the cross would be no more than a reorganisation of consciousness, a mental change in the way the world is viewed. That would mean a mental change without the necessary accompanying radical *praxis* to transform the real and actual conditions of life. Consequently, the theology of the cross would be denounced as a legitimation of the *status quo*. Here suffering is glorified and the promised reign of God is an illusory hope, a consolatory device to curb the "natural" revolutionary tendencies in human beings.[34]

But this is a distortion of the truth about the God of the cross. Whereas for Marx theology of the cross is ideological because it appears to be divorced from (or even devoid of) liberating *praxis,* according to Christian theology, the *praxis* intrinsic to

128

the theology of the cross is the most radical of all *praxis*. Theology of the cross embraces a conception of reality which transcends the depths of socio-economic and political conditions of life, but it also includes these conditions. It is concerned first and foremost with the *praxis* of the God of love who suffered the Son to die on the cross. It is a *praxis* whose efficacy is through the contradiction of love in the crucifixion for the sake of the enemy. In Marx, the proletariat are expected to carry out the revolution to abolish alienation and usher in the future society of freedom and love. But nowhere does Marx tells us how dehumanised human nature will become loving in its revolutionary activity. While love and solidarity might be born out of common suffering, there is no way of guaranteeing the continuation of such love and solidarity after the revolution has been successfully completed (or defeated). Love of human beings for one another does not come from within human beings themselves. Its source is the suffering God, not the human creature. "The believer experiences his freedom and the new possibility of his life in the fact that the love of God reaches him, the loveless and the unloved, in the cross of Christ."[35]

The thrust of this love is freedom. It cannot coerce anyone to love, nor "prohibit slavery and enmity." Instead, it must suffer the contradiction between its freedom to create its own conditions—in which it is open to the loveless—and its impotence to force anyone to love. It suffers grief over this contradiction and, in so doing, protests against it. The love of the suffering God is not an abstract, eternal principle. It is a historical event—the event of the cross. The contradiction in human beings is met by "unconditional love," i.e., by God godself.

> God is unconditional love, because he takes on himself grief at the contradiction in men and does not angrily suppress this contradiction. God allows himself to be forced out. God suffers, God allows himself to be crucified and is crucified, and in this consummates his unconditional love that is so full of hope. But that means that in the cross he becomes himself the condition of this love. ... The fact of this love can be contradicted. It can be crucified, but in crucifixion it finds its fulfilment and becomes love of the enemy.[36]

Here we are not talking about a God who has taken flight from the world and left humankind in its predicament. Rather, we are presented a picture of God who is *pro-human*, whose suffering for the sake of humankind infinitely surpasses human beings' suffering, including their suffering for the sake of others. The suffering

God is not the occasion of human suffering—human beings are. On the contrary, God is the only hope for human beings in their suffering and beyond their suffering. This is the message of the cross and resurrection of Jesus the Christ.

Talk about the God of the cross is not simply another form of theism in which the nature and activity of God are the objects of speculation. The theology of the cross is Trinitarian. It is not a theology which is reduced to Christology.[37] This will be clearer when we discuss the doctrine of the two kingdoms. In the cross, "The loving Father has a parallel in the loving Son and in the Spirit creates similar patterns of love in man in revolt."[38] The event of the cross is the event of the Triune God. When we posit human freedom as rooted in God alone, we thereby conceive of a dynamic God, whose activity in history is perceived as fully dynamic and comprehensive only when it is Trinitarian in essence. The Trinity is not the occasion for a speculative discourse on the "substance" of God's nature. Rather, it is the occasion for proclamation of the activity of God, both within godself and within history. "Evangelical" talk about the Triune God who acts in history is simultaneously talk about the God who acts within godself. In Jesus Christ and through the power of the Spirit, God enters history and takes history into godself.

> Between the Trinity in its origins before time and the eschatological glorifying and unifying of God lies the whole history of God's dealings with the world. By opening himself for this history and entering into it in his seeking love through the sending of Christ and the Spirit, God also experiences this history of the world in its breadth and depth.[39]

Moltmann insists that "we must drop the philosophical axioms about the nature of God." Such axioms distort the truth about God, for they represent God in static, abstract terms as One incapable of feeling, especially of experiencing suffering. God must be described in dynamic terms which point to the centrality of suffering in God's being.

> God is *not unchangeable*, if to be unchangeable means that he could not in the freedom of his love open himself to the unchangeable history of his creation. God is *not incapable of suffering* if this means that in the freedom of his love he would not be receptive to suffering over the contradiction of man and the self-destruction of his creation. God is *not invulnerable* if this means that he could not open himself to the pain of the cross. God is *not*

perfect if this means that he did not in the craving of his love want his creation to be necessary to his perfection.[40]

Thus the concept of the Trinity is integral to our talk about the suffering God, for it connotes the dynamic within the Godhead whose *praxis* as Father, Son and Holy Spirit is not divorced from human suffering. In the Divine *praxis*, the Triune God fully embraces this suffering, taking it up into godself.[41]

Trinitarian talk about God conceives of God as embracing the whole of reality, for God is both immanent and transcendent. But Christian theology must not stop here—even Hegel's God does the same. It must emphasise that, unlike Hegel's God who is incapable of suffering, the Triune God of the theology of the cross shows godself to be the One who suffers for the sake of love. Kazoh Kitamori points out that this distinction is crucial to a Christian understanding of the God who brings salvation to humankind and the whole creation, precisely because God suffers pain, of which Hegel's God is incapable.

> In the gospel message, God *suffers* pain because he embraces. But in Hegel, God *does not suffer* pain although he embraces. Even if Hegel's God allows individuals to wound one another, he remains a universal being, undisturbed and invulnerable. This God protects himself from being disturbed by 'cunning of reason' *(List der Vernunft)*. By cunning of reason, Hegel's God never suffers wounds. Thus the abstractness of Hegel's philosophy lies not in his portrayal of God as embracing the world, but in his portrayal of God as a being without pain. Because of this abstractness, Hegel's rationalism cannot bring salvation to our reality.[42]

The question of speaking about God in response to the challenge of Marx's atheistic and anthropocentric world view imposes a heavy strain upon the Christian faith. The dilemma may be summed up in terms of making the faith relevant to the needs of humankind, the world and the whole creation without losing the identity of the faith in the crucified and risen Christ. We have been pointing out that the churches' response to this dilemma is evangelical when it points to the salutary suffering of God on behalf of sinful, broken and suffering humanity. The theme of the hidden presence of God in the suffering world permeates our study of the theology of the cross as an evangelical response to the challenge of Marx's *Weltanschauung*.

131

Whereas theology of the cross takes with radical seriousness the human condition, which is understood in more than—but includes—the socio-economic and political realities, theology of glory is triumphalistic. It emphasises unambiguous success. To classify Marx's world view as a philosophy of glory is a logical conclusion in light of its express, pervasive optimism about the ultimate success of humanity's efforts at total historical self-transformation. It is clearly justification through human *praxis* vis-à-vis justification through the transcendent grace of the suffering God. Ironically, it is inherently triumphalistic, in spite of Marx's radical concern with the pervasiveness of human alienation and degradation. Admittedly, Marx takes human suffering seriously, but not seriously enough, for his anthropology is severely limited.

On the other hand, a radical anthropology emerges from the radical concept of God in the theology of the cross. Humankind's future is not confined to the history of its own creation but is bound up with the future of the crucified God who transcends history. At the same time, both human *praxis* and the whole of history are given their appropriate meaning in the cross and resurrection. This meaning surpasses that given in Marx's historical materialism. Human freedom is not denied by the freedom of God but is found only through the freedom of the suffering God who suffers the Son to die for the sake of humankind and the whole creation. The suffering God is most present in *nihil*, suffering in and with those who suffer.

We must emphasise that speaking about the suffering God does not lead to the glorification of suffering and that the presence of God in suffering is not reduced to a mere identification of God with fellow sufferers.[43] Indeed, the presence of the suffering God is salvific because the God of the cross is also the God of the resurrection. Therefore, in the suffering of the cross, there is the resurrection hope. At the same time, we wish to point out that talk about resurrection hope apart from its grounding in the cross is illusory and triumphalistic; in short, it is a theology of glory. However, without the resurrection of Jesus Christ from the dead, the cross remains the symbol of tragedy and doom. Thus, in the light of the cross and the resurrection, there is hope for alienated and sinful humankind (and all creation): hope *in* the world and hope *beyond* death and the world.

Theology of the cross does not call human beings to quietism nor to apathy based upon a reactionary ethic of the *status quo*. To speak of the *praxis* of transcendent grace is to exhort to radical *praxis* in order to transform the inhuman conditions which, in many parts of the world, means the transformation of the socio-economic and political realities of life. The acceptance of humankind's ultimate future in the hands of the suffering God is not to dismiss or to reduce the acute need for a more human future premised upon human *praxis*. On the contrary, radical forgiveness through the cross of Christ calls Christians to radical *praxis*. It is *praxis* which is always in danger of becoming legalistic and of reducing the gospel to a form of law through the justification of human beings by their works. *Praxis* for the transformation of the material conditions of life must be complemented by the *praxis* of celebration: celebration of the future of God which is already here in the presence of the crucified and risen Christ Jesus. At the Lord's Table we are called to partake of the messianic banquet, of which the Eucharist is a prolepsis. Moltmann describes this indispensable sense of joy and celebration, which is also characteristic of a theology of the cross. In contrast to Marx's critique of religion as belonging "merely to the realm of necessity as the groaning of the creature in bondage," Moltmann argues that it is only partially so, for religion "also and more properly belongs to the realm of freedom as the play of remembrance, as an expression of joy, and as the imaginative hope of man's basic and final humanity before God."[44] Such talk about joy and celebration in the crucified God in the midst of alienation could arguably be called ideological in the Marxian sense. However,

> religious myths and images are not just ideological tranquilizers which compensate for unbearable conditions or mitigate suppressed misery. They are daydreams of human communities in which the totally-other is made manifest, no matter how inappropriately, and where consequently the transformation of the here and now is already being anticipated. These communities are already celebrating that creative play which heavy-laden and labouring mankind longingly desires when it desires liberty.[45]

We conclude, therefore, that the liberating power of the crucified and risen Jesus Christ is present in the anticipatory celebration of the transformation of sin and alienation. The genuine urge for wholeness emanates from God. It is not the product of historical circumstances. It is not the result of human achievement nor is it sustained nor heightened by optimistic hope in humankind's capacity to transform ultimately the human condition. Through the Holy Spirit, human beings "become" the power and love of God in Christ in the world. Openness to God is completely and totally the gift of the Triune God, who brings the Absolute Future. This does not deny the celebration of the real liberating Divine-human activity in history. To do so would be to distort the theology of the cross into a form of docetism. The cry for wholeness in history is the cry for the salvific presence of God, which is already available to the "eyes of faith." God is not confined to history even as God "participates" in the suffering in history. It is a cry whose primary presupposition, contrary to Marx's atheistic and anthropocentric world view, is not only that God is, but, above all, that God hears the cry of suffering humanity. The epistemological centre of Christian faith is the revelation of God in the life, death and resurrection of Jesus Christ. Thus, Marx's proletarian cry, "The philosophers have only *interpreted* the world in various ways; the point, however, is to *change* it," finds its true and most radical meaning and expression, not in Marx's proletarian revolutionary *praxis-theoria,* but in the loving *praxis* of the suffering God of the crucified and risen Jesus Christ.

B.
Luther's *Theologia Crucis*: A Theology of Radical Reversal

In Luther's theology of the cross, talk about God is simultaneously talk about humanity, its condition and its suffering, its salvation and its future. Luther repeatedly reminds his readers that God, revealed in the cross of Jesus Christ, is God *pro me*. Consequently, humanity is not subsequently brought into the theology of the cross following the discussion about God. Humanity is present from the very beginning.

There is no way to avoid the historical distance between Luther and Marx: Luther lived in the sixteenth century and Marx in the nineteenth century. This is not the only crucial issue which should be considered in any attempt to establish a hermeneutical dialogue between the two thinkers. Of greater significance is the fundamental difference between their respective ways of looking at historical and eschatological reality. On the one hand, Luther the theologian did not question the existence of God. He accepted the existence of God as basic to his own existence. On the other hand, Marx *a priori* and methodologically rejected the existence of God. Luther was burdened by the crucial question: How do I find a righteous and gracious God? For Marx, the question was: How does one find free, unalienated, autonomous humanity?

The undisputed difference between Luther's and Marx's "ultimate" questions is made even more acute when we consider the attitude of Marx the economist to Luther's works. Per Frostin writes:

134

Already in Marx's early works, Luther is an object of his interests. He is described as a revolutionary, who was, nevertheless, unfulfilled. Also, in *Kapital* and the *Grundrisse,* Luther is often quoted, but there in a new perspective. Indeed, Luther is probably the German economist most quoted by Marx in *Kapital*, and this with considerable agreement with his views. According to *Grundrisse,* he is the 'earliest national economist'. In *Theories of Surplus Value,* i.e., in the closing volumes of *Kapital,* Luther is frequently quoted with agreement. For Marx, it is not Luther's moral commitment nor his pathos in the fight against incipient capitalism that is important but his economic analysis. He is portrayed in contrast to Proudhon, who showed no lack of moral pathos during his revolutionary phase. Marx indicates, however, that the sixteenth-century Luther saw something in developing capitalism that Proudhon did not discover in the fully developed capitalism of the nineteenth century, namely, that capital consists of accumulated surplus value.[46]

Marx's preoccupation with economic categories leads him to see Luther's main positive contribution to human liberation in Luther's analysis of the evils in capitalism. Needless to say, his interpretation is far from the central thrust of Luther's concern with a gracious God who is *pro-human.* As we have already shown, Marx, through the influence of Feuerbach, criticises the anthropology of Luther (and others), in which humankind is seen as utterly depraved before the righteous and holy God who alone can save humankind from sin, death and the power of the devil. In his critique, Marx posits his own peculiar anthropocentric and atheistic world view. It is precisely the overriding concern with humanity that opens up the way for a critique of Marx's world view from the standpoint of Luther's theology of the cross.

Luther's *theologia crucis* is a practical method. It is not abstract and speculative. Though his anthropology, as well as his understanding of reality as a whole, differs fundamentally from Marx's *Weltanschauung,* there is, nevertheless, a common element in their existential concern with humankind. Luther's "living" concern draws us to him as we seek to articulate a radical concept of God in the face of the challenge which Marx's world view presents. Thus our concern with Luther's concept of God is existential and is paralleled, not only in the situation described by Walter von Loewenich, in which he notes that we are "today experiencing a return from a theology of glory to a theology of the cross similar to the one we observe in Luther,"[47] but also in the very fact that Luther's theology arose out of the existential need for a gracious and loving God.

Luther refused to reduce theology to anthropology. Yet he insisted that any talk about God is simultaneously talk about humanity. It is "relational" talk: the relationship between God and humanity for the sake of the latter. As Gerhard Ebeling points out, it is impossible to speak about God in such a way that what is said is not at the same time "the direct concern of man." Relational talk occurs because "what is said of God is addressed to man."[48]

Through Christ, God's address to humanity is salvific. This is apprehended through faith in Christ which is the gift of God initiated and sustained through the Spirit and the Word. Faith is "certainty"—certainty that God's address to humanity through the cross of Christ is a gracious call, and certainty that it is God, in the first place, who makes such an address. "For Luther certainty is the essence of God's being with man and therefore of man's being with God. In the presence of God, and there alone, there is no uncertainty. But uncertainty is man's sin, and certainty is salvation."[49]

The conviction that God's address to humanity is salvific conflicts with Marx's argument that human autonomy is lost when it is subject to any heteronomous power. It would be instructive here to look briefly at Norman H. G. Robinson's approach to the thorny problem of autonomy and heteronomy.

Noting that the Christian ethic is "essentially an ethic of redemption," Robinson argues that the "collision" between heteronomy and autonomy is inevitable:

> The Christian ethic is necessarily related in a quite explicit manner to God's remedial activity in Jesus Christ, to the saving Word of God in Christ and so to the revelation of the divine grace. If, however, the Christian ethic is an ethic necessarily and explicitly related to the self-revelation of God that fact in itself is the immediate occasion of questions and difficulties which are largely concerned with the problem of autonomy and heteronomy.[50]

In his own understanding of autonomy, Marx is heavily dependent upon Kant. Kant, Robinson tells us, describes human autonomy in terms of the situation in which "man himself and by himself can produce from his reason or from any other part of himself, the practical principles and the guiding stars by which he should live."[51] Thus, for Kant, as well as for Marx, human autonomy as a free agent becomes, and is, in fact, impaired by positing the autonomy of God who reveals godself in Jesus Christ. In relation to the autonomy of God's will, the human will is made secondary. Human beings stand in a creature/Creator (and Redeemer) relationship *coram Deo*.[52] Robinson therefore concludes that in light of the "gift of the Gospel, which is, when seen from within the original or rather from within *what man has made of it*, the quite unimagined and unimaginable restoration of man by the act and intervention of God and the creation of a kingdom of love within a self-willed world of man's devising," there is a place for creaturely autonomy. He states: "Accordingly the idea of autonomy is right, but it is the autonomy of the *creature*, a secondary and derivative autonomy which combines the valid elements of both sheer heteronomy and pure autonomy, it is the autonomy of one whose nature it is to stand by grace in the presence of God his Creator."[53] Needlesss to say, Robinson's conclusion would represent for Marx a "bourgeois" Christian compromise. Humankind's absolute autonomy is not only not affirmed, but God's autonomous power is not declared non-existent. In the end, humankind's autonomy is subordinated to the will of God whose real existence is a primary assumption in the whole argument.

When we assert that God is *pro-human*, our concern is to demonstrate that in Luther's *theologia crucis* both the Divine and human essence are defined in dynamic, not static, terms. Any definition of human nature which is not derived from and rooted in the crucified and risen God is deficient and dehumanising. To posit any other relationship, as Marx does, in which humankind is the centre of its life, is to distort the fundamental truth about reality: God stands over against humankind, but God is simultaneously *pro-human*. The theologian of the cross must be completely radical in his/her declaration of the truth. "The theologian of glory says bad is good and good is bad. The theologian of the cross calls them by their proper name."[54] The latter is not afraid to recognise reality for what it is: distorted and sinful, seemingly Godforsaken. He/she is convinced that in cross and shame, there humanity actually finds the gracious and loving God.

Despite the basic polarity between Luther and Marx, there is a sense in which their respective radical critiques of reality agree. Admittedly, Marx advocates the doctrine of humanity's "justification" through human creative activity, which finds an indirect parallel in the mediaeval offer of salvation through the sale of indulgences which Luther outrightly rejects. However, when the implication of Marx's atheism is seen in terms of protest atheism, it may be argued that he stands on common ground with Luther, who attacked the religion of indulgences in his theology of the cross. Thus both Luther and Marx attacked forms of religion which were offering counterfeit goods: according to Marx, an opiate; according to Luther, consolation and peace to stricken consciences through the sale of indulgences. The grace of God is not "opium." But Marx did not recognise this, and he could not, given his *a priori* and methodological atheism. Further, the grace of God is not for sale. It does not call human beings away from the world but drives them into it. In the theology of the cross, humanity is reminded that it can courageously face the brokenness and sinfulness of the world and humankind. Humanity does not have to fearfully hide from the sin and brokenness. Above all, human beings are able in faith to behold the healing and saving God in the Christ of the cross. The parallel between Luther and Marx should therefore not be pushed too far. It is a limited and qualified parallel.

Talk about God is not exclusive of talk about humankind; rather, the two are inextricably bound together. The human condition is taken seriously, even as the essence of the "revealed" God is described. Care should be taken, however, to ensure that Luther's insistence upon talk about the God *pro me* does not lead to the reduction of God to a mere human projection, manipulated and manipulable. This is a constant danger which, nevertheless, Luther was able to avoid. According to Luther, to speak about the God who is *pro-human* is a paradoxical statement, for it is of the essence of Divine freedom that God appear weak and impotent when God acts on humankind's behalf through the cross of Christ. In this light we understand Rubem Alves' statement concerning Luther's understanding of the God "for us." Luther, Alves writes, "stubbornly refused to allow the language of theology to be concerned about a God who had not given himself historically to man. To speak correctly about God is to speak about One who does not have any other mode of determination save that of being for man. For Luther, consequently, the language of theology was simply the description of a historical person who exhausts the self-determination of God: Jesus Christ."[55]

Therefore when Luther talks about the God who is *pro-human,* he does not wish to eradicate the qualitative distinction between God and humankind, between Creator and creature. Paul Althaus makes clear "the close connection which Luther establishes between the theology of the cross and man's sinfulness." This "does not nullify the fact that this theology is also intimately connected with and expresses Luther's understanding of God's being God."[56] The salvation of humankind is bound up with the "being" of God. Because God is who God is, humankind's salvation is guaranteed. Humanity's need of salvation occasions the revelation that God is *pro-human,* even to the extent of suffering death, death of the Son on the cross. When Luther speaks about God who is *pro-human*, he is speaking about God who is known through the Christ of the cross.

Theologia crucis is therefore a peculiar theology. It is not one theology among various possible theologies, but the only true theology. Von Loewenich correctly observes:

> For Luther the cross is not only the subject of theology; it is the distinctive mark of all theology. It has its place not only in the doctrine of the vicarious atonement, but it constitutes an integrating element for all Christian knowledge. The theology of the cross is not a chapter in theology but a specific kind of theology. The cross of Christ is significant here not only for the question concerning redemption and the certainty of salvation, but it is the center that provides perspective for all theological statements. Hence it belongs to the doctrine of God in the same way as it belongs to the doctrine of the work of Christ.[57]

Elsewhere in his illuminating work, von Loewenich identifies the thesis which he defends: "The theology of the cross is a principle of Luther's entire theology, and it may not be confined to a special period in his theological development. On the contrary, as in the case of Paul, this formula offers a characteristic of Luther's entire theological thinking."[58]

Luther's most formal, comprehensive description of *theologia crucis* is given in his theses on "The Heidelberg Disputation" (26th April, 1518), in which he contrasts the theology of the cross with the theology of glory. There are other references to a theology of the cross, both before and after "The Heidelberg Disputation." For example, of special note are his "Lectures on the Epistle to the Hebrews 1517–1518" and two of his later writings, *The Bondage of the Will* and "Lectures on Isaiah" (1527–1530). It is beyond the scope of our study to trace the development of Luther's theological method, but we shall confine our attention to a brief description of its main characteristics, some of which have already been mentioned. It should be noted in passing that, nowhere in his writings, does Luther provide a comprehensive formulation of a theology of glory. This is not at all surprising since the theology of glory is speculative and abstract.

In his search for a gracious God, Luther emphasises that knowledge of God which is saving knowledge decisively revealed in the Christ of the cross. God characteristically reveals godself in veiled and hidden ways, since humankind is incapable of seeing the Holy One in God's nakedness. God is always "clothed" in the Divine self-disclosure. Saving knowledge of God reveals that humankind is confronted by God who is clothed in the humanity of Christ, who rests in his mother's arms, and who eventually hangs upon the cross. In contrast to a speculative knowledge of God, derived through reason alone, true knowledge of God in the theology of the cross is available only to faith, which allows God to be God and which seeks God where God is to be found: in the humanity of Christ. God's indirect and "concealed" sef-disclosure is centred in suffering and the cross—both the cross of Christ and the cross of the Christian. The two belong together. Although they must be distinguished from each other, they must not be separated. The theology of the cross is practical and existential. Von Loewenich writes:

> The cross of Christ and the cross of the Christian belong together. The meaning of the cross does not disclose itself in contemplative thought but only in suffering experience. The theologian of the cross does not confront the cross of Christ as a spectator, but is himself drawn into this event. He knows that God can be found only in cross and suffering .... For God himself is 'hidden in sufferings' and wants us to worship him as such. ... If we are serious about the idea of God and the concept of faith in the theology of the cross, we are faced with the demand of a life under the cross.[59]

In his comments on Hebrews 12:11, "For the moment all discipline seems painful rather than pleasant; later it yields the peaceful fruit of righteousness to those who have been trained by it," Luther helpfully illustrates his argument that *theologia crucis* is a theology of faith, which perceives the saving presence of God in the midst of the experience of its opposite.

> Frequently in the Scriptures there are two opposite ideas side by side. For example, judgement and righteousness, wrath and grace, death and life, evil and good. This is what is referred to in the phrase, 'These are the great works of the Lord.'... 'An alien work is done by him so that he might effect his proper work' (Isa. 28:21) .... For in a wonderful way he makes the conscience glad, as it is expressed similarly in Ps. 4:1: 'In tribulation thou hast made me greater,' that means, thou hast made more of me, improved me. Now this is what infusion of grace means. As it says in Rom. 5:4: 'Experience worketh hope and hope maketh not ashamed.' Here we find

> the Theology of the Cross, or, as the Apostle expresses it: 'The word of the cross is a stumbling block to the Jews, and foolishness to the Gentiles' (1 Cor. 1:18, 23), because it is utterly hidden from their eyes. 'It is withdrawn from their eyes and is taught in hiddenness. This means that it is not manifest but is hidden as in the midst of a tempest.'[60]

Luther preserves the sovereignty of God in his talk about the revealed God when he points out that, in *The Bondage of the Will,* there is a double sense in which God remains hidden: as the One who is revealed in the hiddenness of the cross and as the One who remains *Wholly Other* (whose mystery faith does not and cannot penetrate). To faith, there are not two Gods but one. However, the concern of faith is with the God who is revealed in Christ who saves ("proper work"), and not with the hidden God who is awesome and inscrutable ("alien work").

C.
Theologia Crucis Contrasted with *Theologia Gloriae*

Luther claims, in thesis nineteen of "The Heidelberg Disputation," that "he is not worth calling a theologian who seeks to interpret the invisible things of God on the basis of the things that have been created." The knowledge about God derived thereby is not true knowledge, since it arises out of human speculation and is not the consequence of God's revelation in the cross and suffering of Christ. Luther tells us in thesis twenty, "But he is worth calling a theologian who understands the visible and hinder parts of God to mean the passion and the cross." The knowledge of God which the theologian of glory offers through his/her study of "the invisible things of God" is not salvific. The theologian of glory speaks of God's "strength, his divinity, wisdom, righteousness, goodness and the like. Knowledge of all these things does not make a man worthy or wise."[61] On the contrary, Luther insists, "The sort of wisdom which sees the invisible things of God in known good works simply inflates a man, and renders him both blind and hard."[62] The way of the theology of glory is one of triumph and human self-glorification and self-centredness. However, in spite of the great power and awesome majesty of the God posited by the theology of glory, that God is subject to human manipulation and is none other than an ideological tool who legitimises the way of salvation and human liberation chosen by humanity without reference to the decisive and definitive Divine self-disclosure in

Jesus Christ. The God of the theology of glory is a threat to genuine human salvation. This "divine one" stands so far above humankind that God is *de facto* absent from the world of human suffering. Human striving for self-liberation and self-affirmation in the theology of glory is never satisfied and is ultimately dehumanising. In his comment on thesis twenty-two of "The Heidelberg Disputation," Luther helpfully illuminates the distorting thrust of theologians of glory:

> For since it is clear that they know nothing about the cross and even hate it, then of necessity they love the opposite, that is wisdom, glory, power and the like. Therefore by such a love they become more and more blind and hardened. For it is impossible for cupidity to be satisfied with the things it desires when it has acquired them. For just as the love of money grows as fast as the wealth increases, so it is with the thirst of the soul, the more it drinks the more it thirsts. As the poet said, 'The more the waters are drunk the more they dry up.' The Book of Ecclesiastes says the same: 'The eye is never satisfied with what it sees nor the ear with what it hears' (Eccl. 1:8). The same is true of all longings and desires.63

Luther's remedy for the theology of glory is the theology of the cross! The two are dialectically related to each other but must be distinguished from each other, since they are fundamentally opposed to each other. His remedy for a theology of glory is premised upon a reversal of those very things which human wisdom has come to value as of ultimate signficance for human wholeness. He states:

> It is not cured by satisfying it [i.e., the insatiable longing for 'wisdom, glory, power'] but by destroying it. That is, that he who wishes to become wise should not go forward and seek wisdom but should become a fool, go back and seek foolishness. Thus, he who wants to become powerful and famous, to have a good time and enjoy all the good things of life, let him flee from power, fame, enjoyment and a sufficiency of everything and not seek after them. This is the wisdom we are talking about, the wisdom which is foolishness to the world.64

The paradox in Luther's thought on the question of real, saving wisdom rests in his claim that the wisdom of the cross is the very opposite to what worldly wisdom thinks it is. It is reasonable to conclude that Luther's theology of the cross is a theology of "radical reversal."

Since the cross of the Christian is united with the cross of Christ, "the theology of the cross can never be a brilliant statement about the brokenness of life; it has to be a broken statement about life's brokenness, because it participates in what it seeks to describe. Apart from that participation, it would be empty chatter."[65] The language of the theology of the cross is experiential language, for it describes the saving presence of God in Christ in the midst of God's seeming absence and impotence. Essentially, the theology of the cross and the theology of glory are at polar ends.

Our discussion of the theology of glory leads us to conclude that Marx's peculiar anthropocentric world view belongs to the category of theology of glory. Whereas Marx "broods" over the history of alienation and comes up with his peculiar anthropology and philosophy of history, the theologian of glory broods over creation and comes up with his/her attributes of God. Though the former is inherently atheistic in outlook and the latter theistic (or specifically, Deistic, since he/she thinks of God as removed from the suffering of the world), they are both united in their respective means of understanding reality by confining their attention solely to creation. They concentrate upon different aspects but are united in their conviction that ultimate answers to the human situation (and the world as a whole) are found through those means alone.

In light of Luther's *theologia crucis,* the theologian of the cross replies to Marx by claiming that human nature and destiny cannot be fully known by humanity through its own initiative. Human nature and destiny are shrouded in mystery and hiddenness because of humankind's fundamental relationship to the God of the cross. Only God can reveal this hiddenness. Therefore, at best, human insight into humanity's history and destiny is only partial and temporary. The truth about humankind is a gift of grace that finds only partial expression through human knowledge. Moreover, humankind is called to look for the truth about itself by exploring and comprehending the cross of Christ. Similarly, to the theologian of glory, the theologian of the cross replies that God cannot be known as *pro-human* apart from the cross of Christ. The cross of Christ is pivotal for a true knowledge of God and of humankind, i.e., saving knowledge that pertains to humanity and its future.[66] Saving knowledge is contingent upon God's self-revelation. Von Loewenich's interpretative comment on Luther's nineteenth thesis is instructive here:

1. For the theologian of the cross it cannot be a question of brooding

over God's being in itself. For example, he is not interested in a doctrine concerning God's attributes that substitutes quiescent abstractions for living acts. In fact he considers that extremely dangerous. God does not want to be known in his invisible things but in his visible things. True theology must understand clearly that it has to be a theology of revelation. God has spoken, and therefore we are able to speak about God. God has shown himself, and therefore we know where we must look.[67]

God hears the cry of groaning humanity and graciously acts through the pain of the cross. Marx's "ear" for the groaning and sighing of the oppressed proletariat, genuine though it may be, cannot be compared with God's "ear" for the groaning of humanity and the whole of creation. The radical difference lies in the unbridgeable gap between the Creator (God) and the creature (humanity). Further, only God can suffer and die for humanity's salvation. For his part, Marx turns his attention to the creature and the forces of history to find the solution to humanity's "groaning and sighing." It is fair to conclude that Luther's negative attitude toward philosophy applies to Marx's philosophy as well as to the theology of glory. In a poignant summary of Luther's negative attitude toward philosophy, von Loewenich writes:

Philosophy has no ear for the groaning and sighing that run through nature. How could it? It knows nothing of a need for deliverance. It has the view of 'moral man' through and through. Just as the theology of glory prefers works to sufferings, glory to the cross, power to weakness, wisdom to foolishness, so philosophy would rather investigate the essences and actions of the creatures than listen to their groanings and expectations ... . Genuine metaphysics would have to proceed from the principle that creatures are creatures which dare not be absolutized in their being. They are not self-contained. Philosophy overlooks this. It is blind to genuine reality.[68]

Luther's negative estimation of philosophy does not fully apply to Marx's world view. For example, for an accurate appraisal of Marx, we must recognise the depth of his awareness of human misery under nineteenth-century bourgeois capitalism. His perspicuous analysis of human alienation shows that he is not totally blind to "genuine reality." Indeed, it is a tribute to Marx that his concept of alienation continues to be of special significance today in understanding the human condition in socio-economic and political terms. However, Luther's negative critique of philosophy is particularly appropriate to Marx's world view, which proceeds from the principle that the human creature is absolute, i.e., the creature is the centre and standard of human existence. In the face of Luther's criticism of philosophy, Marx's *Weltanschauung* is not a "genuine metaphysics." Despite its acute awareness of humanity's alienation, it is ultimately "blind to genuine reality." What, then, is genuine reality? Genuine reality, which pertains to the "sacred philosophy" of the Apostle Paul, is thoroughly eschatological. Like Marx's philosophy, it embraces history. However, unlike Marx's philosophy, it embraces history in terms of the cross of Christ by which it also transcends history. It is a "philosophy" of grace.

Luther is a very complex thinker. Not surprisingly, his negative attitude to philosophy finds its counterpart in his approving comments about a sacred philosopy. The influence of Luther's theological mentor, the Apostle Paul, is evident here. Von Loewenich explains:

> Paul appears to him to be a true philosopher. True philosophy would, of course, be a complete reversal of the hitherto existing kind. While the accustomed philosophy occupies itself with the *being* of things, this appears to the 'apostolic philosophy' as a foolish approach. For the true being of things does not lie in their existence and condition, but in their final purpose. Therefore the apostolic philosophy is thoroughly eschatological. … Such a philosophy is suitable for theology.[69]

In speaking about the eschatological dimension of the "apostolic philosophy," Luther does not move beyond or away from the cross of Christ. On the contrary, he emphasises and further explicates the significance of the cross as the source of ultimate meaning of human existence.

Reflecting on the meaning of transcendent grace in the face of Auschwitz, Ulrich Simon provides a lucid description of the eschatological dimension in Luther's theology of the cross. Simon writes, "The life of Grace both comes from beyond anything this life can offer and aspires to an eternal consummation which lies beyond death."[70] He is careful to point out the real possibility of the distortion and abuse of this eschatological future. Nevertheless, he insists that the eschatological perspective is indispensable for our salvation, which begins now and in the light of which our decisions are governed.

The theme of the sowing and the harvest cannot be removed from the re-making of life in bondage. Without the eternal perspective our enslavement reaches the proportions of Auschwitz, which Luther seems to have foreseen in his honest, but unattractive warning: 'If you believe in no future life I would not give a mushroom for your God ... do then as you like; for if no God, then no devil, no hell ... ; then plunge into lechery, rascality, robbery, and murder.'[71]

Meaning for human existence is rooted only in God—God who makes godself known in the cross—not in humankind. The cross, which is the paradigm of suffering, is not divorced from real suffering but is a real protest against real suffering. Indeed, in the cross the greatest and only victorious protest was (and is) made, for it is the protest of God godself.

We must sound a cautionary note at this point concerning the equation of Marx's philosophy with that which Luther criticised in his day. Marx saw that philosophy had culminated in the philosophy of Hegel's Absolute Spirit. Thus he argued that the problem was not to promulgate a new philosophy of the mind unrelated to the radical transformation of the socio-economic base of society. On the contrary, the time had come to transcend philosophy by realised practice. The problem before humanity was not to reinterpret the world but to change it, as his eleventh thesis on Feuerbach poignantly makes clear. The call to radical action—*praxis-theoria*—was not the result of any blindness to human suffering. *Praxis-theoria* was posited by Marx's concern to understand and transform the alienated human condition.

The problem with Marx's analysis of the human condition is its unequivocal reduction of all reality to a socio-economic base. Humanity is posited as the definition of itself. At this point the theology of the cross stands diametrically opposed to both Marx's philosophy and the philosophy (or theology) of glory in Luther's day. The latter two have both "lost sight of revelation."

Philosophy crowded out the Bible. Philosophy wanted nothing to do with the way of God; it is offended at the cross of Christ, the great no to all human endeavor, to all opinions of one's own. For that reason philosophy does not speak about this ... . For that reason also Luther declaims against the 'seat of the scornful'.[72]

Luther responded to this situation by attacking philosophy and calling for a return to Biblical faith. He felt that he had been divinely commissioned to undertake such a task for which he was "especially qualified as a philosophically trained theologian." In Luther's view, the epochal moment had arrived for a radical reversal from a theology or philosophy of glory to a theology of the cross. In the words of von Loewenich, the clarion call was: "Turn away from philosophy and turn to Christ the Crucified!"[73] The cross of Christ judges all human attempts at defining humanity in relation to itself alone or in relation to a future bound up with a speculative concept of God in the Divine glory and majesty.

Marx's worker—the proletarian collective—exercises a free will subject to no one or to nothing except himself/herself and the contingency of the forces of production in history. The worker, as *species-being,* is called upon to assume the place of God. In light of Luther's criticism of free will in relation to God and his argument that humankind's will is in bondage *coram Deo*, Luther would have rejected Marx's anthropocentric reductionism with its emphasis upon human autonomy. This crucial difference between Marx and Luther takes us back to their different conceptions of humankind's enslavement. In Marx, enslavement is bondage to the alienated socio-economic base. In Luther, it is bondage to sin, the flesh and the devil, reflective of the basic state of human rebellion against God. Thus, in Luther, the human will which is in bondage, is the will of *sinful* humanity.

Furthermore, in contrast to Marx , Luther sees the will of sinful humankind as also in bondage vis-à-vis the will of God. "Luther is not content with the statement that the human will is under the dominion of sin, and to that extent is enslaved." Instead, he "goes on to make general statements concerning the necessity of everything that takes place, and asserts the impotence and bondage of the human will in contrast to the free omnipotence of the divine will."

Here we have a subtle but crucial difference between Marx's *Weltanschauung* and Luther's theology of the cross. Whereas, on the one hand, Marx envisages a historical future where the worker will autonomously live creatively and harmoniously with the material forces of history (admittedly, Marx does not make clear how this state will be achieved!), on the other hand, Luther insists that the human creature cannot and does not exercise an autonomous will vis-à-vis God. The one who trusts in Christ is not freed from God. For Marx this represents perpetual human oppression and bondage; for the theologian of the cross, it constitutes real, authentic freedom.

Luther's refusal to speak of the free will of humankind in relation to its salvation is bound up with his concept of the sovereignty of God, i.e., with God being God.

To speak of the free, creative will of humankind, as Marx does in his world view, is tantamount to attributing deity to human beings, which is an impossibility in Luther's theology. Ebeling summarises that

> for Luther ... 'free will is a divine name and is appropriate to no one except the divine majesty alone; for the latter can and does do everything it desires in heaven and on earth.' To attribute the term 'free will' to man means no less than to attribute deity itself to him. Consequently this term ought to be reserved to God, and another expression used to refer to man.[74]

However, does not Marx infer a different term for human being by not positing humankind as a god in place of the God of Christian faith? Marx does not explicitly and directly argue for human deification. Nevertheless, Marx's concept of the worker as a free, autonomous human being is *de facto* human deification. Thus his concept of human autonomy is open to Luther's criticism of "free will." For Marx, human wholeness and salvation are inextricably and completely bound up with the immanent, actual and real conditions of life, in which God oppresses and enslaves humankind. In Luther's *theologia crucis*, on the other hand, one is enslaved by sin, and one's assumption of the responsibility for one's own salvation is tantamount to damnation. Only the God who reveals godself in suffering and the cross can release human beings from their bondage and make them fully human.[75]

The complexity of the polar difference between Marx's concept of human autonomy and Luther's concept of Divine autonomy is intensified by Luther's claim that there is a sense in which Christian faith can talk about the free will of the human being. For Luther, the human being is not devoid of a will informed by reason which, when exercised properly, conduces to human dignity. The human being does not exercise a free will in relation to his/her salvation *coram Deo* but in service to the neighbour. Paradoxically, the human will is simultaneously free and in bondage. Ebeling aptly states: "Man can exercise his will with regard to things which are subject to man, and this includes, in a limited sense, the realm of morality, which we may describe as the sphere of activity of secular righteousness, where the concern is with works."[76] These are the works which are done for the sake of the neighbour, which are not and cannot be considered salvific in the presence of God. Ebeling writes:

> As soon as we turn to consider man in relation to God, it becomes

meaningless to speak of free will. In relation to God it is impossible for man to be the subject of action, for here he can only be considered as one who receives, who is acted upon, who is subject to judgement, and who is accepted or rejected.[77]

In short, in relation to God, "at the end as at the beginning, 'we are beggars'."[78]

In terms of this relationship, Luther finds that the human essence is fully defined. It remains the same for the human being even when he/she is seen in relation to his/her neighbour and the world. That is, "the being of man in the sight of God is not something extra and additional to the being of man in, and in the sight of, the world." Moreover, this anthropology is applicable to all human beings, both Christian and non-Christian. Whether one admits it or not, one's "being in the sight of God defines the meaning of his being in the world." Thus, according to Luther, when one speaks of human free will, one must do so in relation to the created, not the Creator. In relation to the common good, human beings are called to exercise their reason and to act responsibly and freely, for it is within their capacity to do so. But even in the sphere where humankind exercises its legitimate caretakership of creation, " 'this too is directed by the free will of God alone, in the way in which he pleases'."[79] Here we come to the ubiquitous question of theodicy, which we shall not pursue further. For our purpose, Ebeling's remark serves to emphasise that the destiny of humankind is found not in itself, its history, or in its creative *praxis,* but only in God who alone acts freely. In the context of the cross, God's activity for the sake of the world is definitively and decisively fully gracious.

In Luther's *theologia crucis,* humanity's essence is not defined *a priori* in static terms. On the contrary, it is defined in relation to "the event that takes place between God and man."[80] It is most clearly expressed not only in the doctrine of Creation, but especially in the eschatological event of the cross and resurrection of Jesus. Humanity, its freedom and what is considered "natural" to it, are no longer taken for granted. A whole new and fundamentally different situation emerges which leads us back to the question of God. "Who is God," Ebeling asks, "if man cannot remain content with defining himself by comparison with the animals, but makes God the one from whom the whole determination of man's being, the whole definition of man is derived?"[81] Ebeling's question is most crucial for the theology of the cross, since we have denied all human claims to freedom and absolute responsibility in determining the ultimate future of humanity.

Returning to Marx, we are reminded of the plight of the alienated worker. Taking the proletariat as paradigmatic of the whole of alienated humanity—alienated in Marx's terms, as well as *coram Deo*—we ask: Who is God? More appropriately we ask: Where is God? What answer should the theologian of the cross give? If he/she is to "call a thing what it is"—in this case, to recognise the situation in which he/she speaks for what it is—then he/she cannot be oblivious to such stark historical realities: the suffering of the proletariat (and of all humanity) and its failure to achieve its liberation through its own initiative; the acute awareness of the absence of God through the Divine impotence to act on behalf of the suffering and exploited; the Marxian immanental and one-dimensional future as well as the transcendent reign of God are still out there in the future. In his/her response, the theologian of the cross claims that faith sees that the reign of God has already come in the cross and resurrection of Jesus Christ and will also come. God is paradoxically present in the midst of human suffering, working on behalf of humankind.

Consistent with Luther's *theologia crucis*, we claim that God is present, standing in solidarity with suffering humanity, effecting its liberation through the cross of Christ. God is known "through suffering and the cross," that is, "the knowledge of God comes into being at the cross of Christ, the significance of which becomes evident only to one who himself stands [i.e., participates] in cross and suffering."[82]

We have reached a crucial point of departure between Marx and Luther (or the theologian of the cross). Whereas Marx finds that alienation is indisputable evidence for the non-existence of any real, liberating God, Christian faith insists that the God of the cross of Christ is the real and living God, who is most present in the midst of human sin and alienation. Christian faith's claim rests on the conviction that God's revelation is always indirect and veiled, manifest in its contrary. Althaus sums up:

> The theology of the cross means that God hides himself in his work of salvation and that he acts and creates paradoxically while camouflaging his work to make it look as though he were doing the opposite. In this Luther feels that God glorifies himself as God. God has power to create out of nothing …. God shows that he is God precisely in the fact that he is mighty in weakness, glorious in lowliness, living and life-giving in death. Thus in Luther's thinking, the theology of the cross and God's being are most intimately connected.[83]

In the foregoing discussion we have attempted to show that Luther's *theologia crucis* is the only meaningful way whereby Christian theology might meet the challenge of Marx's radical *Weltanschauung*. Admittedly, Luther's preoccupation with the question of finding a gracious and righteous God who is *pro-human* and Marx's preoccupation with the question of how to find free, unalienated humanity are two distinct and separate concerns. Nevertheless, we have maintained that the radical concept of God in the theology of the cross contains a more comprehensive and authentic anthropology, which is in sharp contrast to Marx's. God, who is *pro-human*, frees the human being to be a creature who receives its life from God. This is in contrast to Marx's assertion that the worker's future, salvation and freedom are his/hers alone to realise in and through *praxis-theoria*. In consequence, our concern with Luther's concept of God has been primarily soteriological. We agree with Moltmann that "in fact Luther's *theologia crucis* here is a radical development of the doctrine of the incarnation with a soteriological intent."[84]

With reference to Marx's challenge which calls for a radical concept of God, the theology of the cross points to a soteriology in which God enters into human history, participating fully in human liberation as well as in the liberation of the whole creation. God stands in solidarity with the weak, the poor, the forsaken, and the despised. Solidarity, identification and crucifixion are salvific in light of the resurrection of the crucified One. In his focus on the presence of the Crucified One, Douglas John Hall writes:

> The theology of the cross is first of all a way of speaking about the character of God's entry into the sphere of human history. It is not merely a statement about the death of Jesus, but about his life and the meaning of his life for our lives. It is not merely a statement about the human condition; it is testimony to the *assumption* of the human condition by the One who created and creates out of nothing. The basic point of this theology is not to reveal that our condition is one of darkness and death; it is to reveal to us the One who meets us in our darkness and death.[85]

What makes *theologia crucis unique* is not that "it wants to put forward this ghastly spectacle as a final statement about life in this world, but because it insists that God, who wills to meet us, love us, redeem us, meets, loves, and redeems us precisely where we are: in the valley of the shadow of death."[86]

Finally, talk about God is Christological, for it is only in and through Christ that God is encountered and grasped in faith. Ian D.K. Siggins provides a helpful summary of Luther's thought on the subject:

151

> He who wants to encounter God must encounter Him where He may be
> grasped as He cannot be grasped in His majesty: in the incarnate God, Who
> lies in His mother's lap, and in the crucified God. To cling solely to Christ
> as He goes through death to the Father is the only way to find God.[87]

Siggins concludes that, according to Luther, "Since God will not and cannot be found except in and through the humanity of Christ, that humanity is the 'ensign for the nations' of Isaiah's prophecy (Isa. 11:12)."[88] God is available for humankind to grasp God, for Christ is the Emmanuel. Because of Marx's *Weltanschauung*, as well as in spite of it, Luther's *theologia crucis* is crucially relevant to the proclamation of the gospel, in word and deed, in the world today.

The affirmation that the Triune God is *pro-human* is not an opiate but hope incarnated in suffering. It is hope in the crucified and risen Jesus Christ, who heals and makes whole precisely in the midst of suffering. Salvation and liberation are rooted in the incomparable, gracious *praxis* of God alone!

NOTES TO CHAPTER III

[1] Dietrich Bonhoeffer, *Letters and Papers from Prison,* ed. by Eberhard Bethge, trans. by Reginald Fuller, et.al., enlarged edition (London: SCM Press Ltd., 1976), pp. 278–281.

[2] This remains the fundamental claim of Marxists. See, for example, Roger Garaudy, "As Marxists, We are Struggling on Behalf of Man," *Background Information for Church and Society,* No. 34 (Geneva: World Council of Churches, December 1965), 5–9.

[3] Ano J. van der Bent, "Christian and Marxist Responses to the Challenge of Secularization and Secularism," *Journal of Ecumenical Studies,* Vol. 15, No. 1 (Winter 1978), 164.

[4] José Míguez Bonino, *Christians and Marxists* (Grand Rapids, Mich.: William B. Eerdmans Publishing Co., 1976), pp. 55–56. See Giulio Girardi, *Marxism and Christianity,* trans. by Kevin Traynor (New York: The Macmillan Company, 1968), pp. 134-137.

[5] Milan Machovec, *A Marxist Looks at Jesus,* introduction by Peter Hebblethwaite (Philadelphia: Fortress Press, 1976), p. 21.

[6] Henry J. Koren, *Marx and the Authentic Man* (Pittsburgh: Duquesne University Press, 1967), p. 98.

[7] Jürgen Moltmann, *The Crucified God,* trans. by R.A. Wilson and John Bowden (New York: Harper and Row, Publishers, 1974), p. 223.

[8] *Ibid.,* p. 251.

[9] Machovec, *A Marxist Looks at Jesus,* p. 21.

[10] Jürgen Moltmann, *The Experiment Hope,* ed. and trans. by M. Douglas Meeks (London: SCM Press Ltd., 1975), p. 69.

[11] Russel B. Norris, *God, Marx, and the Future* (Philadelphia: Fortress Press, 1974), p. 51.

[12] Thomas Dean, *Post-Theistic Thinking; the Marxist-Christian Dialogue in Radical Perspective* (Philadelphia: Temple University Press, 1975), p. 5; see also, Jürgen Moltmann, *Religion, Revolution, and the Future,* trans. by M. Douglas Meeks (New York: Charles Scribner's Sons, 1969), pp. 7, 219.

[13] Míguez Bonino, *Christians and Marxists,* p. 39.

[14] *Ibid.,* p. 40.

[15] Girardi, *Marxism and Christianity,* pp. 78–79.

[16] *Ibid.,* p. 81.

[17] Koren, *Marx and the Authentic Man,* p. 98; see also, Norris, *God, Marx and the Future,* p. 47.

[18] Girardi, *Marxism and Christianity,* p. 81.

[19] Koren, *Marx and the Authentic Man,* p. 48.

[20] *Ibid.,* p. 97.

[21] *Ibid.,* pp. 45–46.

[22] Donald MacKinnon, "Absolute and Relative in History," in *Explorations in Theology 5* (London: SCM Press Ltd., 1979), p. 55.

[23] Jan M. Lochman, "The Place of Prometheus," *Interpretation,* Vol. xxxii, No. 3 (July 1978), 246–247.

[24] *Ibid.,* 246.

[25] Peter C. Hodgson. *New Birth of Freedom* (Philadelphia: Fortress Press, 1976), p. 334.

[26] Ulrich E. Simon, *A Theology of Auschwitz* (London: Victor Gollancz Ltd., 1967), pp. 157–

158.

27 *Ibid.*, p. 158.

28 Lochman, "The Place of Prometheus," 252–253.

29 *Ibid.*, 253.

30 There is a "School of Hope" among theologians which includes Johannes Metz, Jürgen Moltmann, Wolfhart Pannenberg and Carl E. Braaten in North America, who are among the most prominent scholars in this movement. The movement is by no means uniform, as the perspectives and hermeneutical centres of the various writers reflect significant differences.

31 Marx fails to explain how the negation of the negation in the productive process will be transformed into a positive process. It is a fair conclusion that he assumes this fact as self-evident. This question is tied to Marx's "theological expectation" of an unalienated human future.

32 Lochman, "The Place of Prometheus," 253.

33 *Ibid.*, 253–254.

34 See Karl Marx, *1844 Manuscripts,* in *Early Texts,* trans. and ed. by David McLellan (Oxford: Basil Blackwell, 1971), pp. 115–116.

35 Moltmann, *Crucified God,* p. 248.

36 *Ibid.*, pp. 248–249.

37 Moltmann, *Experiment Hope,* pp. 80–81.

38 Moltmann, *Crucified God,* p. 248.

39 Jürgen Moltmann, *The Church in the Power of the Spirit,* trans. by Margaret Kohl (New York: Harper and Row, Publishers, 1977), p. 62; see also, Moltmann, *Experiment Hope,* p. 78.

40 Moltmann, *The Church in the Power of the Spirit,* p. 62.

41 Moltmann, *Experiment Hope,* pp. 78–81.

42 Kazoh Kitamori, *Theology of the Pain of God,* trans. from the Japanese (London: SCM Press Ltd., 1966), pp. 27–28.

43 Alfred North Whitehead, *Process and Reality: An Essay in Cosmology* (New York: The Macmillan Publishing Co., Inc., 1967), p. 532, cited in Moltmann, *Experiment Hope,* p. 80.

44 Jürgen Moltmann, *Theology and Joy,* trans. by Reinhard Ulrich, with an extended introduction by David E. Jenkins (London: SCM Press Ltd., 1973), p. 75.

45 *Ibid.*; see also, Moltmann, *Church in the Spirit,* pp. 264–265.

46 Per Frostin, *Materialismus Ideologie Religion* (Munich: Chr. Kaiser Verlag, 1978), p. 194 (trans. mine). See also, Martin Luther, "On Trading and Usury," *Works of Martin Luther,* Vol. iv, pp. 12–27, in Hugh T. Kerr, ed., *A Compend of Luther's Theology* (Philadelphia: The Westminster Press, 1966), pp. 183–185.

47 Walther von Loewenich, *Luther's Theology of the Cross,* trans. by Herbert J.A. Bouman (Minneapolis: Augsburg Publishing House, 1976), p. 14.

48 Gerhard Ebeling, *Luther,* trans. by R.A. Wilson, Fontana Library of Theology and Philosophy (London: Collins, 1975), p. 248; see also, Paul Althaus, *The Theology of Martin Luther,* trans. by Robert C. Schultz (Philadelphia: Fortress Press, 1970), p. 27; Martin E. Marty, "Whenever God Dies: Protestant Roots of the Problem of God," in *Speaking of God,* ed. by Denis Dirscherl, S.J. (Milwaukee: The Bruce Publishing Co., 1967), pp. 85–86.

49 Ebeling, *Luther,* p. 248.

50 N.H.G. Robinson, *The Groundwork of Christian Ethics* (London: Collins, 1971), p. 148; see also, pp. 153–154.

51 *Ibid.*, pp. 155–156.

52 *Ibid.*, p. 170.

53 *Ibid.*, p. 223.

54 Martin Luther, "The Disputation Held at Heidelberg, April 26, 1518," hereafter referred to as "Heidelberg Disputation," The Library of Christian Classics, Vol. xvi, *Luther: Early Theological Works*, ed. and trans. by James Atkinson (London: SCM Press Ltd., 1962), p. 291.

55 Rubem Alves, *A Theology of Human Hope* (St. Meinrad, Ind.: Abbey Press, 1975), p. 99.

56 Althaus, *Theology,* p. 34; see also, Ebeling, *Luther,* pp. 232–233.

57 Von Loewenich, *Luther's Theology of the Cross*, pp. 17-18; see also, Ebeling, *Luther*, pp. 226, 234; Douglas John Hall, *Lighten Our Darkness; Towards an Indigenous Theology of the Cross* (Philadelphia: The Westminster Press, 1976), p. 118; Moltmann, *Crucified God,* p. 72.

58 Von Loewenich, *Luther's Theology of the Cross*, pp. 12–13.

59 *Ibid.*, p. 113.

60 Martin Luther, "Lectures on the Epistle to the Hebrews," in The Library of Christian Classics, Vol. xvi, pp. 233–234.

61 Luther, "Heidelberg Disputation," p. 290.

62 *Ibid.*, p. 292; see also, Althaus, *Theology*, p. 27.

63 Luther, "Heidelberg Disputation," p. 292.

64 *Ibid.*

65 Hall, *Lighten Our Darkness*, p. 117. Quotation is used as cited in Gordon Rupp, *The Righteousness of God* (London: Hodder and Stoughton, Ltd., 1953), p. 227.

66 Von Loewenich, *Luther's Theology of the Cross*, p. 69; see also, Althaus, *Theology*, p. 10.

67 Von Loewenich, *Luther's Theology of the Cross*, p. 19.

68 *Ibid.*, pp. 69-70; see also, *Luther's Works*, Vol. 25, American Edition, ed. by Hilton C. Oswald, trans. by Walter G. Tillman (ch. 1–2), and J.A.O. Preus (ch. 3–16) (St. Louis: Concordia Publishing House, 1972), pp. 361–362.

69 *Ibid.*, p. 69; see also, *Luther's Works*, Vol. 25, pp. 360–361.

70 Simon, *A Theology of Auschwitz,* pp. 146.

71 *Ibid.*, pp. 146–147.

72 Von Loewenich, *Luther's Theology of the Cross*, p. 68; see also, *Luther's Works*, Vol. 14, American Edition, ed. by Jaroslav Pelikan (St. Louis: Concordia Publishing House, 1958), pp. 293–294.

73 Von Loewenich, *Luther's Theology of the Cross*, p. 69; see also, *Luther's Works*, Vol. 25, p. 361.

74 Ebeling, *Luther*, p. 217.

75 Martin Luther, "The Bondage of the Will," in *Luther's Works*, Vol. 33, American Edition, ed. and trans. by Philip S. Watson (Philadelphia: Fortress Press, 1972), p. 138; see also, von Loewenich, *Luther's Theology of the Cross*, p. 31; Ian D. Kingston Siggins, *Martin Luther's Doctrine of Christ* (New Haven: Yale University Press, 1970), pp. 82–84.

76 Ebeling, *Luther*, pp. 218–219.

77 *Ibid.*, p. 219.

78 Hall, *Lighten Our Darkness*, p. 117.

79 Ebeling, *Luther*, p. 219.

80 *Ibid.*, p. 224; see also, Aarne Siirala, *Divine Humanness*, trans. by T.A. Kantonen (Philadelphia: Fortress Press, 1970), p. 76.

81 Ebeling, *Luther*, p. 225.

82 Von Loewenich, *Luther's Theology of the Cross,* p. 20; see also, pp. 112–143, 159; Althaus, *Theology*, p. 28; Kitamori, *Theology of the Pain of God*, pp. 4–49.

83 Althaus, *Theology*, p. 34.

84 Moltmann, *Crucified God,* p. 212.
85 Hall, *Lighten Our Darkness*, p. 149.
86 *Ibid.*
87 Siggins, *Luther's Doctrine of Christ*, p. 84.
88 *Ibid.*, p. 92.

CHAPTER IV
PROCLAIMING AND "INCARNATING" THE GOSPEL: THE DOUBLE CRISES OF IDENTITY AND RELEVANCE

A.
Moltmann's Trinitarian *Political Theology* of the Cross: A Radical Concept of God

Both Jürgen Moltmann and the Latin American liberation theologian recognise that the gospel of Jesus Christ has a peculiar relevance to the pressing socio-economic and political problems facing the world today.[1] Each attempts to articulate the relevance in ways that are rooted in and not divorced from the peculiar identity of the gospel. Moltmann articulates an explicit theology of the cross as the fundamental method of talking about God. Latin American theologians articulate more of an implicit theology of the cross as they focus primarily upon the theme of historical liberation from socio-economic and political enslavement and oppression. In both theologies (more especially in liberation theology), talk about God is in fact a theological explication of the Marxian concept of *praxis-theoria*. Moltmann emphasises the loving *praxis* of the Triune God *within godself* and *within history* and the practical-critical activity of the believer in the light of God's *praxis*. In contrast, liberation theologians stress the believers' practical-critical activity *within history*, which is their creative response to the God of justice and liberation. Consequently, when Moltmann's theology is compared with liberation theology, his theology appears abstract and vague about the church's socio-political involvement in any given society. By the same token, when liberation theology is viewed in terms of Moltmann's theology, it appears that God is so actively engaged in humanity's liberation in history that God seems more like humanity's co-agent than sovereign Lord. Both theologies are practical theologies which reflect the tension between the universal meaning of the gospel and its particular, indigenous meaning. Moltmann emphasises the first, while liberation theology emphasises the second.

1.

Political Theology of the Cross

It is obvious from Moltmann's presentation of his theology of the cross that he is greatly indebted to Luther. In Luther he finds the clearest explication of the radical meaning of the Incarnation. He accepts Walther von Loewenich's thesis that Luther's *theologia crucis* is the distinctive and evangelical method of doing Christian theology. But Moltmann articulates his own understanding of *theologia crucis* in order that it not be abstract or speculative. Thus, for Moltmann, Luther's *theologia crucis* is not a mere theoretical and analytical exercise removed from the world of human action. On the contrary, *theologia crucis* is inextricably bound up with liberating *praxis*. In Marxian terms, *theoria* and *praxis* are inseparably held together. In terms of Christian theology, faith in God through Jesus Christ and love of neighbour are a dialectical unity of "faith active in love." With the liberating *praxis* inherent in a theology of the cross in mind, Moltmann argues:

> And yet it only remains *theologia crucis* in the context of critical and liberating practice in preaching and life. The theology of the cross is a practical doctrine for battle, and can therefore become neither a theory of Christianity as it is now, nor the Christian theory of world history. It is a dialectic and historical theology, and not a theology of world history. It does not state what exists, but sets out to liberate men from their inhuman definitions and their idolized assertions, in which they have become set, and in which society has ensnared them.[2]

The truth of the theology of the cross is demonstrated through liberating action on behalf of the oppressed and the dehumanised in society. *Theologia crucis* is therefore not so much an explanation of history but a call to transform history in order to make it more human.

Because of Moltmann's explicit concern with the theology of the cross "as a practical doctrine for battle," his vocabulary, unlike Luther's, is pervaded by *praxis*-orientated terms. This is not to say that Luther was not concerned with practical issues. Such a conclusion would be incorrect. One only needs to read his teachings on the question of Christian liberty, for example, to find that Luther was concerned with "faith active in love" in service of the neighbour as the true expression of Christian freedom. The crucial difference between Moltmann and Luther lies in the nature of the fundamental question faced by each in his particular age. Luther was concerned with the crucial question: How do I find a gracious and loving God? For Moltmann, the question is: How do we speak of God in the face of Godforsakenness and socio-economic and political oppression?

Moltmann does not confine reality to the socio-economic base as does Marx. On the contrary, in his language about God, he seeks to give the fullest expression possible to both God's transcendence and immanence. Nevertheless, he takes Marx with utmost seriousness. Consequently, Moltmann's "crucified God" suffers within godself and with suffering humankind and does not merely call humankind to resurrection hope without participating in human suffering and oppression. The crucified God takes up into godself all suffering, including socio-economic and political suffering and oppression.[3]

Moltmann is careful not to speak of humankind's salvation as simply the result of God's solidarity with humankind.[4] Transcendent hope in the resurrection of Jesus is indispensable to his theology of the cross. Cross and resurrection are bound together. Therefore, in his focus on the cross of Christ, he points out that real, transcendent hope, which characterises Christian faith, is already present in the world, i.e., in the cross of Christ. He summarises thus:

> The cross of Christ is the sign of God's hope on earth for all those who live here in the shadow of the cross. Theology of hope is at its hard core theology of the cross. The cross of Christ is the presently given form of the kingdom of God on earth. In the crucified Christ we view the future of God. Everything else is dreams, fantasies, and mere wish images. Hope born out of the cross of Christ distinguishes Christian faith from superstition as well as from disbelief. The freedom generated by the cross distinguishes Christian faith from optimism as well as from terrorism.[5]

Only the resurrection of the crucified God, Jesus Christ, provides hope in history and beyond history. This does not detract from the penultimate meaning human effort has for humankind's future. However, humankind's future is not the future of its effort but rather the future of the crucified God which is the real and only basis for authentic human liberation.

Moltmann is concerned that talk about God is not divorced from talk about the Divine-human activity in the world. Theology of the cross must be "political" theology of the cross. Explaining the inclusiveness of this theology which he and

Johannes B. Metz have both called *political theology*, Moltmann writes:

> For us the field of politics designates the extensive field of constructive
> and destructive possibilities of the appropriation and utilization of nature's
> powers as well as of human relationships by human society. Nature and
> human history come together in the process of civilization. In it there can
> no longer be a distinction between cosmology and anthropology. For man
> and nature, politics is becoming a common destiny. We take up the ancient
> concept of *theologia politica* or *theologia civilis* to point out the fundamental
> situation in which the God-question is raised and in which Christian God-
> talk must become relevant today.[6]

Continuing the description of his "synthetic" and "wholistic" approach to
theology, Moltmann adds that *political theology* of the cross is bound up with the
question of theodicy. The political question which has replaced the traditional
"cosmological theodicy question about evil and misfortune" demands that Christian
faith in the salvation of God—who liberates the world from its self-imposed
enslavement—show itself to be practically relevant to the situation at hand. The
primary focus of talk about God today must be the political questions which
contemporary human beings face, i.e., the questions of history and the practical-
critical activity of human beings. Christian faith should not be restricted to the
private realm of individual existence, which allows the "godless and inhuman
powers" to have full control over the realm of politics.

The dilemma which Christian faith faces as a result of the dichotomy between the
private and political dimensions of human existence is aptly summarised thus: How
can Christian theology continue to profess faith in God in the face of the obvious
absence of God from the world? When the world is left to its own whim and fancy
and the creative activity of God is confined to the inner, spiritual sphere of the
individual soul, then, for all practical purposes, "God is dead." Unfortunately,
Christian theology is partly responsible for the "death of God" which has naturally
strengthened the cause of Marx and other "protest" atheists. "That faith which no
longer seeks God and his righteousness in the world but only in the soul has allied
itself with a practical atheism which seeks the world without God and righteousness,
and with it has contracted an alliance of death, of the 'death of God' in the world."[7]
It is therefore with the aim of recalling theology to the intrinsic unity between the
activity of God in the soul and the presence and activity of God in the world, that

Moltmann articulates his *political theology* of the cross. As is clearly revealed in the salvific suffering of the Triune God in the event of the cross of Christ, God's concern is for both humankind and for the world.

Undoubtedly, there is always the danger that any attempt to correct the distortion of Christian faith by way of a *political theology* might result in a political ideology. In that case, it is not the truth of the gospel of the crucified and risen Christ Jesus which is presented, but a distortion which is inevitably tied to a political system, order, or class. Taking full cognisance of this insidious danger, Moltmann qualifies his *political theology* of the cross:

> Political hermeneutics of faith is not a reduction of the theology of the cross to a political ideology, but an interpretation of it in political discipleship. Political hermeneutics sets out to recognize the social and economic influences on theological institutions and languages, in order to bring their liberating content into the political dimension and to make them relevant towards really freeing men from their misery in certain vicious circles.[8]

Political theology of the cross takes up Marx's challenge in his eleventh thesis on Feuerbach in terms of the cross of Christ. It is not afraid to subject itself to Marx's critique of ideology. Political hermeneutics does not lead to a dissipation of the substance of Christian faith, even when political hermeneutics asks: "What is the function of" talk about God and what effect does it have? Instead of loss of substance of Christian faith, "faith gains substance in its political incarnations and overcomes its un-Christian abstraction, which keeps it far from the present situation of the crucified God." Therefore, Christian theology must necessarily make clear whether, in its political formulations and activities, "it is disseminating faith or superstition."[9]

Moltmann's *political theology*, which is a dialectical, critical-historical theology, focuses upon both God and humankind. Unlike Marx's atheistic and anthropocentric philosophy, it talks about the God "for humankind," and does not exclude God from the human struggle for liberation. At the same time, unlike theology characterised by an "other worldly" piety and the search for the inner salvation of the soul, *political theology* of the cross talks about human activity in the world for the sake of the world. It is activity rooted in and built upon God's gracious and salvific *praxis* in and through Christ. *Political theology* of the cross maintains the intrinsic dialectical unity between the *praxis* of God and the *praxis* of humankind's response to God's gracious activity in the cross of Christ, by exercising a continual critical appraisal of its talk about God.

Moltmann's concern is that his *political theology* of the cross be a theology of Christian faith and not a reduction to politics or to any form of humanism, Marxian or other. He explains:

> If we would in practice put man in place of the divine, we would theoretically have to put the human essence in place of the divine. If we would change religion into politics, as our 'leftist' friends and Marxists demand, politics would have to become our religion. The state or the party would then become the Leviathan, the mortal god on earth. That would mean abolishing once again the desacralization of politics which Christianity has effected. This divinization of politics is a superstition which Christians cannot accept. They are Christians and hold to the crucified one in order to witness to men of a greater freedom.[10]

Therefore, in facing the Marxian challenge, the church should not capitulate to Marx's anthropocentric and socio-economic and political reductionism by, for example, becoming primarily a political power bloc in society. (The church cannot escape being *de facto* a political reality.) Instead, it should stand at the foot of the cross of Christ where all superstition—of politics, economics, humankind's capacity to end its historical alienation—is exposed and rendered impotent. Christians cannot show the relevance of their faith in the crucified God and maintain their identity as Christians, except by standing with the Lord who is the crucified One.

2.
Trinitarian Theology of the Cross

While the caption *political theology* shows Moltmann's concern with relevance, the caption *Trinitarian theology* shows his concern with identity. What makes theology of the cross evangelical theology? The answer rests in the Trinitarian character of Moltmann's theology of the cross. Marx's atheism (and all forms of atheism) cannot be met seriously by positing theism, for the God of theism is not necessarily the suffering and crucified God of the cross of Christ. To be true to its roots, Christian faith must point to a Trinitarian theology of the cross—an evangelical

theology which explicates the event of the cross as an event of the Father, Son, and
Holy Spirit. It is an event within the Triune God. Moltmann writes:

> It is an event between the sacrificing Father and the abandoned Son in a
> power of sacrifice that deserves to be named the Spirit. In the cross, Jesus
> and the Father are in the deepest sense separated in forsakenness, yet are at
> the same time most inwardly united through the Spirit of sacrifice. From
> the event between Jesus and his Father at the cross, the Spirit goes forth
> which upholds the abandoned, justifies the despised, and will bring the
> dead to life.[11]

Trinitarian theology of the cross is not a reduction to a theology of the Son, the
Second Person of the Trinity. It is characterised by the focus on the inherent unity
which exists between the God who suffers externally for the sake of God's people
and the God who suffers within godself. Thus, Moltmann's Christology is not
reduced either to a monotheism of the Father or to a monotheism of the Son but is
centred in the activity of the Triune God.[12]

In his insistence upon a Trinitarian theology of the cross, Moltmann emphasises
that the church's quest for relevance in the world neither shapes nor gives content to
the message of the salvific work of the crucified and risen God. To raise the
question of God only after the contemporary situation of socio-economic and
political oppression has been described is to fail to understand adequately the human
condition and the world as well as the God's creative presence which describes
God's being. Relevance and identity are complementarily bound together and,
therefore, must not be separated into entities unrelated to each other.

Where the church finds its identity, Moltmann notes, the question of relevance
arises. Similarily, where the church achieves relevance in the world, the question of
identity arises. It seems that only one or the other may obtain at any given moment
in history, but not both simultaneously. Moltmann calls this situation the "double
crises," where each "is simply a reflection of the other."

> Both crises can be reduced to a common denominator. Christian theology
> must be theology of the cross, if it is to be identified as Christian theology
> through Christ. But the theology of the cross is a critical and liberating
> theory of God and man. Christian life is a form of practice which consists
> in following the crucified Christ, and it changes both man himself and the

circumstances in which he lives. To this extent, a theology of the cross is a
practical theory.[13]

When God and humanity are spoken of together in the theology of the cross, there is
the explicit concern with relevance and identity.

Moltmann expresses a profound awareness of and concern for suffering
humanity. He recognises that human suffering includes socio-economic and political
suffering but is not limited to those forms of suffering. His concern for prophetic
witness in a suffering world leads him to interpret the event of the cross in the
context of the prophetic theology of the Old Testament.[14] He reminds us of the
continuity between "the Jewish God-situation" in the Hebrew scriptures and "the
passion of God according to the New Testament:"

> Christian faith does not have a new idea of God, but rather finds itself in
> a different God-situation. It is defined through the passion of God and the
> cross of Christ. It is related to the Jewish God-situation, for the pathos of
> God in the Old Testament is the presupposition for the passion of God
> according to the New Testament.[15]

Despite the continuity, there exists a fundamental difference between "the pathos
of God in the Old Testament" and "the passion of God according to the New
Testament." The crucial difference lies in the "bipolar" nature of the former and the
Trinitarian theology of the latter. Whereas, on the one hand, "the prophetic theology
of pathos proceeded from God's covenant with his people and, on this basis,
developed a bipolar theology between the pathos of God and the sympathy of the
Spirit in man," on the other hand, "those who discern the God-situation in the
crucified one are men from among all peoples." In the latter, the universality of
God's pathos is most acutely accented. Further, the contrasting difference between
the two forms of theology surrounds the way in which each apprehends the Divine
reality. While Israel apprehends God in terms of the covenant, Christians have
"Christ himself, who mediates the fatherhood of God and the power of the Spirit."
The latter is distinctly and necessarily a Trinitarian theology of the cross.

> Christian theology cannot develop (as is often done in process theology) a
> bipolar theology of interaction between God and the Spirit in man. It must,
> for the sake of the crucified one, intentionally become a *trinitarian theology*.

Through the crucified one, that dialogical God-relationship is first opened
up. Through Christ, God himself creates the conditions necessary to enter
upon a relationship of pathos and sympathy. Through the crucified one, he
creates a new covenant for those who cannot meet these conditions because
they are Godless and Godforsaken.[16]

Because the event of the cross is Trinitarian, even the hopeless and the despairing
receive genuine hope in God through Christ.

In his contrast between the bipolar theology in the Old Testament and the
Trinitarian theology in the cross of Christ, Moltmann does not suggest that the
phenomenon of God's suffering (even unto the death of the Son) for the sake of
humankind is lacking in the former. Indeed, bipolar theology is characterised by the
pathos of the suffering God. But the difference lies precisely in "the recognition of
God in Christ, and above all in the crucified one,"[17] who is the very completion of
God's humiliation. God not only enters "into the finitude of man but also into the
situation of his God-abandonness." As the Divine-human representative, Jesus is
Saviour and Liberator precisely in the Godforsakenness in the cross. In the
experience of the Godforsakenness of the Son, the Triune One shows that God is *for*
the forsaken and alienated. Jesus is for God and for humankind because he is of God
and of humankind.

Moltmann summarises the efficacy of God's paradoxical activity:

The Godforsaken Son of God takes the eternal death of the forsaken and the
damned upon himself in order to become God of the forsaken and brother
of the damned. Every person damned and forsaken by God can, in the
crucified one, experience community with God. The incarnate God is
present and accessible to the humanity of every man. No one needs to play
a role or to transform himself in order to come to his humanity through
Christ.[18]

Human beings are freed from having to *do* works in order to *be* free. Through
Christ, human beings are freed from and not further enslaved by the responsibility
for their self-transformation. The dynamic essence of the Triune God is totally and
irrevocably *pro-human*. "Nothing more exists that could exclude the lost man from
the situation of the pain of the Father, the love of the Son, and the life of the Spirit.
Without limits and without conditions, unhappy man is received into full community

with God." Here Moltmann posits the genuine and liberating *praxis* of the sovereign, yet humble and loving God, who freely suffers the pain of God's love for the sake of the salvation of suffering, oppressed and alienated humanity.

We return again to the danger that, in talking about God for humankind, the sovereignty of God is impaired and subordinated to the needs of humanity. Invariably, humankind is involved in talk about the crucified God—language about God is always human language. The dilemma is that in talking about the dynamic of (and within) the Trinity, in relation to the double crises of Christian faith's identity and relevance, it appears that the needs of sinful, alienated humanity are the primary occasion for God's self-disclosure in the Godforsakenness of the cross of Christ. If the latter is true, then God's sovereignty is violated, for God is portrayed as *subject to* humanity's needs. Moltmann attempts to avoid this danger by arguing that to say God reveals godself for the sake of humankind does not necessarily reduce, distort, or dispense with God's freedom and sovereignty. God does what God does because God's essence is freedom and love by which suffering is taken up by God into godself.

Moltmann writes:

> In the cross of Christ, a rupture tears, as it were, through God himself.
> It does not simply tear through Christ, as the doctrine of the two natures
> states. At first, it sounds paradoxical if one says that God himself is
> abandoned by God. God rejects himself. God cries out to God. Or, as
> Luther said: 'There God dies to God.'[19]

The solution to the dilemma is contingent upon whether God's revelation in the cross of Christ is a revelation of the inner-Trinitarian life. For Moltmann, humankind's needs do not occasion a radical transformation in the nature of God but a salvific revelation of the dynamic of and within the Triune God. There is an essential unity and harmony within the Trinity. Only because of this unity and harmony between "the sacrificing Father," "the abandoned Son," and "the Spirit of sacrifice" can the Godforsaken condition of sinful humanity be transformed by the suffering, death and resurrection of Jesus Christ.[20]

Moltmann's argument that the cross is both an inner-Trinitarian event and the external event of suffering love for the sake of humanity and the world echoes Hegel's thesis that Absolute Spirit realises itself by positing itself. But there are significant differences between the revelation of the Triune God in Moltmann's theology of the cross and the self-manifestation of Absolute Spirit in Hegel's philosophy—not least of all is the notable pathos in the former and the lack of pathos in the latter. Moltmann's Trinitarian theology of the cross capitulates neither to Feuerbach's anthropological reductionism nor to Hegel's philosophy of *Geist*. Instead, by embracing the pathos of Yahweh in its description of the Trinitarian event of suffering and crucified love in the cross of Christ, it seeks to be a Biblical theology of the cross.

A word about the crucial question of "change" within God is appropriate here. Moltmann's Trinitarian theology of the cross inevitably raises the question of whether the "dynamic" activity of the Trinity in the cross of Christ suggests "change" in God godself. Moltmann asserts that "the suffering and dying of Jesus, understood as the suffering and dying of the Son of God ... are works of God towards himself and therefore at the same time passions of God."[21] These inner works of God are contrasted with God's external works of "creation, new creation and resurrection" directed "against chaos, nothingness, and death."[22] Accordingly, the event of the cross reveals a *stasis* within the Godhead, a *stasis* linked to the formula, "God is love." The dynamic outworking of love implies a change within God who is Other, i.e., God turns towards humanity and assumes responsibility for its sin. God changes from the God who is Wholly Other to the God who is *pro-human*.

> God overcomes himself, God passes judgement on himself, God takes the judgment on the sin of man upon himself. He assigns to himself the fate that men should by rights endure. The cross of Jesus, understood as the cross of the Son of God, therefore reveals a change in God, a *stasis* within the Godhead: 'God is other.' And this event in God is the event on the cross. It takes on Christian form in the simple formula which contradicts all possible metaphysical and historical ideas of God: 'God *is* love.'[23]

In the Trinitarian event of the cross of Christ, the history of God's suffering for the sake of humankind is in reality a dialectical history involving God's suffering *in* history and God's suffering *within* godself. Thus, the truth of God's salvific suffering is distorted when the dialectic is destroyed and the message of God's suffering in history isolated from God's suffering *within* godself. "To think of 'God in history' always leads to theism and to atheism." However, when history is viewed in a "panentheistic" way, i.e., as existing in God, then, theism and atheism are transcended. "To think of 'history in God' leads ... into new creation and *theopoiesis*. To 'think of history in God' however, first means to understand humanity in the suffering and dying of Christ, and that means all humanity, with its dilemmas and its despairs."[24] In conclusion, Moltmann's Trinitarian theology of the cross views history in a dialectical way: the dialectic of "God in history" and "history in God."

3.

The "Unreligious" Cross in Christianity and the Critique of Religion as Ideology

Talk about God in response to the challenge of Marx's *Weltanschauung* must take constant cognisance of Marx's critique of religion as false consciousness. It is therefore instructive to consider whether Moltmann's theology of the cross is merely a legitimation of the *status quo,* be it economic, political, social or religious. Is not Marx's advocacy of the proletarian cause matched and, indeed, surpassed by God's solidarity with all of suffering humanity? The cross of Jesus refuses to be tied to any worldly system. No one can invoke its salvific efficacy on the basis of merit. It is always simultaneously judgement and grace, law and gospel. To say that the poor are blessed by God is not to say they merit that blessing. The miracle of God's presence with them is a miracle of grace. By the same token, to say that those who oppress the poor and the lowly are judged guilty by the cross of Christ is not to say that God is without mercy for them. The cross is the place of God's sovereignty and wrath, even as it is also the place of God's love. God's sovereignty and wrath prevent the cross from being the ideological tool or weapon of any individual, group or structure. The cross is the only true symbol of liberation. Moltmann captures this inherently elusive, "pilgrim" quality in the cross of Christ:

> A rejuvenation of Christianity when it has grown old and grey is only
> possible on the basis of its own origin, and becomes a dangerous and
> liberating reality when faith becomes aware of the incommensurability of the
> cross of Christ with the revelation of God, and realizing this, becomes
> aware too of its own strangeness and homelessness in its own Christian
> world.[25]

The cross of Christ does not conform to the expectations of either the religious or the non-religious. The "foolishness of God" leads to a "revaluation" of values. The foolishness of God contradicts human expectations and human estimation of what is good and beautiful.

> If faith in the crucified Christ is in contradiction to all conceptions of the righteousness, beauty and morality of man, faith in the 'crucified God' is also a contradiction of everything men have ever conceived, desired and sought to be assured of by the term 'God'. That 'God', the 'supreme being' and the 'supreme good', should be revealed and present in the abandonment of Jesus by God on the cross, is something that it is difficult to desire.[26]

Moltmann insists that there is no logical connection between "the religious longing for fellowship with God" and the peculiar "foolish" revelation of God as the crucified One, who is powerless and abandoned "in absolute death." Conditioned as it is by the world's uncritical acceptance of human triumphalism, religious longing for fellowship with God sees in the cross of the crucified One only abandonment, shame and powerlessness, but not the power of God. Consequently, the history of religion and theology in relation to the cross is replete with attempts to make the cross less the scandal it is and more a symbol of beauty and human achievement. This history of distortion and misinterpretation might be called ideological, because of the obvious manipulation of the event of the cross to suit human desire. Moltmann reminds us, however, that, despite the ideological use of the cross of Christ, it still retains its insuperable resilience as the definitive and decisive event of God—of both judgement and grace.

> In spite of all the 'roses' which the needs of religion and theological interpretation have draped round the cross, the cross is the really irreligious thing in Christian faith. It is the suffering of God in Christ, rejected and killed in the absence of God, which qualifies Christian faith as faith, and as something different from the projection of man's desire.[27]

Thus, even Marx's critique of religion as projection and as an opiate and the challenge of Marx's atheistic and anthropocentric world view, as well as the attacks of those of the school of "modern criticism of religion" on "the whole world of religious Christianity," cannot dull the poignancy of the message of the "irreligious" cross of Christian faith. Furthermore, all forms of human deification, be they religious or secular, are crucified in the cross of Christ. Marx's *Weltanschauung* is not exempt from this judgement but stands at its centre. Speaking about the absolute inclusiveness of the power of negation (judgement) of the "irreligious" cross, Moltmann writes:

> The modern criticism of religion can attack the whole world of religious Christianity, but not this unreligious cross. There is no pattern for religious projections in the cross. For he who was crucified represents the fundamental and total crucifixion of all religion: the deification of the human heart, the sacralization of certain localities in nature and certain sacred dates and times, the worship of those who hold political power, and their power politics.[28]

The cross of Christ reverses human achievement and human speculation about the meaning of existence, of history, and of the future of humankind and of the cosmos as a whole. Neither the religious power politics of the bourgeois capitalist class nor the secular, messianic revolutionary politics of the proletarian class can claim theirs is an inspiration that is totally sanctioned by the irreligious cross without any distortion of the message of that cross. Properly understood, the cross of the crucified One does not allow ideological manipulation. It negates all ideology and brings freedom and new life.

Consistent with his *Weltanschauung*, Marx left unanswered the question of the altruistic transformation of proletarian consciousness. Yet, the future of the proletarian revolution and the possibility of human liberation are dependent upon it. Marx was unapologetically critical of any interpretation of reality which left the mode and the relations of production unchanged or just partly changed. For him, the only transformation that is radical and liberating is that which would overthrow the bourgeois-capitalist system and replace it with the so-called communist mode. It must be *real* change, change premised upon a real change in the socio-economic (material) base of society. Moltmann neither totally rejects nor de-emphasises the need for Marx's materialist transformation. On the contrary, he calls for it, but his premise is the liberating and gracious *praxis* of the Triune God.

The meaning of *praxis-theoria* in Moltmann's theology differs fundamentally from its meaning in Marx's *Weltanschauung*. Moltmann derives its meaning only from the cross of Christ. "The symbol of the cross in the church points to the God who was crucified not between two candles on an altar, but between two thieves in the place of the skull, where the outcasts belong, outside the gates of the city." Moltmann conceives of *praxis-theoria* as directed towards the liberation of those who are oppressed and are without hope. He therefore asserts:

> [The cross] does not invite thought but a change of mind. It is a symbol which therefore leads out of the church and out of religious longing into the fellowship of the oppressed and abandoned. On the other hand, it is a symbol which calls the oppressed and godless into the church and through the church into the fellowship of the crucified God. Where this contradiction in the cross, and its revolution in religious values, is forgotten, the cross ceases to be a symbol and becomes an idol, and no longer invites a revolution of thought, but the end of thought in self-affirmation.[29]

Moltmann places heavy stress upon critical thinking that results in transformation of thought and action. Reflection upon the cross of the crucified God, as the place of refuge, hope and salvation for "the oppressed and godless," leads to inner conversion and outward, visible fellowship among "the oppressed and abandoned." Theology which does not call for true conversion, even when it insists that the cross of Christ is its centre and source of life, is not a theology of the cross but a theology of glory. "Revolution of thought" is replaced by "the end of thought in self-affirmation."

Perhaps, Moltmann's finest and most poignant expression of the paradoxical nature of the theology of the cross is his insistence upon the reversal of the title "Jesus Christ is Lord" to "The Lord is Jesus:"

> It is only through this reversal of emphasis that this image of the ruler is related to the person and history of Jesus and thus radically transformed. For early Christianity to use titles of rule and lordship in order to term Jesus the true Lord and ruler of the world—the Jesus who was mocked because of his helplessness and murdered on the cross by the world's rulers—involves about the most radical reversal of the ideal of rule that can be conceived: the Lord as servant of all; the ruler of the world as a friend of tax-collectors and sinners; the judge of the world as a poor outcast.[30]

Moltmann recognises the danger that in calling Jesus "the Lord," the picture of lordship is divorced from "the man from Nazareth" and, instead, "is derived from the experience of and longing for power." In contrast, the title, "the Lord is Jesus," is modelled after "the crucified Son of man on Golgotha" which gives it a distinctive and new meaning. The gospels show Jesus as the servant "for freedom." Jesus, who is not only the crucified and risen Son of man, but also "Lord of the world," stoops low and "washes his disciples' feet like a house slave (John 13:1–16)." For the sake of human liberation, Jesus empties himself and chooses the way of radical obedience and "self-surrender," instead of the path of violence and oppression.[31]

In keeping with the theme of the revaluation of values, Moltmann also emphasises the "agape" partisanship of Christ's solidarity with the poor and the oppressed. Agape partisanship does not negate the universal scope of the gospel of Christ. On the contrary, it is the paradoxical way of proclaiming the message of universal salvation in the crucified God in the midst of the ambiguities of existence. Though "the goal of glory is intended for all men," God has chosen to bring this about by being partial to the humble. "Because not all are 'people' in the same way, as far as their means, rights and freedom to live are concerned, the fellowship in which all are to see the glory of God 'together' is created, through the choosing of the humble and through judgment on the violent."[32] Thus, the Divine partisanship is inevitable and intentional. Its function is not to ultimately exclude any from, but to include all in, the salvation of God. Hence, partisanship and universality are dialectically related, for they are held together by universal love.

> This form of partisanship does not destroy Christian universalism, nor does it deny God's love for all men; it is the historical form of universal love in a world in which people oppress and hate each other. Jesus turned to the sinners, tax-collectors and lepers in order to save the Pharisees and the healthy as well. Paul turned to the Gentiles in order to save Israel too. Christian partisan support for the oppressed is intentional and its goal is to save the oppressor also.[33]

Divine partisanship is not an end in itself. God's rejection of the oppressor is not the last word of the cross. Love, acceptance, and the will to save all are the ultimate motivations, not the thirst for revenge. Through Divine judgement and wrath *qua* rejection, God ultimately intends a positive catharsis for those who oppress others:

"Masters are rejected because of their oppression, so that they may experience the fulness of the common humanity, of which they are depriving themselves and others."[34]   Oppressors are themselves victims of their own oppression! Nevertheless, the suffering love of God is open to all, including the rich and powerful. Suffering love is not available for use as a legitimation of any acts of revenge by the oppressed. The latter is a distortion which is, in turn, judged by this sacrificing love.

However, to talk about the universal salvation of the crucified God runs the risk of being abstract and speculative unless this partisanship is practised by the church. Moltmann recognises the need for a word of caution here, lest the very attempt at avoiding mere abstraction and speculation simply results in a reversal of roles of the oppressors and the oppressed. When that happens, the church is no longer the broken, forgiven community serving the world in love for the sake of and in the name of Christ—the Lord who is Jesus. Grace is replaced by a new form of law. Moltmann soberly reminds us that Jesus

> did not call upon the poor to revenge themselves upon their exploiters nor the oppressed to oppress their oppressors. Theologically, this would have been no more than the anticipation of the last judgment according to the law, but not the new righteousness of God which Jesus revealed in the law of grace. Instead, its consequences is: 'Love your enemies and pray for those that persecute you.'[35]

Hence, the liberation of Christ which is offered to all people everywhere is aptly described as the revolutionary *praxis* of *agape*. It is the " 'human revolt' of Jesus."[36]

4.
Definition of Human Being

Recalling Marx's theses that human beings make themselves and that history is the process of their creation of themselves, we note the influence of Marx's world view in Moltmann's emphasis upon human beings' realisation of themselves "in mission." Moltmann argues that human beings are defined in relation to the divine mission and call of God. The Divine mission reveals the gap between human beings and their fulfilment of their mission, of which they are incapable.

The dominant question of all anthropology—who or what is man? who am
I?—does not arise in the biblical narratives from comparing man with the
animals or with the things of the world. Nor does it arise simply *coram
Deo,* as Augustine and the Reformers affirmed. Rather, it arises in face of a
divine mission, charge and appointment which transcend the bounds of the
humanly possible.[37]

Moltmann finds support for his argument in the Hebrew scriptures:

> Moses (Ex. 3.11) asks in the face of his call to lead the exodus of the
> Israelites from Egypt: 'Who am I, that I should go unto Pharaoh, and that I
> should bring forth the children of Israel out of Egypt?' Thus, too, Isaiah
> (Isa. 6.5) in face of his call recognizes himself to be personally guilt-laden
> in the midst of a guilt-laden people: 'Woe is me! for I am undone; because I
> am a man of unclean lips, and I dwell in the midst of a people of unclean
> lips.' Thus Jeremiah in face of his call recognizes what he is and what he
> was: 'Ah, Lord God! behold, I cannot speak: for I am a child' (Jer. 1.6).[38]

Moltmann concludes that in the face of their discovery of the obvious gap between
the "divine mission" and their "own being," human beings learn what they are, what
they are to be, and, above all, that by and of themselves they cannot be.[39]

The human being is not defined by past and present but by the future. His/her
nature is not fully revealed but remains hidden with Christ in God. He/she is *homo
absconditus.*

> The very call to the possibilities of the future which are as yet obscure,
> makes it clear that man is hidden from himself, a *homo absconditus,* and
> will be revealed to himself in those prospects which are opened up to him
> by the horizons of mission. The mission and call do not reveal man simply
> to himself, with the result that he can then understand himself again for
> what he really is. They reveal and open up to him new possibilities, with
> the result that he can become what he is not yet and never yet was.[40]

In the scriptures, the call of those who are given special tasks includes a "new name
and a new nature and a new future." The hidden nature of human beings is not fixed

and static but dynamic, and it will unfold itself in the future to which God has called humankind. What human beings discover about themselves through their participation in this future will be new and different from what they thought they were before they became aware of God's call.

In speaking about humankind's future, Moltmann does not wish to deny the significance of the past and the present for humankind's identity. Indeed, his concept of human being includes the past and the present but defines human being from the perspective of the future. Thereby, Moltmann points beyond the possibilities of humankind's creative activity to the creative and gracious call of the crucified God, who alone can lead humankind out of enslavement and sin to freedom and a new, complete humanity. In the context of God's gracious call, humankind's total passivity is simultaneously a call to a totally human and liberating *praxis* of radical obedience. The crucified God not only calls forth the believer but also dwells within and stands alongside him/her. Both the believer and his/her world are totally embraced by God. Consequently, "in his call man is given the prospect of a new ability to be. What he is and what he can do, is a thing that he will learn in hopeful trust in God's being with man. Man learns his human nature not from himself, but from the future to which the mission leads him."[41] What human beings are will be revealed in the history of the call of God which they experience within the wider and totally inclusive embrace of the twofold *history* of the Trinity. The unfolding of human nature in history is the result of grace—the *praxis* of love. Paradoxically, human beings are also engaged in the unfolding of this mystery as creatures of response.

In spite of Moltmann's attempt to maintain the dialectic of the freedom of God (grace) and the secondary and creaturely freedom-in-bondage of human beings, the problem still remains whether humanity has not been circumscribed within political history which is (partially) calculable and manipulable. In answer to the question of transcendence which arises here, Moltmann points out that real eschatological history is both "God in history" and "history in God." He therefore departs from Marx, Bloch, and other Marxists, who limit history to human projection and achievement, by centring his anthropology within the domain of orthodox Christian theology. Humanity's future is firmly planted in the "history" of the Trinity in the crucified God. There is therefore an indispensable tension between immanence and transcendence, history and eschatology.

Human beings are oppressed when their nature is defined exclusively in terms of the socio-economic and political forces in history. Wherever such oppression occurs, the hope for genuine liberation rests in that future which transcends those forces and which is inextricably tied to the mission humankind receives from the crucified God. At the same time, human nature is not docetic, i.e., totally separated from those historical forces.

In the context of the cross, God understands human suffering to the extent that God suffers within godself for the sake of humankind. The *"praxis* of pathos" in the event of the cross takes with utmost seriousness the pervasiveness of human sin, meaninglessness and death, and offers forgiveness, reconciliation, hope, and life, both within and beyond history. Even now, the believer, in the midst of suffering, can celebrate in the "Spirit of sacrifice," who is the *arrabon* (2 Cor. 1:21; 5:5), the salvation which has come, and which will come, through the suffering, death, and resurrection of Christ—the Lord who is Jesus.

5.
A Critique of Moltmann's Radical Concept of God

There is no doubt that speaking about God in terms of the theology of the cross presents a radical concept of God. We have repeatedly referred to the pathos in Marx's description of the suffering of alienated humanity in capitalist society. We have argued that, in spite of its one-dimensional character, Marx's anthropology must not be bypassed by Christian theology but must be faced seriously in its entirety.

By engaging in such a dialogue, Christian theology places itself in a situation in which faithfulness to the gospel means that it must articulate a radical concept of God found only in the cross of Christ. In this dialogical situation, Christian theology is challenged by the question of the relevance of its talk about God in relation to human suffering. The human condition includes socio-economic and political oppression but is not limited to these forms of suffering. For Christian faith, the question of sin, evil, and death is most crucial.

According to Moltmann, in the face of suffering, Christian faith is most relevant when its central concept is the crucified God. The crucified God comprehends human suffering and takes it into godself because God's nature is love, which makes God open to pain and suffering. When the tragedy of the human condition is seen in the context of the suffering within God, then, the crises of identity and relevance find their solution. Moltmann writes:

> In the passion of the Son, the Father himself suffers the pains of abandonment. In the death of the Son, death comes upon God himself, and the Father suffers the death of his Son in his love for forsaken man. Consequently, what happened on the cross must be understood as an event between God and the Son of God. In the action of the Father in delivering up his Son to suffering and to a godless death, God is acting in himself. He is acting in himself in this manner of suffering and dying in order to open up in himself life and freedom for sinners.[42]

Moltmann's radical concept of God is not without difficulties, which cannot be overlooked in our attempt to formulate an evangelical theology of the cross. Has Moltmann fully dispensed with "philosophical axioms" about God? Has he dispensed with the mystery of God as Wholly Other? Is there no necessary place for talk about human nature *coram Deo*?

In the face of the meaninglessness and hopelessness that characterise human existence today, Moltmann's emphasis upon the suffering of God for the sake of humanity is of significant pastoral import. It is comforting to hear that God fully identifies with humanity in its suffering, sin and death. Jesus the Son suffers Godforsakenness and death, while the Father does not suffer death but the pain of Divine love in the Son's Godforsakenness and death. The Spirit of sacrifice— Moltmann is not clear on this—"suffers" the pain of such a sacrifice. Suffering is in the Trinity itself—hence the concept of the crucified God in the cross of Christ.

God not only identifies with suffering humanity, God suffers the death of the Son in order to heal broken humanity. Absolute Love cannot do, nor be, otherwise. It must suffer the extremities of pain which are intrinsic to such love. God as Absolute Love is thus not equated with Hegel's *Geist*. Moreover, love must suffer pain because of the existence of "non-love." Moltmann is very careful to place the latter— suffering for the sake of alienated humanity—in the context of the former— suffering of love in itself. Salvation is *sola gratia*. God is dynamic. All three Persons of the Trinity are actively engaged in the cross of Christ for the sake of love and the liberation of humanity.

The problem is: How do we know this? Where is the Totally Other God, the One who remains fully hidden from human scrutiny? Admittedly, God as Totally Other "remains" in terms of the peculiar twofold nature of God's love: love of God in godself and love of God for humanity. Still, Moltmann's dynamic of the crucified

God is unavoidably speculative. Though Moltmann does not capitulate to Hegel's concept of *Geist*, his concept of the dynamic God in the cross of Christ is, nevertheless, influenced by the concept of the all-embracing nature of Absolute Spirit. But, Moltmann's crucified God feels pain. Did not Yahweh feel wrath and love and joy? In the cross the suffering love of God becomes universal love. This is achieved because a *stasis* occurs within God godself. The Wholly Other becomes wholly *pro-human*. The Trinity is no longer enshrouded in total mystery.

It is true that the event of the cross embraces the whole of creation, but in the face of human suffering, sin and death, the believer can only say that God *in Christ* understands and suffers because Christ suffered death on the cross. God who loved the world and allowed the Son to die for humanity and all creation knows the pain of loving. That is comforting to the believer. But the event of the cross does not reveal, even to the eyes of faith, that the "Wholly Otherness" of the Triune God has been totally transformed into being totally *pro-human*. The dynamic of the Trinity in the event of the cross does not exhaust the mystery of God, who, as Totally Other, remains hidden and eludes definition even in such a concept of the Trinity. This hidden God remains in the background and is not our concern. Our concern is with the gracious and loving God whom we meet in the man on the cross. Through the Spirit, humanity is called to reconciliation to and fellowship with the Triune God.

By speaking of the God who is transcendent future, who calls humankind to mission, Moltmann softens the criticism that he distorts the concept of God as Totally Other. As Absolute Future, God remains mystery, which humankind cannot unravel. God is more than the God of loving *praxis*. God is also necessarily the One who is not always active, calling humankind to a liberating future. In spite of this criticism, it is absolutely crucial for humankind that the God who reveals godself is totally *pro-human*.

When Moltmann describes the passion of Christ as the passion of the Trinity (the crucified God), he is not formulating "a new idea of God." Instead, he is pointing to the fact that talk about God today is done in "a new God-situation," i.e., in the realm of politics. Here the process replaces the old theodicy question about evil in the cosmos. In making this transference, Moltmann unwittingly places evil in God. The crucified God (who is unlike Hegel's God who cannot suffer pain) is in fact like Hegel's God who embraces everything. Thus history, its ambiguities and dilemmas, its sin and evil, are now placed within God. But the implication is contrary to orthodox Biblical and confessional theology, where evil is not in God.[43] This problem needs further exploration, which is beyond the scope of this book.

In appraising Moltmann's radical concept of God and its universal scope of the passion in the cross, evangelical theology of the cross sums up the description thus: How do we proclaim the word of hope that the love of God embraces all suffering and distortion, including sin and evil, and transforms them by bringing healing and wholeness through the passion of Christ, without, at the same time, placing not only the potentiality of evil but the actuality of evil in God? Can we resolve this dilemma within the context of the church's historical confession of the two natures in Christ?

Moltmann suggests that we can do so only partially, as is evident from his peculiar Trinitarian theology of the cross by which he attempts to go beyond the traditional explication of the suffering love of God in the cross of Christ. God who loves unreservedly and unconditionally is "the other." It is impossible for humankind to be this God; indeed, humankind needs this God. Divine love suffers infinite pain, for "God dies to God." In the event of the cross of Christ, the Son of God experiences Godforsakenness and death. At the same time, God the Father experiences the Godforsakenness of the Son. For Moltmann, only a radical concept of God does justice to the intra-Divine love between the Father and the Son.

The implication of this is speculative and, as we have already argued, must be viewed in tension with the concept of God who is totally *pro-human* and at the same time Totally Other, not only in the sense of suffering and embracing love, but also as the Totally Other whose feelings cannot be known directly or indirectly. Theology of the cross does not exhaust the mystery of the *Deus Absconditus*. Therefore, in our attempt to appropiate Moltmann's explication of the cross, we maintain the historical doctrine of the suffering love of God in Christ for, as we have seen, in both Luther and Moltmann, humankind learns about the gracious and loving God precisely through the cross of the Lord who is Jesus. The believer looks to the cross and sees the suffering and death of the Son, who loves both the Father and the world. By implication, the Father, who loves both the Son and the world, suffers as well. Theology of the cross is a practical-critical activity which is done within the context of Christian faith.

Despite Moltmann's refusal to accept the Marxian one-dimensional definition of humankind, his own concept of human nature is significantly influenced by the Marxian concept of historical transcendence. We recall that Moltmann defines human nature in terms of the missionary hope to which God calls humankind. It is an inadequate definition, for he fails to account for the evil in humankind (and in the world)—unless he places it in God! Humankind is not totally perfectable in history. Sin cannot be adequately described in Marx's concept of alienation. It is more pervasive. The gap between sin and grace cannot be bridged by humankind, not even by its participation in missionary hope. Humankind does not have to run after God, who is out there in the future, to know itself. God is already here and humankind *coram Deo* knows itself. Humankind is fundamentally separated from God. Despite the static nature of the concept of original sin, we cannot dispense with it in any definition of human being. To do so would not ultimately liberate humankind but further enslave it. Thus, in defining human nature, we would speak of humankind as basically estranged from and in rebellion against God. God calls humankind to a future which is shrouded in mystery, hidden in Christ.

Such a definition of humankind obviously has implications for the way we talk about the event of the cross. The *praxis* of love is not the transformation of Hegel's *Geist* into a being of pathos who dynamically continues to embrace the whole of creation without end. Rather, the *praxis* of love is primarily that of the Triune God, who experiences the pain of the death of the Son for the salvation and reconciliation of sinful humanity and of all creation. Through the Holy Spirit—the Spirit of sacrifice and fellowship—all are invited to see the gracious God in the cross and resurrection of Jesus Christ. The invitation is also a call to fellowship with God and with all creation which God has redeemed. The crucified God alone is the revealed God who is *pro-human*.

B.
Liberation Theology: A Theology of Human Familyhood[44]

We turn now to two of the pivotal works in Latin American liberation theology: Gustavo Gutiérrez, *A Theology of Liberation* and Jon Sobrino, *Christology at the Crossroads*. Gutiérrez's initial exploration into theology as a critical reflection on human *praxis* in the light of the dawning of the reign of God is taken a step further by Sobrino's formulation of a critical Christology in which the reign of God, and not just communion with God, is seen as Jesus' ultimate focus. The two theologies functionally complement each other.

Unlike the theologies of Luther and Moltmann, Latin American theology comes out of the context of widespread socio-economic poverty and political oppression. Consequently, liberation theology is more pervasively bound up with the problem of socio-economic and political liberation. Its themes of universal brotherhood *qua* familyhood, justice as preferential option for the poor, solidarity among the oppressed, destruction of all that injures or totally prevents the emergence of the reign of God which Jesus claimed has come—themes which are all related to the primary motif of liberation as salvation—significantly reflect the profound influence of Marx's world view upon liberation theology.[45] Liberation theology articulates a radical concept of God who is the God of the Exodus, of justice and freedom, of the cross and resurrection of Jesus Christ. God sides with the oppressed against the oppressor, in the concrete, historical conditions of life, for the sake of both the oppressed and the oppressor.

Liberation theology sees the task of theology as a process of critical reflection which is done in the context of the socio-economic and cultural issues actually existent in society. Critical reflection is done by the Christian community, which attempts to make its talk about God relevant to the needs of the oppressed. But the content of critical reflection is not merely the material conditions of life. It includes that which is peculiarly Christian and theological as well. There is an ongoing dialogue between theology and sociology. The Christian community constantly listens to both the scriptures and the human condition. Presuppositions are altered, corrected, or totally rejected in the light of *praxis*, which is also informed and corrected by the scriptures and the symbols of the church. This is the hermeneutic circle. By maintaining the hermeneutic circle, the church moves away from being a supporter of the oppressive *status quo* to being a community for liberation and justice in society.

According to Gutiérrez, both church and society are criticised to the extent that "they are called and addressed by the Word of God." This Word serves as a critique of any critical theory which emerges out of theological reflection. The authenticity of any theology is determined by its positive evaluation in the light of the Word, especially its call for genuine liberating historical *praxis*.[46] Writing in the same vein, Sobrino distinguishes between inauthentic and authentic theology in terms of "an inherited faith that is rather abstract," on the one hand, and a "concrete faith that is truly liberative," on the other hand.[47] Let us now examine some of the main emphases in the respective theologies of Gutiérrez and Sobrino.

1.

Gustavo Gutiérrez: A Theology of the Neighbour

Consistent with his emphasis on "theology as critical reflection on historical praxis,"

Gustavo Gutiérrez insists that theology is not concerned simply with the liberation of the privileged minority in the church but with the universal liberation of the whole of humanity. Indeed, because of its basic concern with "the liberating transformation of the history of humankind," theology is consequently concerned with "that part of humankind—gathered into *ecclesia*—which openly confesses Christ."[48]

This claim is based on the conviction that as a result of the Divine incarnation in Jesus of Nazareth, the erroneous distinction between the religious and the secular realms has now been dissolved. "Since the Incarnation, humanity, every human being, history, is the living temple of God. The 'pro-fane,' that which is located outside the temple, no longer exists."[49] The God of the Exodus and of the cross of Christ reveals godself to all. Hence, God is available to all everywhere. Every person has new dignity because of Christ. Socio-economic, political, and other distinctions, which hitherto have been used to divide and to separate humanity into superior and inferior classes, are anathema to God. Divisions and separations which exist are therefore to be historically abolished. The mandate to do so comes from God godself.

God not only calls humanity to engage in liberating *praxis,* God leads the way by generating that living faith and hope which are born out of involvement in *praxis* and are continually nourished by God precisely where such liberating activity occurs.

> Where oppression and human liberation seem to make God irrelevant—a
> God filtered by our longtime indifference to these problems—there must
> blossom faith and hope in him who came to root out injustice and to offer,
> in an unforeseen way, total liberation. This is a spirituality which dares to
> sink roots in the soil of oppression-liberation.[50]

Liberating love and faith are "the gift of the Kingdom of God."[51]

Gutiérrez reminds us that love of humanity, of the neighbour, does not violate the sovereignty of God, for it is precisely in the concrete love for human beings that God becomes God. Hence, human beings should be loved for their own sakes and not merely for God's sake. Only in this way can love for humanity not distort human dignity but promote and strengthen it. Humankind is not a means to an end. Human beings are created in the image of God. Human beings must, therefore, not be made into "instrument[s] for becoming closer to God." Only when human beings are loved for their own sakes can there be a genuine encounter with God. Love of humanity and love of God form a dialectic of love which fully embraces the dignity of humankind and the sovereignty of the liberating God. "That my action towards another is at the same time an action towards God does not detract from its truth and concreteness, but rather gives it even greater meaning and import."[52]

Gutiérrez is concerned about God and humanity. He insists that if talk about God distorts human dignity, then it is irrelevant and illegitimate. It is not grounded in the liberating Word. Such ideological discourse about God must be replaced by a "new way" of making God relevant and necessary to the needs of the masses of exploited humanity. Gutiérrez pushes his point so far that it reads thus: the existence of God as love in history is *dependent* upon the concrete *praxis* of love for the liberation of humankind.

Gutiérrez points out that love of humanity for its own sake qualifies as love of God, not only because humanity "has been made in the image and likeness of God," but, more especially, because humankind is *"the sacrament of God."* Human beings cannot come to an authentic knowledge of God by mere theoretical reflection which is removed from the concrete socio-economic and political struggles in society. If human beings wish to encounter God, they must draw near to those whose wretched existence is an offence to God. Both the self-satisfied religious person and the earnest seeker of God are reminded that "to oppress the poor is to offend God; to know God is to work justice among human beings." Human beings know that they are in the presence of God when they join the struggle for the liberation of their neighbours.[53]

When Christian celebration of the presence of Christ in the Eucharist is divorced from radical commitment to liberation, then there is no genuine celebration, but only "an empty action." According to Gutiérrez, the loving communion between the Triune God and humanity is the basis for the familyhood of the poor and the oppressed. God initiates and nourishes that twofold bond of unity—between humanity and God, and among human beings. In the Eucharist, the bond is "effectively recalled and proclaimed," provided that there is "a real commitment against exploitation and alienation." Only on this basis can those who participate in the Eucharist gain God's acceptance of their celebration. Worship and "living" are two aspects of one fundamental activity—living and dying for the sake of others. There is no other way of effectively remembering and celebrating the communion between God and humanity. Gutiérrez writes:

> 'To make a remembrance' of Christ is more than the performance of an act
> of worship; it is to accept living under the sign of the cross and in the hope

of the resurrection. It is to accept the meaning of a life that was given over
to death—at the hands of the powerful of this world—for the love of
others.[54]

The cross of Christ means cross and suffering for the Christian community.
Christian life cannot be anything else and still be Christian.

The cross of the Christian community is not just any cross. It is a specific cross,
a cross of solidarity among the oppressed. Knowing that one encounters God in the
neighbour, the Christian must make his/her neighbour's suffering his/her own and
join in the struggle for liberation. Such an unequivocal call leaves little or no room
for the gracious presence of God among those who fail to maintain the unity between
worship and liberating *praxis*. *Sola gratia* is impaired. There is less grace for those
who are not involved in the specific *praxis* for liberation, than for those who are. To
follow Christ is to walk the way of the cross, the way of grace without merit or
praxis. This sanguine reminder needs to be more clearly sounded in Gutiérrez's
theology.

Furthermore, in any theology of liberation, sin is still more inclusive than
alienation as a description of the human condition. Likewise, salvation includes
historical liberation but points beyond it to the more inclusive reconciliation and
communion with God in God's kingdom beyond this world. When this is forgotten
or its significance reduced, the theology of the cross is turned into a theology of
glory—resurrection glory transforms the cross into an ideology of liberation.

Gutiérrez's reflections on a "theology of the neighbor" and the shortcomings in
histheology must be understood in the light of Jesus' discourse on the last
judgement in Matthew 25:31–46. We turn now to a summary of his interpretation of
that text.

2.

Matthew 25:31–46: Discourse on Christ in the Neighbour

Gutiérrez notes that, to many people, this vision of the judgement with which
Matthew concludes his eschatological discourse summarises the "essence of the
gospel message." In light of liberation theology's preoccupation with the solidarity
of God with the oppressed, it is not surprising that Gutiérrez enunciates a theology
of universal familyhood premised upon Matthew's discourse and upon a reading of

various scriptural texts which speak about love of neighbour.

Reviewing Jean-Claude Ingelaere's elaborate study of this text, Gutiérrez points out two basic questions which Ingelaere finds in the text: "Who are the nations judged by the Son of God and who are 'the least of the brethren' of the Son of Man?" Ingelaere's answer offers three possible interpretations: universal judgement of all people—both Christian and non-Christian—on the basis of their love for the neighbour, especially the one in need; judgement of Christians in relation to "their behaviour towards the disadvantaged members of the Christian community itself;" finally, "judgment of pagans based on their attitude towards Christians." Gutiérrez rejects the third interpretation (espoused by Ingelaere himself) because of the restrictive and selective judgement it describes. Gutiérrez agrees with the majority of the exegetes who support the first interpretation. He argues that "the two restrictions involved in this third exegesis ... go against the obvious sense of the text and the context, which stress the universality of the judgment and the central and universal character of charity." He agrees with the conclusion that "all nations" (v. 32) clearly points to the universal sense in which no distinctions are made between Jews and Christians, and pagans. In short, all people, pagans, Jews and Christians, are included in the term, "all nations."[55]

This conclusion provides the Biblical basis for Gutiérrez's argument that God is encountered in and among human beings, i.e., humanity is the sacrament of God. Furthermore, concerning the meaning of "the least of my brethren" (v. 40), he agrees with the view held by most scholars that here we have another expression of the universal scope of human familyhood. All the needy, Christian and non-Christian, are included in the designation, "the least of my brethren." Consistent with his agreement with the "universalist" school of interpretation, Gutiérrez emphasises three points which pertain to the text: "the stress on communion and fellowship as the ultimate meaning of human life; the insistence on a love which is manifested in concrete actions, with 'doing' favored over simple 'knowing'; and the revelation of the human mediation necessary to reach the Lord."[56]

The question arises: How do we encounter the Lord? We recognise that such a dynamic encounter answers the question: Where do we find God, and how do we get to know God? In light of Gutiérrez's three emphases, his response to these questions is found in a reiteration of the central argument of liberation theology: God is encountered in history through our encounter with fellow human beings, especially the culturally, economically, and politically exploited and oppressed. Gutiérrez concludes that, in Matthew 25:31–46, what Christ reveals to us through his identification with the poor is that the locus of God's salvation in the world is found among the poor. Consequently, "our attitude towards them, or rather our commitment to them, will indicate whether or not we are directing our existence in conformity with the will of the Father."[57]

3.

Jon Sobrino: Christology of Radical Discipleship

Jon Sobrino attempts to talk about God in a meaningful and relevant way in the context of Latin America, in order that the movement from an inherited faith to a liberating faith might occur. Sobrino formulates a radical, "relational" Christology which is Trinitarian in outlook. For Sobrino, it is the only way to do Christology in the face of the material challenges in Latin America today.

> Christology is possible only if the Father continues to be the ultimate
> horizon of reality, the Son continues to be the definitive example of how
> human beings can correspond to the Father, and life according to the Spirit
> of Jesus continues to be the authentic Christian way of acting that makes us
> sons and daughters in and through the Son.[58]

One cannot know God except through Jesus. But to know Jesus, one must follow him in radical discipleship. Thus the Son, the Spirit, and the Father are seen to be related to one another through the *praxis* of love, and both God and humankind are related to each other through the *praxis* of the Father in the Son through the witness of the Spirit of Jesus.

Understanding and participating in the relational dynamic within the Trinity involves liberating *praxis* in the world. Apart from such participation, humanity cannot "understand and appreciate the Jesus who sends the Spirit."[59] Genuine knowledge of God does not arise out of theoretical and abstract reflection upon the "numinous" mystery of God's being; nor does it arise simply from some other reflection on *praxis* tied to the *status quo*. Rather, authentic knowledge of God results from humankind's engagement in the *praxis* which is prompted by the Spirit of Jesus. Knowledge comes from action which is not simply mental activity. God is not a metaphysical being whom humanity knows before and apart from humanity's encounter with the neighbour. The definitive criterion of every *praxis* is the history of Jesus himself. Jesus' love of the Father is not a theoretical or a sentimental love; nor is it a love that is mechanically exercised. On the contrary, it is the love of the Son who struggles against oppression and sin on behalf of the oppressed and suffering. This synthesis between love of God and love of neighbour was historically fashioned throughout Jesus' earthly ministry.[60] The confident love which Jesus displays in his address to God as "Abba" "reaches its culminating point in the agony in the garden. Poles apart from some ideologized optimism, it becomes a confidence that has been thoroughly tried and tested."[61]

Jesus' confident love is well-founded, for it is in God who is "greater" than human beings. For Jesus to have such a God "means responding to the demands laid down by love. It is in and through the historical unfolding of those demands that the reality of God as someone 'greater' is made concrete horizontally in history." The ultimate test of the truth of love is incarnation and *praxis*. Jesus responds to the demands of love placed upon him by God by a life of radical obedience, even to the point of death on the cross. The cross is the culmination of love that is fashioned in the encounter with the material world. Such is the nature of his love which cannot violate the sovereignty of God—the ultimate horizon. "Neither conflict, nor failure, nor rejection, nor death itself can set limits on God's demand. This is the way in which the greatness of God is brought out in history and respected to the very end. At no point in his history can Jesus get a 'fix' on God once and for all."[62] It is precisely through Jesus' historical and existential commitment and obedience to and love of God that the sovereignty of God is historically displayed. This is the *very* revelation of God godself.

In the cross of Jesus we see the triumph of Absolute Love (God). Love that is grounded in God and historically fashioned in the real material conditions of life will not remain negated in suffering and death. It will ultimately triumph because Absolute Love remains its source and horizon. This is the confidence of the love of God in the cross of Christ. But in looking for God, one is not called to reflect upon Absolute Love but upon the historically fashioned love. "In the Christian view [God's] locus is not only the resurrection but also the cross of Jesus." Today, the cross of Jesus (God) "is to be found in the crosses of the oppressed rather than in beauty, power, or wisdom."[63] The crosses of the oppressed are the *praxis* of the love of Jesus in the Spirit.

It is in the context of Jesus' *praxis* of love that the Christian learns about God and comes to know God through the imitation of the *praxis* of love. The Christian must recognise that he/she cannot love God directly—that is impossible—but only indirectly through the mediation of a historical love. This mediating love is an unconditional and unreserved love of the neighbour. Sobrino writes:

> When Christians talk about love of God, then, they are talking *materially* about real, historical love for human beings. It is the *formal* nature of this love of neighbor that determines whether it can also be called love of God. If that love is displayed unreservedly and unconditionally, if it is done in the conviction that those who love to the utmost have lived life in all its fullness no matter what happens, then the historical experience of love for neighbor is formally meaningful as love for God.[64]

Love for neighbour, like the love of Jesus which it emulates, is not *a priori* or mechanically received from the Spirit. Instead, it is born and nourished in the midst of liberating engagement for the transformation of the world. Love of neighbour creates a familyhood which reveals both the genuineness of the Christian's love of God and neighbour, as well as the very existence of God godself. "Brotherhood is not just an ethical consequence deriving from a God already constituted and known; it is *the* very way in which God really is the Father, and in that sense, God. In Jesus' eyes, a God who does not create brotherhood simply is not God at all."[65]

The "existence" of many "false" gods is a real possibility. Sinful humanity is not easily persuaded to participate in liberating *praxis* for the sake of the neighbour and thereby to come to know God. Idolatry was present in Jesus' time, no less than today. Sobrino soberly points out that Jesus presents us with a radical concept of God: "a God who stands in complete contradiction to the existing religious situation. His God is distinct from, and greater than, the God of the Pharisees."[66] Jesus' God loves, unconditionally and unreservedly, all people, especially the poor, those who are without hope and who are therefore in need of a miracle from God to transform their situation.[67] From the standpoint of Jesus' life, the privileged place of access to God—which Jesus widened—is not the temple but people themselves. "More specifically, it is the person who is poor, who has been forced into impoverishment." This salvific partisanship is precisely the way in which we come to know God. To speak of "access" to God is to speak of knowing God in the way God chooses to make godself known to us which is by making contact with the very people whom the religious of Jesus' day saw as completely estranged from God: "the alien, the heretic, the ritually impure person, the sinner, the distinherited, the poor, the orphan, the widow, and the enemy."

The poor are not humanity's way to God but the medium God chooses through which humanity comes to know God. Salvific "contact" with the poor is a consequence of God's sovereign grace. Thus, "making contact" with the poor does not mean that the poor are "simply the 'passive material' on which one works to attain access to God through virtuous dealings with them."[68] One cannot experience the liberating power of God through the poor without an unconditional and unreserved love for them. Nothing short of an actual struggle to transform the material conditions of the poor in order that the poor may have true dignity as persons, as Jesus intends, can qualify as solidarity with the oppressed and as making authentic contact with the poor. Whoever would know God must imitate the way of Jesus.

Sobrino is correct in his emphasis upon the ultimate triumphant power of Absolute Love, but he neglects to emphasise that the grace of God allows for failure and blindness and continues to accept the unacceptable, the proud, the mighty, the self-sufficient, and not just the poor, the humble and the oppressed. Care should be taken that in emphasising the inclusive nature of Jesus' love, in terms of the poor and the outcast—the marginalised—we do not fall prey to an exclusiveness that limits the saving presence of God to the marginalised. The tendency towards such an exclusiveness arises in spite of liberation theology's claim that *all* are the sacrament of God. Consequently, there is the need for a more inclusive concept of the poor that transcends the socio-economic and political factors which delineate the poor. At the same time, such a concept must be radical in its attempt to do justice on behalf of that large majority of humanity which actually experiences material poverty and oppression.

In Sobrino's presentation of the material, dynamic development of Jesus' messianic consciousness characterised by "confident love," we are given a stimulating theological explication of the Marxian concept of *praxis-theoria*. Like Marx's proletariat, Jesus comes to an awareness of his messianic mission through his participation in the real, material conditions of life. His consciousness of his mission is not mechanically given. It does not simply unfold itself as if it were pre-programmed. That is not what incarnation means. Rather, Jesus' mission and his consciousness arise through practical-critical activity. But we should not push the Marxian parallel too far, for Sobrino explicitly states that Jesus' ultimate horizon, which includes humanity, is the Father and the kingdom. It is clear that Jesus' ultimate horizon directly contrasts with the proletariat's.

When we turn to the development of the Christian's life under the cross in the material conditions of life, we find that both Sobrino and Gutiérrez use Jesus' "experience" as the paradigm for imitation. The Christian does not repeat the life of Jesus. Instead, the Christian follows Christ in radical discipleship by seeking out the poor and creating human familyhood. Solidarity and familyhood are found precisely in those very situations that deny their existence and make talk about God seem irrelevant. So far, liberation theology is a theology of the cross. But liberation theology abbreviates the Word of the cross, the scandal, and foolishness of the announcement that in spite of the failure to create familyhood, to love unconditionally and unreservedly, God accepts us. Theology of the cross is both life under the cross and Word of the cross. The two are indispensable. Indigenisation of theology must not silence or eclipse the universality of the cross and the preaching of the Word. Despite Sobrino's and Gutiérrrez's emphasis upon both *praxis* and *theoria*, the paradoxical Word of the cross has been circumscribed within the sphere of radical discipleship.

Furthermore, the abundant life to which God calls us through Christ cannot be equated with living life, in the midst of ambiguities, suffering, sin and death, with human beings' unconditional and unreserved love for the neighbour. Such love is only a foretaste which is received in paradox. There is also the hope of the "resurrection and eternal life" which God offers to all unconditionally. Realised eschatology in terms of such confident love for humankind and, consequently, for God can awaken, correct and transform the longing for the reign of God and communion with God beyond this temporal life. By the same token, it can make such confident love an end in itself, thereby abbreviating hope.

4.

Critique of the Concept of God in Liberation Theology

Theology of universal human familyhood emphasises God's immanence vis-à-vis God's transcendence. Although Sobrino speaks about the Father as the ultimate mystery and horizon beyond Jesus the Son, i.e., the God who as the "other" is "greater," there is no question that liberation theologians are primarily concerned with a God who is present in history among humankind actively engaged in real human liberation. The dominant Biblical paradigm is of the God who participates in the Exodus and in the cross and resurrection—always within history, not above, outside or beyond it. Of course, this does not mean that God is wholly immanent;

such a conclusion distorts liberation theology. Rather, it means that transcendence is subordinated to immanence for the sake of humankind. The liberating God acts on behalf of humankind and is thereby simultaneously revealed. To know who God is and where God is acting, we need to look for "signs" of the kingdom. Where a situation of oppression and dehumanisation exists, there God is to be found. The fragmentary indications of various and partial forms of solidarity among the alienated and exploited masses are expressions of the presence of the kingdom. God as Divine love exists wherever there is solidarity among the poor. It is a peculiar solidarity: solidarity that leads to and is not divorced from genuine liberating *praxis*. God is given a "face" whenever and wherever there is a concrete expression of love for the neighbour. It is the *"praxis* of love" and not merely the ethics of love which says that God is, and that God is love and justice and freedom.

The problem with this kind of discourse about God is that the primary emphasis is placed upon critical reflection and analysis of the human condition to know where God is, i.e., where God is acting. Revelation is reduced to the findings of "critical reflection," and authentic Christian faith is viewed as a consequence of correct practice *(praxis)*. Thus Paul's encouragement to the Corinthian Church: "For we walk by faith and not by sight," is reversed—sight and not faith determines the Christian "walk."[69]

On the critical question of how we talk about God, it is to be noted that liberation theology downplays the motif of the *Deus Absconditus*. If God is not up and around effecting noticeable historical transformations in the oppressive and inhuman structures in society, then God does not exist or, if God does, God is merely the ideological idol of the oppressive class in society. The true God is the One who is characterised less by mystery and more by God's increasing, unambiguous presence among the poor and needy to whom God is thereby revealed. Such a conception, however, does not take seriously the inherent discontinuity between God revealed in the suffering of humankind and God who is always more than what humankind is. God stands above humankind and human suffering, even as God is simultaneously present in the most alienated and sinful situations.

Not surprisingly, liberation theology downplays the "mystery" of God, the *Deus Absconditus*. The consequent distortion of the truth of the gospel seems inevitable when one operates within the framework of Marxian categories, as liberation theology does. Carl Braaten suggests that "the impact of this alliance is to press religion into the straightjacket of political humanism, the idea of transcendence being consequently flattened out and confined to a 'negative dialectic' in the material course of history."[70] In dialogue with Marx's philosophy, the breadth, height and depth of evangelical theology is reduced to those aspects of the Christian faith which are more amenable to the Marxian overriding emphasis upon liberating *praxis* and the human future. Consequently, the indispensable tension between immanence and transcendence is eclipsed through the absorption of the latter in the former.

Liberation theology's emphasis upon the immanence of God, the "God for humankind," sounds a primary note in the theology of the cross. For example, it emphasises that in the theology of the cross, God reveals godself in history as always being "for humankind." Instead of speculating about the hiddenness of God shrouded in mystery, i.e., the "otherness" of God which we cannot see, it points out that we should be concerned with the God who meets us in the cross of Christ in judgement and grace. However, the theology of the cross does not reduce God to the dialectics of history for it proclaims the "resurrection of the body and the life of the world to come." In short, true and ultimate liberation transcends history, even though it begins in history. This is crucial to our talk about God. God—the crucified One—is totally concerned about the historical human condition. God is *pro-human* and comes to humanity and the whole of creation as Absolute Future. But God is simultaneously present in the cross of the crucified and risen Christ. We therefore maintain the balance between Divine immanence and Divine transcendence. History cannot exhaust the transcendence of God and transcendence should not be seen as a check on God's immanence but rather as a check upon the euphoric triumphalism of humanity's hope in its efforts to eradicate all oppression and sin and usher in the age of freedom here on earth. In other words, without the transcendence of God, humankind would be confined to history, whether history as its own creation or history as a co-creation with God. In either case, history circumscribes humankind's future.

When liberation theology presents human beings as God's co-workers for human liberation , the result is that, on the one hand, it is not so much human beings who are chosen by God to be God's co-creators as God who comes to human beings' aid to free them to create. Here God is humankind's co-agent for liberation. On the other hand, the truth that humankind's freedom is a gift of grace is distorted and made into "a sophisticated new form of Pelagianism."[71] The sovereignty of God is violated in both instances. In liberation theology, the freedom to create which is given by grace is so wrapped up with human *praxis* that grace is made partial in humankind's salvation: *sola gratia* is made to read *sola gratia* plus human *praxis*. This is a contemporary form of synergism. While the indicative and the imperative of the gospel must never be separated from each other if theology is to remain evangelical, it is the imperative that arises out of the indicative. Freed by God, we are free to serve the neighbour in love. Hence, we do not serve in order to assist in our salvation.

Unfortunately, as liberation theologians, among others, know only too well, the message of *sola gratia* often has been distorted into an ethical "quietism" that allows inhuman and oppressive structures to remain intact without being seriously questioned and attacked with the practical intention of transforming and humanising them. The truth of this accusation is borne out by the history of the church. In its own attempts to respond theologically to the challenge in the historical context of Latin America, liberation theology has not, however, avoided the equally distorting conversion of gospel into law. Instead of gospel as "cheap grace," liberation theology, in overstating its case for knowledge of God as "doing," presents us with gospel as law—the imperative of the gospel has abbreviated the indicative of the gospel. In spite of the hermeneutic circle in liberation theology, in which the final horizon of theological *praxis-theoria* is the liberating Word of God and the kingdom of God, abbreviation of the gospel does occur. Indeed, it is, more significantly, because of its peculiar theological hermeneutics that such a distortion arises. The reason for this is twofold. On the one hand, since the horizon of liberation theology is not a metaphysical reality which is known apart from *praxis*, but one which becomes known and proves its authenticity through *praxis-theoria*, that horizon is subordinated to the dialectic of history. The dialectic of history *de facto* is given priority over any horizon which is merely a word about objective, vicarious liberation. Accordingly, on the other hand, when the indicative of the gospel is subordinated to the ethical imperative, i.e., made subject to the demands of and for liberation—programmes and strategies for liberation are continually being formulated and evaluated in the light of *praxis*—the result is law, not gospel.

We return to the dilemma of maintaining the necessary tension between the freedom of the will (God) and the bondage and freedom of the will (humanity). To resolve this elusive dilemma, the theologian of the cross maintains that the Word of the cross of Christ and, consequently, the cross of the Christian, must be affirmed and proclaimed. Indigenisation of the cross of the Christian does not encapsulate the whole of the gospel. The Word of the cross is not to be separated from the cross of the Christian—they rightfully belong together. However, the Word of the cross, its scandal and foolishness, is the sovereign Word of grace whose "demand" for liberating *praxis-theoria* is an "invitation" to a discipleship of radical grace and

194

brokenness.

Even before we begin to engage in liberating *praxis*, the Word of grace from the cross is addressed and is real to us in faith. This does not deny that this Word may be and is heard in the midst of the struggle for better socio-economic and political conditions of life. In fact, the Word of grace frees humankind for such action. But that Word remains the Word of grace because it announces forgiveness and hope and new life to all those whose *praxis* has met with partial success or ended in disaster. The loving God whom humanity meets in the Christ of the cross is the sovereign Lord. The Lord is free to have mercy on whom the Lord will. Thus, the Word of grace is also available to the oppressor who is confronted by the Word of judgement. Likewise, the oppressed, despite their chosenness for the kingdom, are no less sinners than the oppressors. To both of them, therefore, the Word of judgement and grace is offered. Gazing at the man upon the cross who is the risen Lord, the church cannot be true to him if it reduces the gospel to law and turns the message of grace into an ideology for liberation, however pressing and imperative the need for real material liberation is. The church must be ever vigilant in its proclamation of the gospel and its separation of law and gospel without dispensing with or minimising the significance of either. It must insist upon the dialectic of the divine indicative and imperative and guard against the danger of capitulating to political or other euphoria which openly or subtly identify with the indicative what is achieved in obedience to the imperative of the gospel. Jesus Christ is not just an example for human beings to follow. He was not a political agitator nor should he be an ideological weapon of oppressed or oppressor, although he has been thus abused. He is the Saviour and Lord of the world.

This brings us to the crucial question of sin and grace. In liberation theology, the oppressed and needy are victims of exploitation and alienation. In Marxian terms, they are alienated from the mode and relations of production, from their fellow human beings, and from themselves. In Latin America, such alienation is pervasive and there is no question that the socio-economic and political structures are largely responsible for the human misery found there. Those structures are sinful for they dehumanise rather than humanise. They do not conduce to "abundance of life" but to the increase in "unfreedom" and wretchedness. But the description of structural and "human" sinfulness does not exhaust the meaning of sin. Sin is more basic, and redemption more inclusive, than socio-economic and political emancipation in history. "The qualitative opposition between sin and grace is more fundamental in the Christian interpretation of history than is the opposition between unliberated and liberated, oppressed and oppressors."[72] Thus, even if humankind were able to achieve socio-economic and political emancipation—with or without the aid of God—and thereby achieve a level of freedom hitherto unattained by humankind, it would still be sinful: for it is in freedom that we all sin. We need constantly to remind ourselves that there is a real and necessary distinction between the *consequences* of sin and sin itself, which is fundamentally a broken-relationship with God. Only God can restore or, better still, create a new relationship. Langdon Gilkey writes:

> The freeing of freedom, liberation, achieves the conquest of the *consequences* of human sin in history (i.e., fate) and so—let us repeat—is an essential aspect of Christian concern and action. Nevertheless, it does not represent the conquest of the sin itself out of which fate and fatedness continually arise. Only a new relation of mankind to God, to self and to the neighbor can achieve that goal, an achievement far beyond the range of political activity.[73]

Undoubtedly, sin separates humanity into classes but this "is not the same thing as the universal solidarity of humanity in the structure of sin against God."[74]

In keeping with the concept of unconditional grace, the message of justification by grace alone is paradoxical in its implications. Liberation theology as a theology of universal human familyhood emphasises the salvific efficacy of human *praxis* to the detriment of *sola gratia* and *sola fide*. In contrast to the demand in liberation theology for manifest signs of the solidarity of familyhood based on the gospel of love, evangelical theology of the cross calls for such manifestation, and it also dares to celebrate familyhood as a *prolepsis*. This celebration constitutes a crucial difference between evangelical theology and liberation theology. What might appear to some as ludicrous, and as a violation of the gospel, is acknowledged as intrinsic to the existential experience of the gospel. Therefore, it should not be dismissed as ideological quietism, even though unfortunately, there are historical grounds for so arguing (but, only in particular instances). Braaten sums up this paradox very aptly:

> According to the message of justification by grace alone, we can already celebrate and practice a unity of brothers and sisters in Christ. We can already declare that in Christ there is no East or West, no rich or poor, no slave or free man, no male or female, no Jew or Greek, no Black or white,

> no Brahman or pariah, no prince or pauper. None of these distinctions counts as the ultimate mark of human identity. Yet this fact is not a self-evident truth. It is a gift of the gospel already shared as a datum of eschatological salvation even prior to its actualization in history and in spite of the ambiguities of present social reality.[75]

It is only in such a paradoxical celebration that the triumph of the cross and resurrection of Jesus Christ is held together and human beings are given the courage to transcend their oppression and alienation in whatever forms they find and experience them, knowing that their justification is in the crucified God and not in the failure or success of human endeavour.

Finally, a word about criticising liberation theology is in order. No responsible critique of liberation theology based on an evangelical theology of the cross should attempt to proclaim "cheap grace" to those who are made uncomfortable by the socio-economic and political critique of society and the consequent radical demand for revolutionary change made by liberation theology. The critique of society based on Marxian sociology is very incisive and cannot be dismissed because it is Marxian. In a real sense, to do that would be to provide salve for stricken consciences by removing Divine wrath, law and judgement. It would be another form of idolatry—having a God whom we can manipulate. Liberation theology has arisen out of a context of real, material oppression, which places humanity in a situation where the extravagance of some means the poverty of many others. In such a situation, no theologian of the cross can summarily conclude God desires it to be so and remain a theologian of the cross. Nor can he/she argue that the "extravagences" of those who have are the blessings of God for them, and that, consequently, there is no need to suffer pangs of conscience for the sake of the poor neighbour whose life is both miserable and really all that he or she has. When we paint the conditions in Latin America (and elsewhere) in such vivid terms, it seems unbelievable that human beings could be so blind and insensitive to their neighbours' needs. Why? Can the church point the way towards a creative, material response? As a result of its peculiar theological method, liberation theology *de facto* attempts to do that: to make the world hear the cry of the oppresssed in and among whom Christ dwells. Liberation theology talks about the God who fully *understands* suffering for that is the meaning of the Incarnation. Liberation theology is not afraid to talk about the God of the oppressed, the Christ who is found in the needy, even if it thereby falls prey to idolatry and ideology. It is confident in the *liberation* of God and in the *God* of liberation.

When, for example, liberation theologians speak positively of their programmes and strategies for the *praxis* of faith and love in their context, should we, from a political standpoint and in a theologically irresponsible way, simply denounce and reject their *praxis* as ideological—as so often happens—by using our own ideological premises? Are we not both forms of ideology judged by the cross of Christ which has no handles for any individual, group or society to grip and control? Before God all of us stand as beggars with open hands, all of us are in need of God's grace. This is the message of the creative Word of freedom, hope and love for all which is active here and now, but which points to its eschatological fulfillment beyond history.

Pointing out the inadequacies and deficiencies of liberation theology without listening to and taking seriously its clarion call to struggle for a better world so that the gospel may be preached and people hear and believe and live in light of the gospel, is unfair to liberation theology and an injustice to the gospel. We are free to hear criticism because it is Christ who makes us free. The theologian of the cross needs to remember, however, that the credibility and efficacy of the gospel does not ultimately depend on how much justice and freedom and solidarity (or lack thereof) are found in society. The efficacy of the gospel is the work of the Holy Spirit. Furthermore, the reign of God is present in the most sinful situation and may even be ultimately fulfilled when all the "signs" point to the absence of God and God's reign. This is the paradox of the kingdom.

NOTES TO CHAPTER IV

[1] Liberation theology is the name given to the theological method that characterises the movement within the Latin American church which came to prominence in the late 1960s, with the Medellín Conference (Second General Conference of Latin American Bishops), Medellín, Colombia, in 1968. A comprehensive treatment of liberation theology is found in the seminal work of Gustavo Gutiérrez, *A Theology of Liberation,* rev. ed., trans. and ed. by Sister Caridad Inda and John Eagleson (Maryknoll, New York: Orbis Books, 1988).

To date, the variety of material written by Latin American scholars reflects a growing diversity of interests in and approaches to the task of "theologisation" inthat region of the Americas. It is significant that there are both Roman Catholic and Protestant scholars, including so-called conservatives among the latter, who have been contributing to the wealth of literature that is commonly referred to as espousing and/or advocating some particular aspect of liberation theology. Besides Gutiérrez, other writers of note include Hugo Assmann, Leonardo Boff, José Míguez Bonino, Orlando E. Costas, Enrique Dussell, Ignacio Ellacuría, José P. Miranda, Juan Luis Segundo, Jon Sobrino, S.J.

For an informative summary of the development of the themes of liberation and of liberation theology, see Hugo Assmann, *Practical Theology of Liberation,* trans. by Paul Burns, with a Preface by Ernesto Cardenal, and an Introduction by Gustavo Gutiérrez (London: Search Press Ltd., 1975), especially, pp. 43–56.

[2] Jürgen Moltmann, *The Crucified God,* trans. by R.A.Wilson and John Bowden (New York: Harper and Row, Publishers, 1974), p. 72.

[3] *Ibid.,* pp. 178–195.

[4] Jürgen Moltmann, *The Experiment Hope,* ed. and trans. by M. Douglas Meeks (London: SCM Press Ltd., 1975), p. 80.

[5] *Ibid.,* pp. 57–58.

[6] Jürgen Moltmann, *Religion, Revolution, and the Future,* trans. by M. Douglas Meeks (New York: Charles Scribner's Sons, 1969), pp. 218–219.

[7] *Ibid.,* p. 219.

[8] Moltmann, *Crucified God,* p. 318.

[9] *Ibid.*

[10] Moltmann, *Experiment Hope,* pp. 117–118.

[11] *Ibid.,* p. 81.

[12] *Ibid.,* p. 80.

[13] Moltmann, *Crucified God,* p. 25.

[14] In *Experiment Hope,* pp. 75–78, Moltmann expresses his appreciation of and indebtedness to rabbinic theology, especially Rabbi Abraham Heschel's explication of it. The motif of "The Pathos of God and the Sympathy of Man" in this Old Testament theology already contains an implicit theology of the "cross." Hence, Moltmann claims, there is a continuity between the "crucified" God in the event of the cross of Christ and the suffering God in the Old Testament.

[15] *Ibid.,* p. 78.

[16] *Ibid.*

[17] *Ibid.*

[18] *Ibid.,* p. 79.

[19] *Ibid.,* p. 80.

[20] *Ibid.*, pp. 80–81.

[21] Moltmann, *Crucified God*, p. 193.

[22] *Ibid.*, pp. 192–193.

[23] *Ibid.*, p. 193.

[24] *Ibid.*, pp. 246–247.

[25] *Ibid.*, p. 37.

[26] *Ibid.*

[27] *Ibid.*

[28] *Ibid.*

[29] *Ibid.*, p. 40.

[30] Jürgen Moltmann, *The Church in the Power of the Spirit,* trans. by Margaret Kohl (New York: Harper and Row, Publishers, 1977), p. 102.

[31] *Ibid.*, pp. 102–103.

[32] *Ibid.*, pp. 351–352.

[33] *Ibid.*, p. 352.

[34] *Ibid.*

[35] Moltmann, *Crucified God*, p. 141.

[36] *Ibid.*, p. 142.

[37] Jürgen Moltmann, *Theology of Hope,* trans. by J.W. Leitch (London: SCM Press Ltd., 1967), p. 285.

[38] *Ibid.*

[39] *Ibid.*

[40] *Ibid.*, p. 286.

[41] *Ibid.*, pp. 285–286.

[42] Moltmann, *Crucified God,* p. 192.

[43] See Carl E. Braaten, "A Trinitarian Theology of the Cross," a review of Jürgen Moltmann, *The Crucified God,* in *The Journal of Religion,* Vol. 56, No. 2 (April 1976), 118–119.

[44] This discussion was published in a slightly modified form: Winston D. Persaud, "The Article of Justification and the Theology of Liberation," *Currents in Theology and Mission*, Vol. 16, No. 5 (October 1989), 361–371.

[45] See Juan Luis Segundo, *Liberation of Theology,* trans. by John Drury (Maryknoll, New York: Orbis Books, 1976), pp. 7–38; also, Robert McAfee Brown, "Reflections on Detroit," in *Christianity and Crisis,* Vol. 35, No. 17 (October 27, 1975), 225–226; Ignacio Ellacuría, *Freedom Made Flesh,* trans. by John Drury (Maryknoll, New York: Orbis Books, 1976), pp. 15–18; José Porfirio Miranda, *Marx and the Bible,* trans. by John Eagleson (Maryknoll, New York: Orbis Books, 1974).

[46] Gutiérrez, *A Theology of Liberation,* p. 9; see also, pp. 10–12.

[47] Jon Sobrino, S.J., *Christology at the Crossroads,* trans. by John Drury (London: SCM Press Ltd., 1978), p. 87.

[48] Gutiérrez, *A Theology of Liberation*, p. 12.

[49] *Ibid.*, p. 110.

[50] *Ibid.*, p. 118.

[51] *Ibid.*, p. 12.

[52] *Ibid.*, p. 116.

[53] *Ibid.*, p. 168.

200

54 *Ibid.*, p. 150.
55 *Ibid.*, p. 112.
56 *Ibid.*, pp. 112–113.
57 *Ibid.*, p. 116.
58 Sobrino, *Christology at the Crossroads*, pp. xxiv–xxv.
59 *Ibid.*, p. xxv.
60 See *Ibid.*, pp. 162, 201–217.
61 *Ibid*, p. 174.
62 *Ibid..*
63 *Ibid.*, p. 201.
64 *Ibid.*, p. 172.
65 *Ibid.*, p. 357 (emphasis mine).
66 *Ibid.*, p. 207.
67 *Ibid.*, pp. 49–50.
68 *Ibid.*, p. 207.
69 2 Corinthians 5:7. Revised Standard Version (RSV), copyright 1946, Division of Christian Education of the National Council of Churches of Christ in the United States of America.
70 Carl E. Braaten, *The Flaming Center* (Philadelphia: Fortress Press, 1977), p. 154.
71 Orlando E. Costas, *The Church and its Mission: A Shattering Critique from the Third World* (Wheaton, Ill.: Tyndale House Publishers, Inc., 1974), p. 256.
72 Langdon Gilkey, *Reaping the Whirlwind* (New York: The Seabury Press, 1976), p. 237.
73 *Ibid.*, p. 236.
74 Braaten, *Flaming Center*, p. 156.
75 *Ibid.*, p. 152.

CHAPTER V
CHRISTIANITY, MARXISM, AND THE CARIBBEAN

Caribbean society presents an acute challenge to Christian theology. The challenge may be fruitfully explored in terms of the critical question of who the so-called Caribbean man and woman are. What are their history, consciousness, vision or lack thereof, longings and aspirations like? This question eludes easy answer, for we are dealing with subtleties and nuances which are easily and often lost to the casual observer of Caribbean society and Caribbean man and woman—whether the observer is from within or outside the region. The task is made more difficult by the fact that the discussion involves three parties: Caribbean man and woman, Christian theology *as well as* Marx's *Weltanschauung*.

Christianity has both a dialogical and proclamatory character. R. J. Neuhaus's comment on Theme 5 of the Hartford theses concerning the false dichotomy between the prophetic and priestly ministries of the church is instructive here:

> Christianity must have a dialogical relationship to other ways of putting the world together. But Christianity is proclamatory as well as dialogical. As embarrassing as it may seem in a world sated by the deceits of subjectivism, Christian claims present themselves as objective and normative. Related to many cultural idioms, historically conditioned in ways beyond number, seen through the prism of myriad world views, the Word nonetheless goes out: Jesus Christ is Lord.[1]

The Church cannot neglect evangelism in its pursuit of its ministry to the socio-economic needs of people. In this vein, Neuhaus soberly warns:

> To abandon that Word and the mandate to proclaim it, is to lose all claim to Christian identity. Christians proclaim it, not necessarily in order to prevent other people from going to hell but because they believe it as true, because they believe it is the most important single thing to be said about human existence, and because they are commanded to proclaim it. The failure to proclaim that Word with clarity and courage is one of a part with the

capitulation to political agendas that are designed either in indifference or in overt hostility to the lordship to Christ.[2]

These insights are very relevant to our response to the challenges facing the church in the Caribbean today. The challenges may be summed up in terms of the interrelated crises of identity and relevance which are peculiar and intrinsic to the church's presence and ministry in the world. Though identity and relevance have been separated innumerable times from each other in the history of the church, it is essential that they always be held in dialectical unity if the church is to be true to the gospel that has called it into being and continues to sustain it. Thus, it is only through dialogue and proclamation that the church can attempt to establish and maintain the dialectical unity of identity and relevance.

Furthermore, to meet the challenge of Marx in the Caribbean (and elsewhere), Christian theology must have a genuine openness to the cry of the human condition as expressed in the region. It must admit failures and defeats, be willing to be corrected on its false assumptions about Caribbean man and woman and their society, and must criticise the false assumptions and shortcomings of its dialogical counterparts. However, and most importantly, it must also proclaim and mirror in its life the Lordship of the suffering Christ if it is to be faithful to its roots, its source of energy and power. It must bring to the dialogue its "whole" perspective, and not merely that part of it which is seemingly more amiable and which could be conducive to compromise.

A.
Alienation, Marxism, and the Caribbean: A Challenge to the Church

It is obvious that Marx is historically, philosophically, and in many other ways removed from the contemporary Caribbean situation. Simply to apply his anthropology and theory of history, however critically, to twentieth-century Caribbean society without paying due consideration to this hermeneutical distance would be ahistorical and unfair to both Marx and Caribbean man and woman. Indeed, such a transference would be ideological in the negative sense used by Marx.

It does come as a great surprise to the student of Caribbean history that Marx paid no attention to plantation slavery. Instead, he concentrated primarily on proletarian alienation in industrialised European societies. Anyone who studies the sociology of

"New World" slavery—where the slave was a part of plantation property, a mere chattel who did not even own himself or herself, let alone their offspring—and compares the situation of the slave with that of the proletarian worker would have to conclude that the slave was no less alienated than the proletarian worker. Some would argue that the slave vis-à-vis the proletariat was more alienated. Nevertheless, it is useful for an understanding of Caribbean man and woman today to use Marx's concept of alienation, albeit with considerable reservations and qualifications.[3]

Who are the Caribbean man and woman? What are their characteristics? Are they descendants of African slaves, or of East Indian, Chinese, Portuguese or European indentured immigrants? Are they of mixed parentage—for instance, European and African? Are they descendants of Aboriginal Indians, who were there before Columbus came to the West Indies? Are they enigmas? If they are alienated, from whom or what are they alienated? Who or what is alienated from them? What precisely does the concept alienation mean in the context of the Caribbean? The answers to these and other relevant questions are partly found in the history of the Caribbean. There can be no serious attempt to describe Caribbean man and woman which does not take seriously the history of the region. For instance, of central importance is that period of Caribbean history which began with the arrival of Europeans, followed by Africans and then by Asians, all of whom contributed to the tribal, national, linguistic and cultural diversity within plantation society. Such a detailed study is beyond the scope of this work. However, it is difficult to avoid describing in some detail some of that history. Recognising that there were over four hundred and fifty years of domination and exploitation under colonialism which have shaped the consciousness, the language, and the cultural and religious expressions of the Caribbean peoples, we ask again: Who are Caribbean man and woman?[4]

1.

Alienation and the Caribbean Man and Woman: A Historical Overview

The history of the Caribbean is a history of colonialism, of the plantation system, of slavery and indentureship. It is a history characterised by the domination and exploitation of the masses by a disproportionately smaller elitist ruling class motivated first and foremost by the desire for economic gain.[5] The legacy of this history hangs like a millstone around the neck of Caribbean man and woman. It is a legacy that eludes transcendence and even leaves Caribbean man and woman without any lasting answer to the question of who they are. Philip Mason succinctly sums up this predicament:

> But it is the essence of colonialism, and indeed of most forms of rule of the many by the few, that the few impose on the many a spiritual yoke which comes to govern their day-to-day actions, more constantly and pervasively, if less obtrusively, than the physical force which lies in the background. Nowhere did this happen more completely than in the Caribbean. Whole societies were persuaded to imitate a way of life that was quite unfamiliar to them, one they had little hope of attaining and not in itself particularly estimable; what was more serious, they came to despise themselves and their own way of life.[6]

Because of the grouping together of peoples from Europe, Africa and Asia during the centuries of colonialism, the subject peoples were directly and indirectly forced to imitate the values and patterns of behaviour of the plantocracy. Their consciousness of themselves, of their roots vis-à-vis those of the ruling class, was determined by the ruling class. Their values were alien to them, having been imposed upon them through coercion at first, and later, through servile and dehumanising imitation. Whatever values slaves or indentured immigrants brought with them from their ancestral lands were relegated to an inferior status relative to European values, mores, and patterns of behaviour. Barbadian novelist George Lamming provides another negative appraisal of colonialism:

> It is the brevity of the (British) West Indian's history, and the fragmentary nature of the different cultures which have fused to make something new; it is the absolute dependence on the values implicit in that language of his coloniser which has given him a special relation to the word, colonialism. It is not merely a political definition; it is not merely the result of certain economic arrangements. It started as these and grew somewhat deeper. Colonialism is the very basis of the West Indian's cultural awareness .... A foreign or absent Mother culture has always cradled his judgements.[7]

This mentality of dependence, which always looks to the outsider for its cue and which despises the "local" and exalts the "foreign," left Caribbean man and woman in a quandry as to how to govern themselves once they have gained political independence from the *mother* country. In his novel, *The Overcrowded Barracoon*, V.S. Naipaul, with characteristic pessimism, vividly describes Caribbean man's and woman's predicament:

> These Caribbean territories are not like those in Africa and Asia, with their own internal reverences, that have been returned to themselves after a period of colonial rule. They are manufactured societies, labor camps, creations of empire; and for long they were dependent on empire for law, language, institutions, culture, even officials. Nothing was generated locally; dependence became a habit. How, without empire, do such societies govern themselves? What is now the source of power? The ballot box, the mob, the regiment? When, as in Haiti, the slave-owners leave, and there are only slaves, what are the sanctions?[8]

Any return to ancestral roots in Africa, Asia, and Europe, even if that were possible (and it is doubtful whether that is really a viable possibility), will be, at best, only a partial solution or, more particularly, an aid to a solution to Caribbean man's and woman's search for their identity and for sanctions with which to govern themselves with dignity and increasing humanity. Whatever is imported today from outside of the Caribbean, i.e., from Europe, North America, and even Japan, does not automatically apply to the Caribbean. It must still be "Caribbeanised." Consequently, the Christian church, like other institutions in the Caribbean, must be firm in its insistence upon an empathic understanding of and attempt at a solution to the problem of alienation in the Caribbean. The good of one group must not be promoted and realised at the expense of the marginalisation of others.

Both Lamming and Naipaul insist that colonialism as an alienating experience has left an indelible mark on Caribbean man's and woman's consciousness. Caribbean man and woman have never known real freedom, for they have never been responsible for the selection of the criteria which defined (and even now continue to define) them as persons. They possess a slave mentality which sees people as things or objects, rather than as persons, independent and other. Both master and slave, under slavery, were alienated. But it was the master who dominated the slave. In a curious way, however, the master's identity was bound up with the master-slave relationship in which he had placed himself and his slaves. Hegel's observations of the phenomenon of the master-slave relationship are helpful for our purposes. For example, in his *Phenomenology of Mind*, he says that in the master-slave relationship

> it might seem that the master has now obtained recognition as an
> independent being. But since this recognition is accorded him by the slave,
> who is *not* an independent being but merely does his master's will, it does
> *not* constitute an objective confirmation of the master's identity. ... The
> slave, on the other hand, realizes himself and objectifies himself through
> *work* for the master. In shaping and forming the natural world, he can find
> in the product of his work an objective and lasting expression of his own
> identity, whereas the master, whose relationship to the natural world is
> entirely one of desire and consumption, is incapable of doing this.
> Moreover, the slave has experienced *fear*, fear for his life, and therefore
> knows that his whole existence has been at stake; through the experience of
> *service*, this fear has spread itself over his whole life; and consequently he
> has experienced to the full that consciousness of his own existence which
> can be given objective expression in work.[9]

We need to be careful here that we do not push Hegel's analysis of the master-slave relationship too far. He did not have plantation slavery in mind but the concept of slavery in classical Greek and Roman societies. Furthermore, Hegel's analysis is philosophical and, therefore, it does not take full cognisance of the pervasive influence of socio-economic and political factors, which were so characteristic of plantation slavery. Again, Caribbean societies were characterised by absentee-ownership, which meant there was a great geographical distance between the slaves and the real plantation owners. The culture in which the master was immersed was one in which slavery was absent. Despite these differences, however, Hegel's description of the master-slave relationship, in which the master was in a curious way dependent upon the slave for his (master's) plantation identity, is still helpful to our analysis.

In terms of plantation slavery in the Caribbean, slaves, far from realising and objectifying themselves through their work for their master (who was not necessarily the plantation owner), were alienated from their work, in Marxian terms.[10] Under slavery, they experienced almost total loss of self. Moreover, the master was not dependent on the slaves for his identity, in Hegelian terms. The master perceived himself in terms of European values which gave him his sense of cultural, and other, superiority vis-à-vis his slaves. But the master's consciousness of himself as political ruler invested with economic and sociological power was, nevertheless, enslaved by the unshakable conviction that freedom for the slaves would be tantamount to ruin for the colonies. He did not know how to rule when the sanctions that bolstered slavery no longer existed. It was therefore not surprising that he tried to cling tenaciously to his power during the short-lived apprenticeship system (1834–1838)[11] Moreover, the "slave mentality" of the former master persisted during the period of indentureship, aptly called "a new system of slavery." The alienated master mentality also persisted even after slavery had been legally abolished by an Act of the British Parliament.[12] This is the mentality that has characterised colonialism.

But it was not only the plantocracy that was unprepared for Emancipation; the slaves were unprepared as well. The apprenticeship scheme was an inevitable failure, and the newly freed slaves were left without any liberating pattern of behaviour which they might emulate in order to be and to act as free men and women. All they had were the centuries of schooling in imitating European ways without any hope of gaining full and equal status with, and recognition from, their former master. A reading of reports of ex-slaves' views about the meaning of freedom reveals an odd mixture of visions of being like "Massa," being free of agricultural labour. There was certainly no clear picture of returning to a primordial African paradise, or even of creating such a paradise in the New World.[13] There was a lack of a Marxian proletarian solidarity among the ex-slaves, as well as any concerted effort to achieve a primitive communist utopia.[14] Slavery had taken care of that. It is against this background that Eric Hobsbawn perceptively writes that the Caribbean region is "a curious terrestrial space-station from which the fragments of various races, torn from the worlds of their ancestors and aware of both of their origins and of the impossibility of returning to them, can watch the remainder of the globe with unaccustomed detachment."[15]

Commenting on Hobsbawm's observation, Sidney Mintz raises the question of Caribbean man's and woman's vision of their future:

> Indeed, if enslavement disjoined once-free men from a past they would have preferred to cling to, then renewed freedom—freedom from slavery—must prove a very different state from preslavery. The special enigma of Caribbean peoples may well lie in their never having settled for a vision of history as something that must or should repeat itself.[16]

Freedom from slavery has left Caribbean man and woman with an ambiguous mixture of ingredients with which to carve out a new and liberated future. Although they do not wish to repeat the past, they cannot avoid its debilitating legacy. It is sobering to recall that the principal ingredients that make up contemporary Caribbean society were not selected either by the ancestors of the Caribbean peoples or by the Caribbean peoples themselves. Mintz explains that the "unusual ethnic and physical heterogeneity of the Caribbean region ... reveal the economically motivated intents of distant rulers." He concludes that "it would be fair to say that almost no one who was not European ever migrated to the Caribbean region freely; and surely no non-European born in the region was ever consulted about the advisability of additional migration."[17]

It is no wonder that politicians, academicians, literary artists, church leaders, among others, who have emerged from the ranks in the Caribbean, have been calling on their people to begin building their own liberated future. They insist that it is only the people themselves who are capable of creating their own destiny. The truly independent and free Caribbean man and woman will only emerge through their own self-assertive, self-sacrificial efforts. They must extricate themselves from the enslaving colonial legacy. Only they can do so by drawing upon that legacy those liberating cultural fragments which have been passed down through the centuries.

Political and ideological sloganeering, however, is a far cry from true human dignity.[18] Political independence is a mere step, however necessary, in the direction of achieving total human liberation. We do not need Marx to remind us of this. We need only look at the history of the independent territories since the achievement of independence to realise that alienation still persists. The majority of the Caribbean populace today do not think of themselves as first and foremost a Caribbean people, who are more united by shared commonalities—such as values, history, culture, political structures, and ethnic and class affinities—than by differences—such as nationalism, geography, ethnicity, and economic viability. The persistence of alienation, despite emancipation and post-colonial independence, suggests that the term Caribbean peoples instead of Caribbean people more accurately points out that each separate society is a macro-cosmic view of the fragmented, alienated Caribbean man and woman. For example, there is a greater feeling of being Antiguans, Barbadians, Guyanese, Jamaicans, and Trinidadians, than of being West Indians. Moreover, even in each separate society, it would be inaccurate to say that we have a strong nationalist feeling which is unmistakably greater than and takes precedence over any ethnic, colour or class "in-group" feeling.

Governments in the Caribbean are acutely aware of the deep-seated racial, colour and class distinctions and rivalries within their respective societies. Observe, for example, the various national mottoes which purport to promote, if not magically create, oneness and unity among the various, differing (and oftentimes even conflictual) sectors in Caribbean societies. David Lowenthal writes insightfully:

> Guyana, once the 'Land of Six Peoples,' now proclaims it is 'One People, One Nation [and One Destiny]'; Trinidad's coat of arms reads 'Together We Aspire, Together We Achieve,' and the ruling party's slogan is, 'All o' we is one'; Jamaica proclaims 'Out of Many, One People,' and the island's Five-Year Independence Plan insists that 'racial integration, in our society, is not merely an ideal; ... it is in fact a part of life.' 'Nowhere in the world,' asserted Jamaica's premier in 1961, 'has more progress been made in developing a nonracial society ... in which color is not ... psychologically significant.'[19]

Viewed in terms of the objective realities of Caribbean societies, such claims to national unity still represent aspirations and ideals which, to many, are more elusive now than at the time when they were each enthusiastically promulgated.

Let us now look more closely at the multifaceted fragmentation within individual Caribbean societies (and, of course, within so-called *Caribbean Society* as a whole). It is a fragmentation which is far more complex than a simple Marxian two-class stratification of owners and controllers of the means of production, on the one hand, and lack of ownership and control of the means of production, on the other hand, would indicate. To describe Caribbean society using Marx's analysis of class structure, without paying due attention to factors such as race and colour, which militate against the development of genuine working class consciousness and solidarity, would be ahistorical and even non-Marxian.

2.

Alienation and Pluralism

When Caribbean society is compared with North American society, there are two striking demographic contrasts. First, in the former (with the exception of Guyana and Dominica) there are hardly any aboriginal inhabitants while, in the latter, significant numbers of Native Peoples from various tribes still exist. Second, whereas in the Caribbean the European grouping of the total population is significantly small, in North American society, in spite of a large African-American minority, the European grouping forms the bulk of the population. Throughout the period of colonial rule in the Caribbean, plantation society was characterised by absentee-ownership. Fewer and fewer European owners lived in the West Indies. The majority elected to stay at home and appoint deputy managers to take care of their affairs. This practice of absenteeism was a determinative factor in the development of Caribbean societies.

Bearing in mind that the Europeans formed the ruling class, while the bulk of the population was comprised of African slaves, we are able to understand the pyramidical social structure that eventually emerged.[20] At the top of the pyramid were the European ruling elites and at the base were the African slaves. In the middle stratum, forming a buffer between the Europeans and the Africans, were the people of mixed blood. Thus, instead of a two-tiered class sytem, there eventually emerged a three-tiered social hierarchy.[21] During slavery, indentured European immigrants were part of the lowest stratum. However, when their contracts were over, they were free to move up in the hierarchy. The absenteeism practised by plantation owners served to enhance the importance of Mulattoes who, because of their European blood, came to regard themselves as superior to the Blacks, who were invariably below them. The Europeans allowed the Mulattoes certain privileges which were denied the Blacks. The colour consciousness meant that whiteness and close proximity to it in terms of skin colour and texture of hair were preferred. In contrast, blackness was despised. Such preference and denigration became increasingly acute following emancipation in the 1830's. Aspirations of upward social mobility meant imitating European ways.

Soon colour was an important criterion for deciding one's suitability for important jobs and positions in society. As Mason explains, the termination of the legal distinctions between free (white or mixed) and non-free (black) resulted in an increase in prejudice based on the "formal distinction based on colour." Mason continues: "When the legal barriers go down, the psychological defences go up. We should expect, and do in fact find, that when slavery came to an end there would be an increase in discrimination based on shades of colour." There is no denying that Caribbean people are both race and colour conscious. Mason provides a useful summary of the general picture of the social structure in the Caribbean at the time of Emancipation. He does so as he notes the growing significance colour came to play in the social structure:

In the Caribbean, the main distinction at first was between slave and free, but this broad distinction was quickly modified by considerations of race and colour. The European indentured servants worked out their time and became free; some of the children of African women and some of the more skilled and trusted Creole slaves were released, and an intermediate class of free blacks and free coloured arose. It became a society of many grades and distinctions—but the distinction of slave and free continued to be of overriding importance until slavery showed signs of coming to an end. At this stage, the free part of society first closed its ranks against the slaves and then when emancipation became a fact, established strong barriers of discrimination against the former slaves, for whose identification colour became the principal badge.[22]

Following Emancipation, the ensuing shortage of labour for the plantations eventually led to the establishment of indentured immigration from Europe, China, Madeira, Africa and India. Through the process of trial and error the planters, among others in the ruling class, soon realised that Indian (or East Indian as the immigrant from India came to be called) immigration was the most viable form of immigration. Thus East Indians came to form the largest immigrant community in Caribbean society as a whole following Emancipation. They were transported to the region between 1838 and 1917. It is the coming of East Indians, in contrast to any other ethnic group (with the exception of the Chinese in Jamaica), which led to the further complexity in Caribbean social structure. In Guyana and Trinidad, their numerical preponderance and near preponderance in the population, respectively, became a significant factor in the interracial rivalry between themselves and the "Africans". Alhough East Indians initially occupied the lowest rung in the hierarchy, which was vacated by the ex-slaves, they perceived themselves as superior to the Africans, whom they came to dislike. Likewise, they were despised by both the European and Black communities. In fact, the former regarded them as despicable heathens, while the latter pejoratively labelled them "coolies."[23]

What emerges are societies in which race, colour and class were fundamental criteria for determining cultural values, people's social perceptions of themselves and others, and their general outlook on life. Naturally, these factors militated against cohesiveness and integration within each of the societies and, indeed, in the society as a whole. Whereas significant similarities were found between lower class

Africans and Chinese in Jamaica, there were significant and divisive differences as well. "Colour and ethnicity are not neatly correlated with class membership."[24]

Despite this obvious conflictual situation, a growing measure of consensus emerged among the various ethnic groups comprising the population in each society. It was a consensus which was the result of an acceptance of certain common values known as "creole" values, which were greatly influenced by values from outside, i.e., from Europe. The sad truth is, however, that in spite of perceived improvement toward greater consensus—about common values, for example—a basic situation of divisiveness and conflict still persists. There is still a cultural gap between the "poor" class and the more affluent class.[25]

One of the primary problems that emerges from this complexity is the extreme difficulty in classifying Caribbean society. In tackling the problem of classifying Caribbean society, many social scientists have opted for the "plural" mode which was developed by the Dutch scholar, J. S. Furnivall.[26] In summary, when the plural model is applied to the Caribbean, the aim is to take full cognisance of separate and different, even conflictual, social groupings, whether they are based on cultural, ethnic or colour differences. It is not our intention to argue for or against the analytical and sociological appropriateness of the plural model as a description of Caribbean society. Rather, we wish to draw attention to it in so far as it serves to accentuate the fragmentary and "conflict-ridden" character of Caribbean society. More precisely, it invariably draws attention to the fact that Caribbean man and woman are alienated from their fellow citizens either because of economics, race, culture or colour, or because of a configuration of these and other factors. It cannot be denied that such alienation persists and that a significant degree of inter-class and interracial suspicion and mistrust also exists. Suspicion and mistrust do not follow rational and logical patterns.[27]

The failure to recognise the plural nature of Caribbean societies is often the result of an unrealistic feeling of optimism about the efficacy and growth of creole culture and a naive expectation that the legacy of history could be easily transcended without undue conflict and loss of individual freedom. The relinquishing of freedom, whether willingly or through coercion, in order to gain more (total) freedom often leads to a decrease in personal freedom. In short, the opposite effect is created. Here it is not simply a judgement on anybody or group, nor is it a questioning of motives. It is rather an attempt to make a realistic appraisal of historical realities.

In a lucid study on socialism in Guyana, viewed from the perspective of the pluralist model, Paul G. Singh reaches some very sobering conclusions which are worth noting. Summing up the inevitable and disastrous failure of socialist experiments in Guyana, he writes:

> Each ideological approach (transplanted Fabian labourism, Jaganite Marxism/Leninism, Burnhamite co-operation) failed to take sufficient cognisance of the forces of pluralism. There was a common gross neglect or common gross under valuation of these pluralistic forces .... Socialism has failed to have the desirable impact both as an integrative force and as a method for bringing about radical changes in society. It lacked the power to enthuse, to inspire, to pull the sharply differentiated cultural groups into a common will and a more universal acceptance and participation in new beliefs and new values.[28]

Noting that Guyanese Marxian socialists have tended to view society in terms of only one basic social division, i.e., between the capitalist and the proletariat, Singh points out that such socialists were under the illusion that race prejudice could be eliminated by simply abolishing its root cause: capitalism. Their "simplistic conclusion" is without historical foundations, for nowhere has the abolition of capitalism and the emergence of some form of Marxian socialism resulted in total solidarity among various societal groupings. Admittedly, Marxists might insist that nowhere has there been a "true" Marxian revolution; hence, social divisions remain. But their reply does not remove the fundamental criticism of Guyanese socialists. Regrettably, Singh notes, the situation in Guyana is characterised by "the absence of unified pressure from the working class" and the unlikelihood that such a consciousness might emerge in the near future to give impetus to radical and concerted action to eliminate inequalities and poverty. He admits that these are national and global problems and that they call not only for working class solidarity but, also, solidarity among all peoples, both capitalist and proletariat, on behalf of humankind.[29]

Singh's discussion illumines the fact that the pluralist forces in Guyanese (and Caribbean) society do not allow for an uncritical transference of Marx's theory of the class struggle to the region. The Marxian prerequisites for the proletarian revolution simply are not present there. Of course, certain partial requirements such as class struggle do obtain.

> The Marxist alternative of seeking integration by the mechanism of struggle and contradiction assumes a degree of class consciousness which is

largely absent from the plural society. Furthermore, the dialectic in Marxism achieves synthesis by the liquidation of the separate identity of the preceding thesis. As such it is essentially anti-pluralistic, and politically it means that conflicts can be resolved only in terms of absolute victories and the elimination of the defeated cultural group. The conflict between proletariat and bourgeoisie ends in the total victory of the proletariat and the utter annihilation of the bourgeoisie.[30]

In contrast to the Marxist alternative to the plural society, Singh advocates the "concept of compromise." Instead of the Marxian elimination of the so-called exploitative class in order to end pluralism, he calls for "acceptance of pluralism" and "a reduction of violence." These will be achieved through "the proposed form of democratic regionalism [which] produces a climate of peaceful reconciliation between the conflicting interests." Furthermore, he argues that the lesson to be learnt from the Guyana experience is

> the necessity for socialists in plural societies to give as much emphasis to de-pluralisation as to egalitarianism. The revolt in the plural society is a revolt against privilege of class as well as race. A planned socialist programme, with clear egalitarian objectives and utilising democratic regional and neighbourhood units to place socialism at the doorstep of the differentiated cultural groups, is a positive approach towards easing the situation.[31]

This is the essence of Singh's "concept of compromise."

It would be fair to say that he envisages that "radical" socialism would take root in Guyana if its introduction and growth in the country are accomplished democratically. Thereby, the ostensible and apparent central concern of socialism, alienated man and woman, would be its genuine, real concern. Thus, rather than further abusing and dehumanising human beings by offending their dignity and constricting their freedom, through the coercive imposition of another alien ideology with its own system of values, democractic socialism would conduce to a gradual de-pluralisation which would result in the achievement of an ever-approaching approximation of egalitarianism.

3.

Towards a More Specific Delineation of the Characteristics of Alienation in the Caribbean

It is important to note that the following list of characteristics of alienation in the Caribbean is both partial and tentative. It may therefore be enlarged, modified or even reorganised in order to allow for greater precision and comprehensiveness.

(i) Caribbean man and woman are strangers to their environment, an environment to which their ancestors did not freely choose to come. Thus it is appropriate to ask: To which part of the globe do they belong? Africa? Asia? North America? The *mother* country of England? Posed differently, Caribbean man and woman are lonely. In response to the question, "Do you see any themes in Caribbean literature that interest you, or any common themes?," Richard Ho Lung, a Jamaican Roman Catholic priest, asserts that there are a number of themes: "the loneliness of Caribbean man, the sense that he does not belong to the old simple world of ... calypso-style life."[32] Trinidadian novelist V. S. Naipaul persistently and perspicuously writes about the theme of "strangeness," of the Caribbean man's and woman's search for an identity in a "home" environment. In his novel, *The Mimic Men,* he tells of a West Indian politician who had failed in the West Indies and so had to turn to London as a place of refuge. Naipaul writes: "I know that return to my native island and to my political life is impossible .... For those who lose, and nearly everyone in the end loses, there is only one course: flight. Flight to the greater disorder, the final emptiness: London and the home counties."[33]

(ii) Caribbean man and woman suffer separation from their fellow inhabitants in the region. They do not fully understand them and, by the same token, they are not fully understood by them (at least to the extent of relating at various levels in society without the negative and debilitating use of stereotypes). Caribbean man and woman are unable to appreciate empathically the cultural, economic, racial, colour, religious, political, and social differences among the various groups of people in society. Social intercourse is characterised by a high level of subtle but real suspicion and hostility.

(iii) In the region, fragmentation and disunity are more dominant than wholeness and unity. Territorial insularity takes precedence over the feeling of oneness as a people shaped by a common history. Even within each separate political unit (including the independent territories), there is the notable absence of a national identity and national unity.[34] National mottoes espousing oneness and unity, as we have already noted, reflect aspirations for future realisation rather than describe existing historical realities. Indeed, the declaration of such sentiments in the mottoes is an acknowledgement of the lack of unity and of the need for national identity. To reject this appraisal of the situation is to descend from noble ambition to ideological fantasy.

(iv) The region suffers an ambiguity in its classification on the world scene. Today it is common to speak of "First World" and "Third World," indeed, of various worlds, with distinctions made on the basis of criteria such as economics, political stability, cultural advancement, and education level of national population. Noting the enigma of "the so-called Third World," Mintz argues that "the Caribbean region can only be part of it figuratively."[35] He rejects Naipaul's view "that the islands are merely the 'Third World's third world'," and explains the peculiar amibiguity in placing the Caribbean in a global perspective:

> These lands were being force-fit into the First World, the European World, before the Third World even existed. It is being rural, agrarian and poor that makes Caribbean folk look like Third World peoples elsewhere; it is being so anciently heterogenized, enslaved, colonized, proletarianized— yes, and Westernized—that makes the Third World label inappropriate for them today.[36]

(v) Finally, Caribbean man and woman suffer from political alienation. As we have already seen, their ancestors were never free to decide whether to come to the Caribbean, or not. The reins of government were never in their hands. It was not until recently that members of the rank and file began to assume positions of leadership and importance in the political apparatus in their respective countries. Sehon Goodridge recognises this fact: "The Caribbean man finds himself today part of a state order based on a borrowed political philosophy and characterized by the absence of ideological choice on the one hand and on the other, an escalating constriction of the avenues of constitutional change."[37] Goodridge draws attention to the glaring and depressing political failures of the 1950's and 1960's, which have left the Caribbean region plagued by the lack of employment, human dignity, freedom, and the continued presence of corruption. He observes that, "as a concomitant to ideological barrenness, our political systems are becoming less accommodative of change. A basic premise of the Westminster-originated political system is that a regular interchange of power will normally occur between the major parties."[38] Unfortunately, historical experience contains scant evidence of such "a regular interchange of power," and the possibility of it occurring more frequently in the future is very difficult to predict accurately.

> The dark days ahead for the constitutional orders in the Commonwealth Caribbean are evident from the increasing prevalence of what have been called 'constitutional dictatorships'—the continuing hegemony of one party through frequent reordering of voting regulations and the restructuring of constituency boundaries. Racial and interest group differences among the masses are exploited frequently, all adding up to make change through constitutional means more and more unlikely.[39]

In the discussion of alienation in the Caribbean, we did not attempt to present a precise definition of the concept. Our conceptualisation of the meaning of alienation was not characterised by an empirical specificity of criteria. In fact, none of the writings quoted above uses the word alienation. We have persisted in using the term, because it describes precisely the predicament of Caribbean man and woman. Certainly, from the peculiar features of their history, it is evident that Caribbean people are different from any other people, be they from Europe, North America, Asia, Africa or Latin America. This is not to deny that Caribbean man and woman share a common humanity with the rest of humankind. What we are saying is that Caribbean man and woman are still in search of themselves and their "home."

Alienation in the Caribbean qualifies as another popular usage of the concept alienation. With respect to the Caribbean, we did not speak of alienation in terms of a separation between "essence" and "existence." Neither did we claim that Caribbean man and woman are alienated because they chose, of their own volition, to be separated from European culture. In other words, their condition does not parallel that of a religious Jew or Christian who may wilfully separate himself/herself from the world and its corrupting influences. Caribbean man and woman are victims of colonial circumstances and their enslaving legacy. The problem of contrasting Caribbean man and woman, as passive victims of alienation, with the Christian, who actively separates himself/herself from the world, is further complicated by the fact that the majority of the Caribbean people are nominally Christian. Consequently, the thorny question is: What is the meaning and function of religion in the Caribbean?

Consideration of this question is further complicated by the particularly inviting and salutary appeal of Marx's concept of proletarian *praxis,* which helpfully illumines Caribbean reality. Alienated Caribbean man and woman live in an explosive situation. Historically, they were forced to "misshape" themselves and, if we accept the Marxian thesis that only Caribbean man and woman can ultimately emancipate themselves, then all that they need to do is to act. When they look around, they find that what they produce primarily benefits others, not themselves. The rich at home and abroad are the beneficiaries. They do not own the means of production, neither do they control the distribution of what they produce. They have inherited an economic system in which the relations of production and the concomitant hierarchy among the workers were determined by a small administrative class. Because of race, colour and class, and other differentials, they have been denied freedom of upward mobility—economically, socially, and politically. Only a few ever move up and, then, only by hard work and favour. Attempts from the top to alleviate the situation are moderate and futile because they are based on the premise that the existing system must be preserved at all costs. The system is primary; people are secondary. All talk about improving the lot of the masses is mere ideology. Such an explosive situation is fertile for revolutionary realisation of Marx's eleventh thesis on Feuerbach: "The philosophers have *interpreted* the world in various ways; the point, however, is to *change* it," and his clarion call, in *The Communist Manifesto*: "The workers have nothing to lose but their chains; workers of all lands unite."[40]

But the situation in the Caribbean, however explosive it may be, does not possess the principal characteristics for the *kairos* that Marx envisages. In fact, nowhere in the world, even in real and so-called communist and socialist countries, where "proletarian" revolutions have occurred, followed by the introduction of socialism and communism, has Marx's vision come to fruition. There has been no situation where a revolutionary vanguard and elitist party did not promote and usher in the revolution. Today those societies are still in a state of continual revolution. The proletariat and non-proletariat feel betrayed because of the persistence of elitist ruling groups in their societies, instead of the emergence of genuine democratic, proletarian governments. In the Caribbean, not only is there the absence of a genuine proletariat, in Marx's sense, but there is the notable and obvious lack of natural resources and ever-advancing technological development in the region. The Caribbean simply does not fit the scheme for Marx's alienated proletariat. This is not to deny that the plight of Caribbean man and woman is in need of radical, immediate redress. But it is certain, from the experience of other nations and from the uniqueness of the Caribbean situation, that Marxism, whether in its pure or in its

Marxist-Leninist form, will not conduce to greater freedom for Caribbean man and woman; nor will it conduce to the emergence of a Caribbean identity without the loss of freedom and human dignity by and the denial of fundamental political and economic power to the majority of the people. In addition, the destruction of their cultural and religious uniqueness seems inevitable.

Notwithstanding the differences that exist between the *Sitz im Leben* of Marx's proletariat and that of Caribbean man and woman, the revolutionary call to alienated man and woman to accept the challenge and responsibility to transform themselves and their actual conditions of life accentuates the twofold crisis of identity and relevance which the Caribbean church faces today. It is once again being called upon to reaffirm that its identity is found only in the gospel of Jesus Christ and that its utmost relevance to the total condition—past, present and future—of the whole human person is definitively and decisively bound up with that gospel. The church must not be afraid to face this challenge nor too proud to acknowledge its failure to proclaim boldly and to seek relentlessly to make concrete the message of the love of God in the crucified and risen Christ. Its history in the Caribbean shows many things of which it can be proud, as well as many other things which cause it to hang its head in shame and admit its guilt. But it knows that it was born out of the forgiving love of God and that its present and future emanate from this forgiving love. The life of the church is therefore one of continual dying to "self" and rising in Christ. But what relevance does this have for the mission of the church in the Caribbean today?

B.
Doing Theology in the Caribbean: Caribbean Voices

To speak of the liberation or salvation of humankind through the activity of God does not mean that there is no place for human participation in God's kingdom, which is proleptically present in the world. Indeed the commandment to love the neighbour which is inextricably linked to love of God makes unambiguously clear that the church is called to care for the neighbour. In the context of the Caribbean, the church is called to mediate this love of God-for-the-neighbour by both modelling its life after love and justice and by pointing to (and calling for) structures in society where power is justly exercised. In the command to proclaim that Jesus is Lord and to serve as unto the Lord who is Jesus, the church knows that its response should be based on loving and willing obedience and not simply on fear of punishment or on guilt. Even when it thus responds, the church still runs the risk of being described, in light of Marx's concept of ideology, as reactionary and as an advocate for a dehumanising and alienating base in society. It is therefore instructive to reiterate the question: Does the church vis-à-vis Marx argue for a more authentic humanity? As is evident in a theology of the cross, the answer is in the affirmative. The Caribbean church's task is to articulate an indigenous evangelical theology of the cross.

In its attempt seriously to apply itself to the task of articulating an indigenous Caribbean theology, the church in the Caribbean must listen to the criticisms, reflections and suggestions that are emanating from the people of the region, both Christian and non-Christian, if its concern for indigenisation is to be more than an empty word. The church needs to take due cognisance of the unique contributions of Caribbean man and woman. Thereby, the process of theological formulation will necessarily include cultural forms which are more Caribbean than European or North American. Also, the church will announce through its theology that there are many religious, cultural, social and even political and economic expressions, which have arisen out of Caribbean's man's and woman's historical experience, which are legitimate forms of expression for Caribbean man and woman, in the same way as European expressions are legitimate for Europeans. There is no way that the church can avoid doing this in response to the challenge to "incarnate" the gospel among the people. Such a process is intrinsic to the task of indigenisation. Its theology must reflect the *Sitz im Leben* of Caribbean man and woman if it is to be an authentic indigenous theology. In the past, indigenisation was done partially and often unconsciously; the task now is to engage in "theological indigenisation" in a more complete and explicit way.

But indigenisation of theology is not simply a matter of allowing the situation to be reflected in the church's worship and liturgy, pastoral care and ministry, social action and preaching. That is only a necessary *part* of the process. The church must also maintain its distinctive character and message, for it has a peculiar origin, source of life and identity in the gospel of Jesus Christ. Identity must not be submerged by relevance. The two must continually form a dialectical unity. The quest for relevance in the Caribbean must not lead to the situation in which the conditions of Caribbean man and woman, and of society as a whole, not only provide stuctures for but give content to the message of the gospel. Otherwise, the church will lose its peculiar essence as the church of Jesus Christ. At the same time, the church should not proclaim a message that is irrelevant to the real, concrete historical hopes and fears, joys and sorrows of the Caribbean people. Such a message would be nothing but docetic. Furthermore, it would lead to the unconscious or even conscious imposition of particular "foreign" cultural patterns upon the people, whose own cultural values would thereby be rejected or made inferior. The content of the message of the gospel must be presented in cultural forms and expressions of Caribbean people.

The task of maintaining the dialectic of identity and relevance is difficult, and it must be tackled critically and with openness. Moreover, the Caribbean theologian needs to remember that the gospel always comes wrapped in a cultural package and it is therefore impossible to strip it, for example, of all its western cultural packaging and then re-wrap it in a Caribbean form. Likewise, the opposite applies equally as well. The process of indigenisation (or "incarnating" the gospel) calls for vigilance and openness—vigilance in discerning law from gospel and openness to both law and gospel, judgement and grace.

With these suggestions in mind, we consider the reflections, criticisms and suggestions of Michael Campbell-Johnston, Idris Hamid, C. S. Reid, and Paul G. Singh which are directly pertinent to the concern of how to do theology in the Caribbean in the light of the alienating and explosive situation that prevails. Campbell-Johnston, Reid and Singh focus attention on the specific question of a Christian-Marxist dialogue in the Caribbean, while Hamid concentrates primarily on the question of theology and alienated Caribbean man and woman.[41]

1.

Paul G. Singh: On Synthesising Christianity and Socialism[42]

According to Singh, there is an indispensable need in the Caribbean for "a radical God" and "a revolutionary Marx." The two are functionally necessary for the ongoing development of the Caribbean and for the present and future welfare of the people. His conclusion is based upon a historical appraisal of the needs of the Caribbean people which have arisen out of the historical experience of exploitation under colonialism, slavery and indenture. Today, Caribbean man and woman are faced with the problem of satisfying basic human needs: food, clothing and housing.

In this situation, Singh argues, Christian-Marxist dialogue is of particular significance to the Caribbean. Noting that there is an unfortunate absence "of an indigenous philosophical tradition which clarifies the meanings of such basic concepts as justice, freedom, equality, democracy, brotherhood, truth within the

Caribbean construct," he suggests that such a dialogue could lead to the creation of a humanising and unifying tradition. He adds that in the transference of cultural values from Europe to the Caribbean, those values were significantly distorted. The hope is that Christian-Marxist dialogue might generate a peculiarly Caribbean ideology which is not only appropriate to the needs of "a new Caribbean," but which is also acceptable to an overwhelming majority of Christians and socialists. In the eyes of the socialist, such an ideology must reflect the fundamental concern with the condition of the working class which has been exploited under "colonial capitalism," while, in the eyes of the Christian, it must reflect the "functionally deeper religious experience" of the people which cannot be easily dismissed "as a mere 'opium of the people'."[43]

It is obvious that Singh is thinking of a particular brand of socialism, as well as a particular theological expression of the Christian faith. On both sides there must be the desire for neither confrontation nor accommodation *per se* but synthesis.[44] It is only through a synthesis that Singh finds the ideology for development emerging. This synthesis will not emerge from a dialogue between "both the imported forms of conservative Christianity and vulgar Marxism." Both "conservative Christianity" and "vulgar Marxism" need to be transformed and thereby be made open to each other, in order that a creative synthesis of the two might emerge.[45]

In this synthesis, whereby a "radical God" and a "revolutionary Marx" meet, the overriding concern is with the needs of Caribbean man and woman. According to Singh, this meeting will allow for a wholistic anthropology. At the same time, neither Christianity nor socialism will be easily distorted if, ultimately, they are both concerned first and foremost with human beings in their particular historical situation. In the creative synthesis where the "radical God" is needed to give the people "greater hope, courage and spiritual strength," and the "revolutionary Marx" is needed "to provide them with a quicker and bigger supply of better food, housing and clothing," the two are mutually complementary. Basic human needs are separated into two realms existing simultaneously: the inner, spiritual realm, and the external, material realm. Neither is dispensable in this life, but the Christian message transcends temporal existence and completes and fulfils the partial and fragmentary redemption and happiness enjoyed in this world. Moreover, Singh points out, eschatological hope acts as a check against naive optimism in the possibilities for human liberation which socialism offers. Here, eschatological hope is not "opium of the people." Singh writes: "Poverty cannot be eliminated in a hurry. Planned Socialism can definitely hasten the process of alleviation. But while this is going on from generation to generation, people must live and die, fortified by the superior Christian hope of absolute redemption and eternal happiness."

In his discussion of the question of Christian-Marxist dialogue in the Caribbean, Singh shows an acute awareness of the danger that, despite its present dominance, Christianity may disappear from the consciousness of the people. The danger stems from the fact that Christianity has allowed itself to be too closely and uncritically allied to exploitative capitalism. Thus the worker, who has traditionally thought of the two as synonymous, in rejecting capitalism comes to reject Christianity as "an opium of the people."

It is not surprising that Singh opts for a sacramental theology. Such a choice is inevitable, considering his argument for a synthesis of Christianity and socialism. In sacramental theology, human beings in their daily life have a satisfying experience of God. In order that Guyanese might meet God in the material world which is outside of the formal structures of church and worship, theology must use non-religious terms. Singh does not, however, elaborate on what he means by human beings meeting God in the material world. Instead, he reminds us of the dilemma facing the church as it theologises in the Guyanese context:

> Those Christian leaders who do not wish to see religion being swept out of human experience have two options: either reconcile Christianity with Socialism and hope that the worker will meet God in his secular condition, or make people aware of the transcendent presence in the midst of life and work in such a way that the secular becomes the possibility of the sacramental when faith opens their blind eyes.[46]

Singh rejects the former which reduces Christianity to a subservient role to socialism, and he shows his obvious preference for the latter when he notes a further positive function it might play in correcting certain inherent excesses in socialism. That is, in addition to satisfying "certain social, psychological and spiritual needs," sacramental theology, which upholds the total dignity and freedom of humankind, therefore functions

> to remind over-zealous Socialists of what has been overshadowed by the over-emphasis on conformity, co-operation, togetherness, groupness: the view that the human person ought to be independent, self-directing, autonomous, free—that is, an individual, a unit distinguished from the

social mass rather than submerged in it.[47]

Undoubtedly, Singh wishes to preserve talk about God in Guyana and in the Caribbean as a whole. He is also concerned that a democratic form of socialism be implemented for the development of the region. Both are necessary for and in the interests of the future of Caribbean man and woman. Therefore he advocates a synthesis between a positive Christianity and a progressive Marxian socialism. Singh anticipates that the theology that will emerge from the synthesis he calls for will be sacramental and indigenous. Unfortunately, Singh fails to make clear how the sovereignty of the "radical God," who forms a synthesis with "a revolutionary Marx," is maintained. His failure is noticeable in his emphasis upon the primacy of the condition and future of Caribbean man and woman in the discussion on the question of Christian-Marxist dialogue in the Caribbean. It is precisely *this* emphasis upon Caribbean *man and woman* that leads to the impairment of the concept of the sovereignty of God.

2.
Michael Campbell-Johnston, S. J.: *Christian-Socialism*[48]

In appraising the critical question of how the church in Guyana might respond to the growing challenge of socialism, Michael Campbell-Johnston argues for a particular, synthetic socialism: *Christian Socialism.* He is convinced that properly qualified, "the basic aspirations of socialism are profoundly Christian in their inspiration." Consequently, he finds that "there is no reason why a Christian cannot be wholeheartedly a socialist." According to him, as long as socialism promotes those values which are intrinsic to human development, then the Christian should not be afraid of wholeheartedly supporting it. Therefore, in Guyana, the church could freely join, and even play a leading role, in building a socialist society without losing its Christian identity. Campbell-Johnston describes the Christian-socialist society by quoting from Pope Paul VI's letter on "The Development of Peoples." It is

'a world where every man, no matter what his race, religion or nationality, can live a fully human life, freed from servitude imposed on him by other men or by natural forces over which he has not sufficient control; a world where freedom is not an empty word and where the poor man Lazarus can sit down at the same table with the rich man.'

Christian-Socialism, in contrast to other forms of socialism as well as the existing capitalism in the Caribbean, allows for the total development of human beings and not only for the satisfaction of physical and material needs, however important and basic they are. Campbell-Johnston criticises capitalism for its preoccupation with "private gain and profit" and socialism for its preoccupation with "merely economic growth and material standards of living." Both systems do not ultimately focus on the "fully human life" but only on significant facets of it. Consequently, where socialism attempts to correct the inherent evil of capitalism, it errs by reducing human beings to mere material and socio-economic needs and their satisfaction. It is only in *Christian-Socialism* that "man does not live by bread alone" and, instead, "a person is valuable for what he is rather than for what he has." Moreover, under *Christian-Socialism*, the liberating benefits of technology are maximised while the potential for human enslavement under technology is held in check. The primacy of humankind over structure and technology is unceasingly championed to ensure such a balance.

Reflecting on the divisions within Guyanese society, which are made on the basis of race, colour, and class, Campbell-Johnston points out that "the fully human life" about which Paul VI speaks in his letter means that in *Christian-Socialism* all forms of discrimination are anathema. He argues that any programme for the redistribution of the wealth in society on a more equitable basis cannot be determined by either race, colour, class, or political affiliation. Rather, it must be "based on the assumption that all men are equally entitled to it." *Christian-Socialism* insists upon a radical equality among all members of society. It is in this vein that Campbell-Johnston soberly warns that "as long as race continues to be a major divisive element in our society, then the road to true socialism will be effectively blocked." The situation is made worse when the issue of racism is overlooked or downplayed, as it is in classical Marxism where society is divided only along class lines.

Campbell-Johnston acknowledges that socialism as an ideology did not have its origins in Guyana or anywhere else in the Caribbean. It is a "foreign" import. But it is essential that socialism emerge from below—become indigenised—so that it might be true socialism relevant to the needs of the Guyanese people. Rejecting that form of socialism which is characterised by the "dictatorship of the proletariat" or by "the dictatorship of the Comrade Leader of the Peoples," because it destroys rather than builds up the individual and intensifies oppression rather than abolishes it, Campbell-Johnston maintains: "True socialism cannot be forced upon a people nor can it flourish in an atmosphere of mistrust, fear or hatred. It has to grow from below in a climate of brotherly sharing, mutual respect and love."

Moreover, the Marxian assumption that the abolition of private property would lead to the eventual eradication of socio-economic exploitation and oppression has not been verified by historical experience. State ownership of the means of production and state control of distribution of the wealth produced in any given society which are achieved through nationalisation are not synonymous with real and effective control of the productive and distributive processes in society. Almost invariably, socialistic nationalisation has led to various kinds of state exploitation and enslavement of the worker. Cognisant of this, Campbell-Johnston asserts that the "Christian socialist" must opt for a "mixed" economy of state control and private ownership. He explains that the mixed economy he has in mind will "both guarantee an individual's right to own and possess the fruits of his labour and also ensure that his private property is not used to exploit someone else." He adds that Christians should diligently work to ensure that the socio-political climate engendered in the society is characterised by a balance between individual and societal freedom. Moreover, fully aware of the historical context in which he speaks, he emphasises that his concept of freedom is inclusive of certain basic freedoms: "Freedom of thought, freedom of expression, freedom of association, freedom of education, freedom of travel, freedom of election."

Finally, *Christian-Socialism* is where "the poor man Lazarus can sit down at the same table with the rich man." A concerted, unrelenting effort must be made gradually to erode economic distinctions among the people so that the gap between rich and poor might be gradually bridged. The purpose behind the struggle to bring about genuine fellowship between rich and poor is twofold: to "guarantee the widest possible participation in decision-making at all levels" and, contingent upon that, to provide an effective means of preventing a new elitist class from emerging and occupying "the positions of power and privilege vacated by the former oppressors."

3.
C. S. Reid: Towards Critical But Friendly Collaboration Between Christians and Marxists[49]

Unlike Singh, who calls for a synthesis of "a radical God" and "a revolutionary

Marx," and Campbell-Johnston, who advocates *Christian-Socialism*, C. S. Reid cautiously suggests that Christians and Marxists should cooperate with each other in tackling basic problems such as the alleviation of poverty. Where such cooperation occurs, both parties need to recognise and appreciate what binds them together—concern for the poor and the oppressed, for example—and not delude themselves into believing that there are no fundamental and irreconcilable differences between them. The two parties will need to recognise that there is a basic theological disagreement between them: Christians are inspired in their social concern by faith in God, while Marxists, who are atheists, are motivated by love for humankind. Thus, for there to be a significant and meaningful cooperation between them, both must be guided in their attitude and action by the tenet "that one of the precious rights which makes man human is the right to *dissent* from the next man!"[50]

Reid criticises the false assumption which Marxists in particular make "that to be a Christian is to become innocuous, or a non-person." At the same time, Reid reminds Christians that even when Marxists are seen as the "enemy," Christians are commanded to love and not despise them.

> Christians who enter into collaboration with Marxists must know with whom they are dealing and keep their eyes wide open. Marxists are not men of God—but they are men for whom Christ died. Therefore, they are not to be seen as Social lepers. And their agitation and action have brought great gain to the peoples of the world. Even where they have not gained power, the force of their existence and Criticism has created conditions for Change. The Psalmist says, 'He maketh the wrath of man to praise Him.'[51]

On the question of whether the church in the Caribbean has been irrelevant to the needs of the people, Reid challenges Marxists to re-examine the historical record of the church from a peculiarly Caribbean perspective. Caribbean Marxists should not be "textbook Marxists," who merely imitate Marx's and Lenin's polemics against a reactionary church. Rather, they need to show that they are progressive and open in light of the significant differences in the conditions in the Caribbean vis-à-vis those in Marx's Europe or Lenin's Russia.[52]

Referring specifically to Jamaica, Reid notes that Marxists need to face honestly the fact that the church has played an invaluable role in education, in land reform programmes, and "in every working-class institution for the betterment of the masses." If Marxists are really concerned about the poor and the oppressed, they should not distort the church's past in order to gain political power. Such an act would not lead to an indigenous Marxism. Instead, Marxism would continue to be a "foreign" import and an exploitative imposition.[53]

The "alienness" of Marxism in the region is accented further by the way in which "successful" poor people are condemned and ostracised by Marxists. Successful poor people are treated as if they form part of a large and widespread bourgeoisie. But, Reid correctly notes, "We are not cursed with too great a body of bourgeoisie in the Caribbean." It is the poor who are widespread, not the successful poor. The latter have been helped by their poor parents "to be *less poor*" and, therefore, with their "success" they carry with them the burden of many obligations to others. In Reid's view, Marxists (and others) need to see in the success of the poor "the symbols of the ability of man to rise out of the dust of poverty" rather than the grounds for abusing and ostracising the poor.[54]

Reid stresses the unique obedience of Christians to Jesus who is the transcendent Lord. It is Christianity and not Marxism that is more indigenous in the Caribbean. He insists that Caribbean people have had a unique history which does not fit Marx's or Lenin's analyses of society. On the crucial question of theological reflection in the Caribbean, he implies that it should be done in light of the church's discipleship to the Lord who calls it to love the "enemy." But this does not mean that the challenge of Marxism must be made of central importance. Dialogue with Marxism calls for significant cooperation on socio-economic issues and not for a creative synthesis, Singh's or Campbell-Johnston's.

4.

Idris Hamid: Towards a Theology of Human Development in the Caribbean[55]

Idris Hamid's contribution to the development of Caribbean theology is seminal. He offers one of the most radical critiques of the dehumanising influence of colonialism, slavery, indenture, and neo-colonialism in the Caribbean. He is severe in his criticism of the church for being an accessory in the crime against Caribbean man and woman.[56] During the centuries of colonial exploitation, the church played a critical role in the domestication of the slaves and the oppressed masses. Hamid observes that "when domestication meant a channeling of our energies and instincts into creative ways, this was not altogether wrong, but this was not the kind of domestication that took place."[57] What took place was equated with Christian conversion, which was often regarded not as a process "of quickening of the spirit but of accomodation."[58]

It is not surprising that the church participated in such debilitating domestication. In the theology of the established churches, God was often presented as the One who subscibed to and preserved the *status quo*. God was made captive to the politics, economics, sociology and culture of the ethos of colonialism. God was foreign to and even absent from the suffering and oppressed masses. God was presented as partial to the exploitative ruling class. As an instrument of colonialism, albeit very often an unwary instrument, the church, for the most part, failed to listen to and heed its own prophetic voices. Not surprisingly, the end product of its labour is "*Colonial Man [and Woman]*," who are still with us today.[59]

Hamid points out that when the open and crude forms of violence of the earlier period of colonialism were replaced by equally dehumanising but subtler and less blatant forms of violence, the church, for the most part, failed to assume its prophetic role. Through the pervasive, blinding and debilitating influence of colonialism, the vision of liberation which was born among the oppressed was transformed into one of "assimilation." Hamid writes: "Now the oppressed were worshipping at the same altars of the oppressors, striving to imitate their life styles, and accepting their values. Liberation now meant beating the oppressor at his own game—even wanting to be an oppressor!"[60]

The message of God's partiality towards the powerful and dominant was emphasised by the "conspicuous absence of the Exodus event as a meaningful symbol among the main-line churches."[61] The distortion of the message of liberation and freedom through the omission of the Exodus was consistent with the church's capitulation to the ethos of colonialism. "The Churches that accepted the ethos of colonialism could not have used the Biblical Exodus motif with its implications for deliverance without calling into question that ethos."[62]

Despite the distortion of the message of the gospel in the main-line churches, the subjugated experienced the presence of God the Liberator, the mighty Deliverer, who accepted the people as they were and who worked to free them both historically and spiritually. Hamid asserts that paradoxically God was more present among the subjugated than in the established churches. God was more partial towards the poor and the oppressed than towards the mighty and dominant in society.

> In the innumerable and intangible ways in which he gives grace to men he gave to the oppressed and the down-trodden. He was present more in the

canefields than in the cathedrals, more in the barracoons than in the basilicas, more in the 'protest' than in the 'obedience', more in their sorrows than in the sacraments of the Church.[63]

The suffering masses experienced God in ways consonant with their historical experience, which, inevitably, contrasted with those prescribed by the theology of the ecclesiastical establishment in the Caribbean.

> When the Church preached many listened through the ears of their experience. God and Jesus Christ were understood in ways far different from that presented. This Christ is the one who sustained the people of the Caribbean when they were in the grip of civilized barbarity. He quickened their weary hearts to work for freedom, to hope in the midst of despair, to fight when the evil was overbearing. Thus God was working to undermine the establishment, not to stabilise it. And in so doing he worked against and in spite of the church at times.[64]

Hamid's argument is problematic, because it implies two Gods. His description of the God of the oppressed is apt and evangelical, consistent with theology of the cross. But he fails to make clear whether the "two" Gods are not in fact one God. The law-gospel dialectic may be illuminating here, for it would recognise that a theology of glory has emerged where the gospel is transformed into law to legitimate the ascendancy of the ruling class over the masses. At the same time, the law-gospel dialectic would highlight that theology of the cross where God is paradoxically present among the poor and the oppressed, working for their salvation which includes, but is not limited to, concrete, historical liberation. In the latter, the Divine Sovereign surprises both the ruling elite as well as the subjugated class by refusing to be tied to the *status quo* and by befriending the poor and powerless. However, The Divine Sovereign is one Lord, not two, and God's presence among the dominated class is not the occasion for revenge on the dominant class. God cannot be made the ideological weapon of the poor and still remain sovereign Lord whose nature it is to love. Hamid fails to overcome this danger.

In light of his argument that the suffering masses experienced and responded to God in Christ in their own peculiar ways, Hamid concludes that "in a sense there has already been an indigenous theology at work in the Caribbean."[65] This "radical" response was a constant cause of disappointment among missionaries, who were too tied to the ethos of colonialism in which faith was expected to produce domestication and accomodation among the masses instead of the desire for and orientation towards freedom in the cultural and structural forms in society.[66] The fragments of an indigenous theology, which he finds in the history of the church in the Caribbean, are crucial for Hamid's own description of a theology of human development in the Caribbean. If, as Hamid persuasively argues, the situation in the Caribbean today is one characterised by "an inherited foreign structure, with a laity whose vision is largely colonial, and with a theology which is the theology not only with blind spots but also colonial orientation,"[67] how do we do theology in the Caribbean?

Hamid suggests that we begin with a decolonialisation of theology, which is a process which recognises that political independence of individual countries is not equivalent to real and complete human emancipation. However, the former is a necessary step towards the achievement of the latter. The church as a distinctive community needs to recognise this, in its attitude towards society as a whole, as well as in its theological reflections and *praxis*. Hamid explains: "Decolonialization seeks to come to terms with this violent history and the new surge of social energy for deliverance. Decolonialization means the death of the Church as it is now: or to say it more mildly—it means radical transformation of the Church as it now is."[68] It is a negative and positive process, both death and resurrection. It is simultaneously a movement away from one undesirable state of things and a movement toward a desired state of things. The church "has to move from the posture which produces a Colonial man and a system of values, theology and so forth, which validates the Colonial ethic, to forging a vision of a new man and providing the spiritual resources and theological underpinning for such a vision."[69] Moreover, Hamid insists that the theme of freedom or liberation must be central to talk about God in the Caribbean, for it is the only way in which a truly historical Caribbean theology may be fashioned to meet the current challenges in society. Hamid reiterates that only when Caribbean man and woman themselves engage in theological reflection, in which the primary focus is on alienated Caribbean man and woman and their need for genuine and wholistic liberation, can there be a distinctive Caribbean theology of human development.[70] Hamid's emphasis upon the conditioning influence of the social context on "all forms of human thinking" leads us to ask the question: What does Hamid see as the catholic, universal core of theology, and how is it related to the social context? Hamid's "answer" further illustrates his emphasis upon the "redemptive" nature of the decolonialisation of theology.

In summary, he explains that the universal core of theology is the "living WORD" concerning "the activity of God." Theology is a human activity of thinking and acting—of reflection and response—in a particular historical context. Every theology is temporal, but the Word is eternal. In addition, theology is usually done "within a community of faith and experience." Hamid perceptively notes, however, that the theology of any believing community which, it is hoped, emanates from the prompting and guidance of the living Word, "never becomes that living WORD." The distinction here is crucial if theology is to be distinctively Christian. Thus the decolonialisation of theology "should not be considered an attempt on the part of the Church or churchmen to keep up with the current field, but rather as an attempt by the Church to come to an understanding of its mission in the new situation."[71]

Hamid does not make clear what exactly he means by "living WORD." His lack of clarity is understandable in light of the suggestive and tentative nature of his writings, which are brief. Nevertheless, his challenge to speak about the activity of the liberating God in the context of the Caribbean is crucial. It is a challenge which the church should not ignore or minimise in its struggle to be faithful to its mission. Put succinctly, "the church is not in the world to service the world and keep it up. Rather the church, drawing its inspiration and stimulus from the future which God promises, challenges this world and calls into question the present world." Thus, instead of developing a definitive understanding of the concept of the "living WORD," Hamid points us in the direction of eschatology and, to a lesser extent, in the direction of Christology as the possible routes which Caribbean theology must begin exploring in depth. Here eschatology and Christology, viewed from a soteriological standpoint, are placed in the service of ecclesiology and missiology, which are Hamid's main concern. In spite of the primacy of these two foci, he correctly does not indicate a separation between any of the major doctrines of the church. They are intertwined. He finds the eschatological dimension of the Christian faith especially applicable to the Caribbean situation:

> The future we abandon is the fruitless and futile futuristic hope. We now see the future as closer—as tomorrow. So close that it impinges on the present and draws it forward. It does not lead to resignation but to action. He calls us to create a new vision of the future. This means the weight of the past injustices and the present dilemma is not left fatalistically for history to correct itself but that the Christian Community will labour toward the future.[72]

Hamid envisages a revolutionary participation of Christians in the struggle for a more just and human world. In the struggle, the traditional divisions between faith and works, individual and communal freedom, material and spiritual, profane and sacred, body and spirit, will be dispensed with in preference for a more liberating unity which is closer to the truth of the living Word. In the context of the Caribbean, a new approach to the Incarnation must be guided by the central concern to destroy the false dichotomy between body and spirit. But Hamid fails to take seriously the fact that even modern eschatological theology suffers from a distorting dichotomy between the Absolute Future, which is coming and is already proleptically present, and the past, which is being transformed by the radical inbreaking of the Absolute Future. Langdon Gilkey poignantly states:

> The qualitative opposition between sin and grace is more fundamental in the Christian interpretation of history than is the opposition between unliberated and liberated, oppressed and oppressors, and a fortiori more fundamental than the temporal oppression between past and future within history.[73]

Gilkey's criticism is appropriate in view of Hamid's undue optimism concerning the imminence of the liberated future which is as close "as tomorrow." There is "a qualitative opposition between sin and grace" which still remains after, and in spite of, the attainment of human liberation. Not surprisingly, Luther's doctrine of two kingdoms is relevant to theological decolonialisation in the Caribbean today.

In his emphasis upon an indigenous Caribbean theology, which abolishes the false dichotomy between faith and works, theory and *praxis*, Hamid boldly claims that the church must "take the risk of preaching a theology of works!" A theology of works would mean that the church's theology is relevant to the material needs of the Caribbean people. Hamid points out, "Once we sweated in labour of non-creative activity; in the era of independence we are faced with prospects of inactivity. From mal-employment to unemployment!" The process of decolonialisation of theology calls for a theology of works by which the church might show that it is seriously concerned about the question of "human creativity within the purpose of God and the fact of the destructiveness of that gift in our history."[74] Whereas during slavery and colonialism, work was an enslaving activity, now, in the situation of political independence and post-colonialism, it must become a creative and liberating activity inseparable from the faith and worship of the believing community. Aware that this synthesis does already exist "in the best of Christian theological understanding," Hamid does not call for "the mere setting up of new attitudes to work," but for the redemption of "work itself in the community; involving such things as for whom and to what end work is used."[75]

Like Latin American theology of liberation and Moltmann's *political theology*, Hamid's theology is primarily concerned with *praxis-theoria* and the human future. He shares an affinity with liberation theology in his argument that the process of theologisation involves taking alienated man and woman—from the Caribbean—and their social context seriously, i.e., to the extent that the starting point of theology is alienated man and woman themselves. His concern with talk about God is fundamentally soteriological. But the direction in which his understanding of soteriology moves shows that he is particularly interested in soteriology as human liberation and development. Talk about God for humankind has as its primary objective the humanisation of human beings. Unfortunately, in Hamid's theology, immanence eclipses transcendence, and theology is reduced to an ideology of liberation. In his attempt to theologise in the Caribbean in a responsible and relevant way, Hamid mitigates the message of *sola gratia* and *sola fide*.

The fundamental Christological centre of evangelical theology, that God meets us in Christ even before we ever begin our militant *praxis*, is described in such a way that the God of the oppressed is not quite the God of the oppressor. This contradicts the message of the church that when God reveals godself in the paradox of the cross of Christ, God does so for all people, both rich and poor, powerful and powerless. Not only are the poor and powerless surprised to find that God is partial to them, but the rich and powerful are also surprised that the truth of God's partiality does not exclude them as well. God is also for the powerful who experience the Divine partiality as wrath. Judgement and *grace* are for them, as well as for the poor and the oppressed. The proclamation of the message of the presence of God in Christ, who liberates all of creation from sin and the powers of evil, is a call to life under the cross, where real and ultimate, immanent and transcendent, hope is found. The call to liberating *work* is therefore always a call to the response of grace. It is a call to hope in God in the shadow of the cross, instead of hope in the results of human effort to make God's tomorrow arrive today. That is impossible to do! An indigenous Caribbean theology must be a theology of the cross, in which the identity and relevance of the Christian faith form an intrinsic unity. Only a theology of the cross takes Caribbean reality with utmost evangelical seriousness.

C.

Towards a Theology of Alienation and Reconciliation in the Caribbean

One of the ways in which the church might creatively and meaningfully respond to the challenge to articulate an indigenous theology of the cross in the Caribbean is by exploring the theme of a theology of alienation and reconciliation.[76] This theme naturally suggests itself in view of the history of alienation in Caribbean society. Furthermore, it provides a unifying centre for an evaluation of Marx's *Weltanschauung*, the theology of the cross, and the task of theologisation in the Caribbean.

In spite of the qualitative difference between *theologia crucis* and Marx's anthropology, Marx's emphasis upon human beings' liberation of themselves and society through *praxis-theoria* has significantly influenced many modern theologies, not least the theology of liberation. Although Marx's influence upon theological reflection in the Caribbean is still in its nascent stage, nevertheless, his call for historical liberation from all forms of socio-economic alienation—the root of all alienation—challenges the future of not only Caribbean man and woman but also of the Christian faith. Concern for the material welfare of human beings and the proclamation of the gospel go together—in the form of relevance and identity. However, the two must not be equated nor the distinction between them dissolved.

In the face of the pressing need for the liberation of Caribbean man and woman from the enslaving legacy of colonialism, there is the constant danger that the church might reduce the message of the gospel to the task of ending alienation. Such a reduction would result not only from the more obvious and blatant accommodation of the gospel to the Marxian ideals but also, and more significantly, from the attempt to form a synthesis of the gospel and Marx's philosophy for the sake of human beings. Here we ask the crucial question: How do we define the "nature" of humankind? Are sin and alienation the same?

In Marx's view, human beings do not have a fixed "essence" but one that is constantly changing in relation to the mode and the relations of production. To posit a constant, static essence is to distort and dehumanise human beings and keep them in perpetual bondage. Marx therefore rejects any concept of "original" sin, even as he rejects the Christian (and religious) belief in the existence of God. He argues that the only radical criticism of human beings is that which restores them to their rightful place, i.e., at the centre of historical reality. Since such radical criticism ends with the call to abolish alienation, Marx's anthropological reductionism goes beyond Feuerbach's by calling for the revolutionary transformation of the socio-economic base of society.

When Marx's concept of alienation is made the functional centre of any theological approach to anthropology, it is difficult for the church to avoid the danger of ultimately contributing to the further enslavement of human beings by reducing them to creatures of real, material needs which can and will be historically satisfied. The danger occurs even when we talk about the *praxis* of the liberating God of love. In fact, when God is brought into the picture, it seems that God is the instrument for humanisation, manipulable and manipulated by humankind. All forms of triumphalistic *praxis-theoria* are judged by the cross of Christ. They are not to be their own self-legitimating principle. Where they are, Divine sovereignty is mitigated.

An indigenous theology of the cross needs repeatedly to emphasise that the miracle of Divine love is that God unconditionally loves the poor, the outcast and the downtrodden, whose lives can only be transformed through such a miracle. But God also loves those who are classified as exploiters and oppressors. Only through the miracle of God's love can they, too, be saved from idolatry and sin. If God's love is partial towards the poor and the oppressed, then, is God's love universal and fully gracious? When today's oppressed become tomorrow's oppressors, can it be said that the love of God intends that? In the New Testament, the miracle of Jesus' love for the poor is not that he loves them instead of the Scribes and the Pharisees. Rather, it is that he loves those who belong to the Establishment, but also those who are "disestablished" by the Establishment.

In contrast to Marx's radical socio-economic immanentism, significantly present in liberation theology, evangelical *theologia crucis* is about the gospel of reconciliation through Christ. It declares that the crucified and living God is both present in the world and is also coming as Absolute Future to transcend and heal all brokenness, alienation and sin. Hope in Yahweh's faithfulness to the Divine promises anticipates the kingdom of God in history as a gift which is coming from beyond history. There is a tension between "in history" and "beyond history," between the "already" and the "not yet."[77]

Talk about the prolepsis of God's reign can and does obscure alienated human beings and their present historical condition. However real the obscurity might be, it is not intrinsic to the theology of the cross. Humankind's total alienation *coram Deo* is more fundamental and pervasive than its alienation from the socio-economic and political conditions of life. Humankind's past, present and future must be seen from the perspective of its relation to God from whom it is separated. Human beings' separation from God is experienced as separation from themselves, from others and from the creation. The end of socio-economic alienation *qua* the dissolution of inter-human separation through human effort, with or without the help of the *praxis* of God, does not constitute total humanisation and reconciliation of humankind. Humankind still is sinful and separated from God. This does not mean that the church must not engage in the struggle for human liberation. On the contrary, it is a call to such a struggle, but with the recognition of the fundamental separation between humankind and God which humankind cannot bridge or heal. Only God can do that. This separation must not be confused with the creatureliness of humankind and the Creatorhood of God which constitute a qualitative difference between humankind and God. Humankind is separated from God because of its sin and not because of its finitude as creature. To be a creature is not dehumanising. To strive to be God is!

Caribbean man and woman with their peculiar history are, like all people, alienated from God. This needs clearly to be stated in any attempt to indigenise theology. In true egalitarian style, Caribbean man and woman also stand before God as sinners. They stand alongside their colonial and neo-colonial exploiters and oppressors, as they (both oppressed and oppressor) are confronted by the cross of the crucified and risen Jesus Christ. Before God they stand as beggars—with open hands—displaying no merit or grounds for God's favour. That God should choose that the Son, the exalted Lord, should be served in the least of the brothers and sisters is God's prerogative, not humankind's.

We are arguing for a more inclusive concept of alienation than that posited by Marx. Recognising the indispensable need to include the Marxian sociological account of alienation, we insist that sin embraces the individual, psychological, ontological and cosmic dimensions of alienation. In short, it takes us back to the primary alienation from God. Admittedly, such a concept does suffer from the inadequacy of presenting the human condition in static, not dynamic terms. However, in spite of its inadequacy, it still serves as a check on any fanatical and overly-enthusiastic expectation that the kingdom of God, whether in its religious or in its secular form, will be achieved through human activity. It is a check which is still valid, even when it is argued that humankind is God's co-creator in a derived sense. Its usefulness is not only functional, but is essential to a theology of the cross.

Our argument for a more inclusive concept of sin vis-à-vis the concept of alienation is premised upon the concept of original sin. The end of socio-economic and political alienation will not mean total "humanisation" of humankind, because the human condition transcends such alienation. Alienation is a primary but partial description of the human condition. On the question of original sin, Article II of the Augsburg Confession states:

> It is also taught among us that since the fall of Adam all men who are born according to the course of nature are conceived and born in sin. That is, all men are full of evil lust and inclinations from their mother's wombs and are unable by nature to have true fear of God and true faith in God. Moreover, this inborn sickness and hereditary sin is truly sin and condemns to the eternal wrath of God all those who are not born again through Baptism and the Holy Spirit.
>
> Rejected in this connection are the Pelagians and others who deny that original sin is sin, for they hold that natural man is made righteous by his own powers, thus disparaging the sufferings and merit of Christ.[78]

Articulation of a soteriology based upon divine-human cooperation to transcend sin as alienation will be evangelical only if it is juxtaposed with the concept of original sin. The ensuing dialectic is considered from the perspective of justifying faith which, in conjunction with reason, distinguishes between law and ideology, on the one hand, and gospel, on the other hand. But distinguishing between law (and ideology) and gospel, or engaging in *praxis* which it thereby prompts, does not constitute justifying righteousness before God. Article IV of the Augsburg Confession on Justification is instructive here:

> It is also taught among us that we cannot obtain forgiveness of sin and righteousness before God by our own merits, works, or satisfactions, but that we receive forgiveness of sin and become righteous before God by grace, for Christ's sake, through faith, when we believe that Christ suffered for us and that for his sake our sin is forgiven and righteousness and eternal life are given to us. For God will regard and reckon this faith as righteousness, as Paul says in Romans 3:21–26 and 4:5.[79]

Can justifying faith become active in love for the neighbour at the individual and societal levels of human existence without faith becoming tied to the *status quo*? Can it do so by talking about Jesus as the "Liberating One," the One whose name means "Freedom,"[80] without reading the conditions of alienated (Caribbean) man and woman into the life, death and resurrection of Jesus? Would it mean that it is the condition of human beings and their society that explicates, shapes and gives content to the message of hope and salvation? The church's creeds and confessions, used as hermeneutical aids in interpreting scripture, can certainly serve to recall the church from any dehumanising distortions of the gospel.

Christology is the key to doing theology in the Caribbean, and elsewhere. Any talk about the power and presence of God in the midst of Caribbean man's and woman's predicament must be Christological, embracing the cosmic as well as individual dimensions of the Divine work of reconciliation through Christ. John Macquarrie helpfully articulates the need for talk about cosmic reconciliation in the face of widespread alienation and sin in the world. "As I see the situation, the problem for religious communities is to find the best means (which will no doubt vary from one area to another) of bringing their vision of a cosmic overcoming of alienation to bear on the alienation of contemporary societies."[81] In specifically Christian terms, the emphasis must be placed on God's reconciling work in Christ. In this vein, Wolfhart Pannenberg argues that the "unity of one history" that has been affected through the event of Christ embraces "antiquity, modern times, and their future."[82] The history of Caribbean man and woman is not isolated and alienated from the hope of its transformation in Christ's cosmic redemption. The Christian tradition is a "unifying bond" which keeps antiquity, modern times and their future from falling apart. Caribbean man and woman should therefore not reject their present because of its alienated and alienating antecedents. In critical awareness of their past, they can, in light of the vision of the future transcendent reconciliation, work creatively to proclaim hope in and beyond the world. Their hope is not rooted in a future separated from the present but in a future that is already present in the cross of Christ. Resurrection hope of liberation in, through and, ultimately, from suffering are seen through the "eyes of faith" in the cross of the gracious God.

Pannenberg argues that humankind, as creature, is inherently dependent upon God. Humankind is created to be in a relationship of trust in God, not in a relationship of control of its own future. Thus, in contrast to Marx's concept of humankind as its own creator, Pannenberg points out that

man always perceives himself as dependent on something before which he

> stands: beyond the world on God and within the world itself on the material
> basis for all technological development. He is dependent on the social and
> intellectual traditions out of which he lives, *even where he turns against*
> *them.* He is dependent on what happens to him from day to day and from
> hour to hour without his cooperation. He is dependent on the men who are
> with him, and upon everything that is given to him through them. In all that
> and beyond that he is dependent on God.[83]

Moreover, humankind's essence is not limited to the socio-economic conditions in society, for "just as exchange and the division of labor do not necessarily lead to the loss of man's essence, so the pressure of serving mammon is not a fateful power."[84] Pannenberg directly refutes the Marxian thesis that humankind is alienated through the division of labour and by seeking the monetary rewards of its labour, instead of finding its fulfilment in the enjoyment of what it has produced. Pannenberg does admit, however, that "money frequently becomes an idol to which a person sacrifices everything else." But he refuses to accept the definition of human nature in terms of the existence of money, for example. Money, he insists, is merely an expression of the more pervasive evil: greed. He explains that

> greed is always present first as the dominating impulse. It is not man's
> alienation through money which brings to power the sense of possession,
> as Marx thought. It is rather the latter which sets the former process in
> motion. Only where greed for money already completely fills a man can
> money attain such power over him that everything else, things as well as
> men, has significance only in relation to money. Only where man has
> become entirely enslaved to covetousness does the automatism of the
> economic development of capitalism, which Marx described so
> impressively, take place.[85]

At its root, such covetousness is a consequence of human separation from God. Therefore, while economic and political systems need to be radically transformed—they have demonically enslaved human beings and distorted their humanity—in order that they may conduce to human enjoyment of a more humane existence, separation from God through rebellion can only be overcome by the gracious act of God. According to Pannenberg, human control over the world must be distinguished, though not separated, from humankind's relationship of trust in God. Control is derived from trust. "Only faith in the infinite God of the Bible, who is beyond everything finite, has given the world of finite things completely into man's control." In other words, "the power to control the world has its origin not in man himself but in trust in the infinite God, through which man soars out beyond the limits of his finitude."[86] Pannenberg concludes that "where control over the world becomes its own end, *the perversion has already taken place.*" Consequently, "life becomes absorbed in procuring the means of life; *life is no longer received as a gift.*"[87]

In his description of the "unity of history," Pannenberg paints a picture of the Biblical hope in the transcendence of all separation, alienation and sin. Unlike the Marxian vision of an unalienated future in history created by humankind alone, Pannenberg's is a vision of "the future of God," a future centred in and promised through Christ. "Through Jesus men have a future of salvation with God beyond all earthly suffering, which was concentrated in Jesus' cross." Participating in this future through faith, the Christian *loves Jesus for the sake of the neighbour.* "Such a person can now open a future for other men in a similar way, through the loving devotion that corresponds to what he ... has already experienced from God."[88]

The power of the message of hope for humankind, including Caribbean man and woman, is not exhausted by human suffering. Aware of the problem of theodicy that arises in the face of so much inexplicable and demonic suffering in the world, Pannenberg, nevertheless, maintains that in the unity of history rooted in the God of Israel, who uniquely revealed godself in Jesus of Nazareth, "man's destiny attains its unified configuration, which incorporates each individual man with his uniqueness and his particular path."[89] Reconciliation is given through the death and resurrection of Jesus Christ. In the unity of the destiny of all humankind, the individuality, the personhood of each unique individual, is not destroyed nor damaged, but fulfilled and recreated. In Pannenberg's view, the "unity of history as it is established in Jesus' fate makes it possible for each individual to attain the wholeness of his own life by knowing that he, together with all men, is related to that center."[90]

In the specific context of the Caribbean, the church's call to faithfulness to the gospel must find expression in a theology of alienation and reconciliation, whereby the response to the historical experience of alienation by Caribbean man and woman is included in a contemporary articulation of sin as separation from God. To meet this challenge, both the individual and cosmic dimensions of the Incarnation must be included.

The question of humanity's creaturely care for the finite, human and non-human world calls for a consideration of the concept of the "two kingdoms." We will turn our attention now to a critical description of Luther's doctrine of the two kingdoms. We do so recognising the need to place humankind's activity in its proper perspective vis-à-vis God's work of redemption and reconciliation through Christ. In the Caribbean, the church is confronted with the task of finding a way of participating meaningfully in creating the future, liberated Caribbean man and woman and their society. Is this a task that is firmly planted within the kingdom of the world? How might the church theologically reflect upon this issue as it seeks faithfully to proclaim the gospel and administer the sacraments?

D.
Luther's Doctrine of the Two Kingdoms[91]

We have already noted that when Marx writes, "The philosophers have *interpreted* the world in various ways; the point however is to *change* it," he issues a critical challenge not only to philosophy but also to theology. Responding to the task involves describing the world as it is and, more particularly, formulating and implementing a comprehensive strategy for the radical transformation of it. Simply to talk about the state of the world without engaging in revolutionary *praxis* is to indulge in ideology and to provide further legitimation for the *status quo*. Theory which does not lead to liberating *praxis* may and can only bring partial freedom which, according to Marx, will be eventually overshadowed by the actual intensification of alienation.

Thus, in order to achieve the historical transcendence of alienation, there must and will be a creative synthesis between theory (*theoria*) and *praxis* among the proletariat, the most dehumanised class in society. Out of this synthesis, human beings will be able to create real *human* history and genuine and dynamic, human "nature." In Marx's ethics, humankind is the measure of itself and is answerable only to itself. There is no transcendent Creator, who is the ground and source of humankind's life and its creative capacities, to whom it is answerable. The truth about humankind is that it is its own and only creator. According to Marx's anthropology, human beings' response to their needs, their accountability to themselves, is a response to human necessity, not to grace. Human beings create their own merits, their own "righteousness," through human effort in order to "justify" themselves in the community of production. Therefore, they do not depend upon the graciousness of God or any other transcendent being as they seek authentic, unalienated existence.

In theology of the cross, however, human beings are seen as creatures whose freedom is bound up with their response of faith to the God whom human beings experience as gracious and loving in the crucified and risen Lord, Jesus Christ. As creatures, human beings are dependent upon God, and in their sin, they are incapable of transforming their condition of rebellion against God. Only God can heal the broken relationship which stems from human rebellion against God. When God heals the brokenness, through God's gracious act of suffering the death of the Son for the sake of humankind, God reaffirms humankind's condition before God as a creature of response. Human beings always stand before God as creatures whose response is either faith or "unfaith." Acceptance or rejection of the grace of God does not abolish this fundamental condition of human beings as creatures vis-à-vis God the Creator, Redeemer and Sanctifier. Whatever humankind's response may be, God, who meets humanity in the contrariness of cross and suffering, is also sovereign Lord. It must be said, however, that it is only to those who respond in faith in Christ that Jesus is *de facto* Lord. To those who reject Jesus, he is still *de jure* Lord: Jesus' Lordship remains hidden.

The response of faith is not without implications for the Christian in society. Indeed, such "saving" faith is characterised by love for the neighbour. The two—faith in God through Christ and love of the neighbour—are inextricably bound together; they form the dialectic of Christian existence in the world. Properly experienced in the life of the church, this dialectic does not inherently call for an ethic of quietism and of withdrawal from the world through a total concentration on the development of an exclusively inward piety, which has no direct bearing on the life of the Christian in society. Neither does it inherently call for a *praxis* for justification by concentrating on the transformation of the world into the kingdom of God (or its closest approximation). The former contains a dichotomy between "other worldly" and "this worldly" piety, and thus God is seen to be absent from the world, which is seen to be in the hands of evil powers. In the latter, the dichotomy or dualism is replaced by an equally distorting monism in which the kingdom of the world is, fully and totally, the only kingdom of God. In an evangelical theology, both dualism and monism are distortions of the gospel. Hence, evangelical theology insists upon maintaining the dialectic of faith and love, the transcendent and the immanent, as the authentic expression of the encounter between God and humankind.

In his doctrine of the two kingdoms, Luther explicates the dialectic of Christian existence in the world. His ethics of faith active in love emerges from his doctrine of justification. Acts of love which the Christian performs are directed towards the neighbour and not towards God, who does not need them. Yet, in acting on behalf of the neighbour, the Christian is simultaneously exercising his/her faith "in terms of obedience, and of thanks and praise to God."[92] At the same time, the Christian is responding in the freedom of the gospel since he/she no longer needs to worry about his/her own salvation. Christian freedom rooted in justification by God is made concrete in care for the neighbour. Paul Althaus explains:

> The man who does something to gain his own salvation really cares only for himself. However, God has already provided for my needs—therefore I do not need to be concerned about myself. Indeed, God gives me what I need in advance when I, through faith, receive his grace and favor. Beyond that, nothing more is needed.[93]

Luther's doctrine of the two kingdoms is practical and experiential, not theoretical and speculative. It is concerned with the activity of God in the life of both the believer and the unbeliever, for both are God's creatures.

Luther concludes, from his study of the scriptures, that God exercises a twofold rule over and in the world.[94] There is a spiritual rule and a secular rule, corresponding to a spiritual kingdom and a secular kingdom, respectively. He writes:

> We must divide the children of Adam and all mankind into two classes, the first belonging to the kingdom of God, the second to the kingdom of the world. Those who belong to the kingdom of God are all the true believers who are in Christ and under Christ, for Christ is King and Lord in the kingdom of God as Psalm 2 [:6] and all of Scripture says.[95]

While it is through the church, which proclaims the Word and administers the sacraments, that people are called to faith in Christ by the Holy Spirit, Luther does not equate the church with the kingdom of God. Even to the "eyes of faith," the kingdom of God is only partially revealed, for Christian existence is always under the paradox of cross and suffering. It is essential to an evangelical critique of ecclesiastical triumphalism that we continually make the distinction between the church and the kingdom of God.

Luther uses clear language to assert that the two classses of humanity stand before God in different relationships. He uses the law-gospel dialectic to describe the nature of humankind's relationship to God. Whereas those in the kingdom of God are "under Christ," those in the kingdom of the world "are under the law." Luther claims that if there were only Christians in the world, then there would be no need for the restraining influence of the law. He suggests that the believer who lives out the freedom of the gospel is less tempted by evil than the unbeliever: "There are few true believers, and still fewer who live a Chirstian life, who do not resist evil and indeed themselves do no evil." Because there are both Christians and non-Christians in the world, God has had to make provisions to restrain those who would be given to the practice of evil, i.e., the unbelievers. Luther writes:

> For this reason God has provided for them a different government beyond the Christian estate and kingdom of God. He has subjected them to the sword so that, even though they would like to, they are unable to practice their wickedness, and if they do practice it they cannot do so without fear or with success and impunity.[96]

Here, in his description of God's dealings with the creation, Luther uses the concept "government" as well as the concept "kingdom." He relates the two to each other: God's rule in God's two kingdoms is exercised through two governments which God has established. In the kingdom of God, there is the spiritual government, and in the kingdom of the world, there is the secular government. Whereas the term kingdom might suggest Divine withdrawal, the term government suggests a more dynamic Divine presence in the spiritual and secular realms. For Heinrich Bornkamm, "both duality and unity thus seemed to be preserved."[97] Commenting that God has established both governments, Luther states:

> God has ordained two governments: the spiritual, by which the Holy Spirit produces Christians and righteous people under Christ; and the temporal, which restrains the un-Christian and wicked so that—no thanks to them— they are obliged to keep still and to maintain an outward peace.[98]

We return once again to the use of the law-gospel dialectic in God's twofold rule in the world—by the law in the secular government and by the gospel in the spiritual government. Again, we emphasise that the relationship between political government and God's secular government, as well as the relationship between the church and God's spiritual government, is neither natural nor unambiguous, but is dialectical. Furthermore, the terms kingdom and government must not be separated from each other nor be placed in opposition to each other. Rather, as Bornkamm argues, both their duality and their dialectical unity must be preserved in order that they may "indicate the two inseparably intertwined aspects of the whole, the realm of lordship ('kingdom') and the mode of lordship ('government'), and [that] they may be used to distinguish these aspects."99 Luther's originality, Bornkamm adds, is precisely that he combines both perspectives of two kingdoms and two governments. There is "the ruthless separation of the world and the kingdom of Christ as well as, on the other hand, the governance of both of them by the will of God according to the two modes of his love."100

In distinguishing both kingdoms and governments from each other, the Christian must remember, at the same time, that they are both necessary. Only Christ's government makes people righteous. Thus the temporal government must not be allowed to usurp the place of Christ's government. Noting the indispensable nature of Christ's government which extends beyond history into eternity, Luther argues that where Christ's kingdom is abolished or becomes absorbed by and is, therefore, indistinguishable from the temporal government and only the latter "or law alone exists," "there sheer hypocrisy is inevitable, even though the commandment be God's very own."101 Here a theology of glory, not a theology of the cross, emerges. Luther adds that "where the spiritual government alone prevails over land and people, there wickedness is given free rein and the door is open for all manner of rascality, for the world as a whole cannot receive or comprehend it."102 According to his understanding of the function of the spiritual government, the absence of spiritual government will not mean that God's righteousness, which justifies the sinner, will become impaired. Instead, its absence will result in libertinism and its accompanying wickedness and violence. The body may be harmed but the soul will remain unscathed.103 Luther emphasises, however, that the kingdom of the world is established to serve the kingdom of Christ. By preserving peace and preventing chaos, the temporal government allows for an atmosphere in which the gospel may be preached and the sacraments administered. But even where such peace is absent and chaos reigns, the church is still called upon to carry on its ministry, for its existence is always *sub cruce*.104

Luther's teaching concerning the two kingdoms contains some serious ambiguities and contradictions. For example, he speaks of Christian existence as being under the gospel and not under the law, while non-Christian existence is under law, not gospel. Such a separation of law from gospel (and vice versa) is a false and dangerous dualism between Christian and non-Christian existence and eclipses the fact that the Christian is *simul justus et peccator*.[105] The Christian, who is simultaneously righteous and sinful, needs both law and gospel. As sinner, he/she needs to be restrained by the civil and political law—and not judged by the "spiritual" law alone—so that he/she might not injure or neglect their neighbour. We are not denying that the Christian is freed from the law as a means of righteousness before God nor that he/she has the guidance of the Holy Spirit. In contrast to the non-Christian, he/she is called to a higher obligation to the secular government in the kingdom of the world because of freedom through the gospel. The Christian constantly needs to hear this message and be reminded that, in the kingdom of the world, he/she is serving God and not someone else. This is precisely how the unity and duality (not dualism) of the two kingdoms are maintained: through the life of the Christian in both kingdoms. God uses those who have not as yet come to faith in Christ to carry out God's will and purpose.

Luther's use of "proper" and "alien" to describe God's activity in the kingdom on the "right" and the kingdom on the "left," respectively, is a helpful way to understand God's work in God's two kingdoms.[106] The first and the second Articles of the Creed, on Creation and Redemption, respectively, form a unity.[107] In terms of Luther's *theologia crucis*, the personal word of grace for humankind is understood in relation to Christ, while the preserving work of God is understood in terms of God's provision for the continuance and sustenance of life. Bornkamm provides a useful summary of Luther's understanding of the unity of God's love for and work in the world:

> The fundamental tenet of Luther's political ethics grew out of the center of his theology. It rests upon faith in the unchangeable *relation of God to the world,* which has not suffered alteration in will or purpose because of the abyss that sin has opened up between them, but has only changed in means. Because of sin, the free community of love which God had wanted humanity to be, and which gleams again in the life together of true Christians, has changed into an order of law and coercion. The distinction is similar to that between God's 'strange work' and his 'proper work' about which the young Luther liked to speak.[108]

Luther's thought concerning the problem of the proper understanding of the use of the law-gospel dialectic in both kingdoms contains another ambiguity in relation to the Lordship of Christ in the two kingdoms. We spoke of both kingdoms as the realm in which God's activity occurs. Thus, the kingdom of the world, and not only the kingdom of God, is also the sphere of God's *love* as well as God's wrath. However, we did not refer to this kingdom as Christ's. Does this mean that the Lordship of Christ, that is proclaimed in terms of cross, resurrection and exaltation, does not embrace this realm as well? Althaus points out that "God—and not Christ—institutes" the secular kingdom, which is indeed God's not Christ's. "Christ is concerned only with the spiritual kingdom. He concerns himself about secular government as little as about God's working in nature—as about storms, for example."[109] Does this not lead to a false and debilitating dichotomy between the presence of Christ's Lordship in the spiritual kingdom and the absence of his Lordship in the secular kingdom? We return once again to the distinction between the *de facto* Lordship in the former and the *de jure* Lordship in the latter. Christ's universal Lordship is real but hidden, for it awaits eschatological fulfilment. Christ's Lordship is inevitably described in paradoxical terms because in this world Christ's kingdom is in the heart of the believer. It is a kingdom that emerges through the activity of the Holy Spirit who moves people to faith through the proclaimed Word. The Holy Spirit builds up the kingdom of Christ through the Word, the sacraments, and brotherly and sisterly consolation. Through these means, the *de facto* Lordship of Christ is achieved.[110] It needs to be pointed out, however, that building the kingdom of Christ is not to be equated with the triumphalistic Christianisation of society by gradually absorbing everyone into the visible church. In the light of the theology of the cross, the "growth" of Christ's kingdom can be perceived only partially. The surprise of those chosen in the final judgement, according to Matthew 25: 31–46, is a clear warning against any definitive identification of those who belong to the kingdom of Christ.

Since Christians, in view of their membership in both kingdoms, have a higher obligation to serve the neighbour in love as unto Christ himself, what sort of ethic of the cross is to be suggested for Christians? Since the Christian is called to renounce all claims to self-glory and attempts to merit God's favour and grace, can this ethic ever be a mere *imitatio Christi*? In answer to the second question, it must be pointed out initially that *imitatio Christi*, whether it leads to "worldly" triumphalism or to suffering, shame and even death, is not a way of salvation. Also, replicating Christ's life is not possible under any conditions, historical or contemporary. Certainly, an ethic of the cross calls the Christian to bear his/her cross, but in the particular situation of his/her own existence. Mere *imitatio Christi* is static and runs the risk of making Christ and his gospel into law. Yet, the truth is that the Christian is called to follow Christ and to experience anew daily his/her baptism, i.e., a continuous dying to self and rising to life in the crucified and risen Christ. Douglas John Hall writes:

> The beginning of the *ethic* of the cross is the identification of this people [i.e., Christians under the cross] with the Crucified One. It is the reduction of this people to nothing, beggarliness, and brokenness. Only through that reduction, continuously accomplished, is it possible for this people to be truly identified with God's work in the world.[111]

The ethic of the cross embraces the duality of Christian existence which is *simul justus et peccator*. The Christian is free to stand in solidarity with all people, irrespective of their race, religion and class, in the struggle to bring greater dignity, humanity and wholeness to human living in the world. The Christian is not afraid to admit his/her beggarliness before God, nor does his/her "hiding" in the righteousness of Christ mean that he/she is to be blind to the experience of total sinfulness *coram Deo* in common with all humankind.[112] As Hall notes, the Christian, on the basis of the social ethic of the cross, even dares to stand with the Marxist—of course, from a responsible, critical perspective.

> Thus the point of departure for *this* social ethic may be the only one that is finally legitimate, even in terms that secular men, such as Marxists, can recognize: namely, *a real solidarity with those who suffer.* Only as the Christian community permits itself to undergo a continuous crucifixion to the world can it be *in* the world as the friend of those who are crucified. ... Real solidarity with those who suffer recognizes that their condition is our own: we are all beggars together.[113]

We agree with Hall that an ethic of the cross of Christ means that Christians are to see their crosses as calling for their suffering with those who suffer. Expanding the meaning of suffering to include both spiritual suffering—i.e., in relation to God—and material suffering—i.e., socio-economic and political suffering—we conclude that the crucified and risen Jesus Christ is present, though veiled from human eyes, in both forms of suffering. Through the proclamation of the gospel, God is revealed to the eyes of faith. The Christian therefore bears his/her cross in the world because he/she believes in Christ *in* the world and *for* the world. Once again, we arrive at a dialectical unity: the unity of the Lordship of Jesus Christ in the two kingdoms through the presence of Christians in both kingdoms, that is, the paradoxical unity between the cross of Christ and the cross of the Christians in the world.[114]

How does God continue "to keep alive a world which has fallen prey to death, after the new aeon in Christ has already been inaugurated in its midst and has become a reality in the life of Christians through the Holy Spirit?"[115] The creative dialectical harmony between the kingdom of God and the kingdom of the world for which we have been arguing is not free of conflict or struggle between the two. The truth of the matter is that there is a real struggle which the Christian should feel all the more because of his/her twofold existence.[116] The church must be vigilant in maintaining the struggle not as an end in itself but as a reminder that the kingdom of Christ has not been fully revealed: "Just this is the sign of the eschatological situation, which is not yet the end itself."[117]

In his description of existence in the secular kingdom, Luther speaks positively about the role of reason. "This is the radical element in Luther's theological-political thought. The ecclesiastical legitimation of the state is overturned and replaced by the legitimation of reason."[118] At first glance, the idea of "the legitimation of reason" in Luther seems to contradict his emphasis upon a theology of the cross. But it is not a contradiction but a tension, for reason has a rightful place in the secular sphere where both Christian and non-Christian are called to act "through law and justice, to preserve the world from chaos."[119] When they act, they participate in the sovereign power of God—another mode of God's love which is often experienced as wrath because of sin. That is, "there is an inherent and necessary element of coercion which contradicts the free order of love in the kingdom of God."[120] When reason is used in the secular kingdom, all social structures are relativised and freed for rational analysis. They are not devalued, nor is God no longer present in the realm in which they exist and operate. Christians are free to serve their neighbour in love through a recognition that all structures are relative and temporary. Only the kingdom of God is eternal.

But does radical relativisation not lead to withdrawal from the world and from the process of humanisation? Does "penultimacy" not result in a reduction of Christian commitment to the world? Unfortunately, the history of the church often suggests that it does. But this does not invalidate the necessity for the doctrine of the two kingdoms. Indeed, as we have repeatedly emphasised, the tension between the two kingdoms, between reason and revelation, law and gospel, is intrinsic to an evangelical theology of the cross. Accordingly, Carter Lindberg, writing on the temporalising influence of reason on the social structure of Luther's day (and those that have since emerged), states:

> The Christian is to take seriously the task of world-building and the maintenance of culture, society, and civilization, but always with the condition that every culture, every system of justice, and every political structure is only relative and instrumental for the humanization of persons. Tradition is to be conserved with insight into its dehumanizing aspects and its penultimacy. Reason and love are to be active in the continual task of socialization in the recognition that God, not the Law, nor the past, nor the empire, nor the church, is sovereign in history. For Luther, faith alone grants the security to live within the insecurity of relative structures. It is only by faith that persons can avoid the defensive sanctification of past, present, or future goods and values. Faith enables persons to be persons because it lets God be God.[121]

Reason, when exercised in relation to the neighbour and to socio-economic and political structures, i.e., in relation to the secular government and kingdom, does not contradict nor conflict with God's universal love for humanity nor God's specific love in Christ. On the contrary, reason acts in harmony with God's twofold love.

Viewed from the standpoint of Luther's doctrine of the two kingdoms, Marx's *Weltanschauung* is correctly placed in the secular realm, the realm of reason. He is concerned about humankind, society and nature which in a theology of the cross are temporary and transitory. They will pass away. Marx himself recognises this, but he is not accordingly open to the transcendent power and kingdom of God. Instead, his understanding of historical and dialectical materialism, prompts him to posit an eternal and dynamic process of mutation in human history which, under the "free" future, will be unalienated and will continually produce an unalienated human world.

Though Marx's *Weltanschauung* correctly belongs to the secular realm, it is diametrically opposed to theological talk about human beings *coram Deo* because of its atheistic base. His ethics, for example, is not built upon a theological but an anthropocentric, materialist base. Moreover, his radical immanentism, in which there is a monistic, not a dualistic view of reality, is an antipode to the theological concept of the two kingdoms. Thus, the theologian of the cross rejects his naive optimism about the emergence of the liberating proletarian revolution (and, equally, naive optimism in Marxist movements). In doing so, the theologian of the cross recognises that he/she must not minimise the centrality of celebration in Christian worship and existence. The theologian of the cross must guard against using the concept of the two kingdoms as an ideology of the *status quo* which seeks to preserve the "old order" because it is considered binding (since it was ordained by God) and/or because the transformation of the "old order" will mean an end to the privileges and dominance of a particular class or elitist group in society.

It is not only Marx's atheistic and anthropocentric world view that is judged by the doctrine of the two kingdoms. Any theological formulation that would suggest that sin is not basically a separation from God from which all other societal forms of alienation are derived is likewise judged and condemned by the law. The reduction of sin to primarily socio-economic and political alienation does not fully conduce to human liberation, since such reductionism does not allow God to be God. "Deified" reason has usurped the place of faith. In the quest for an indigenous expression of the Christian faith, the church must guard against reducing the gospel to law by turning the imperative into the indicative of the gospel.

Finally, the church is called to be the church of Jesus Christ and not merely an agency for social action. While it works for the humanisation, and not the Christianisation of the world, it must be ever vigilant in its proclamation of the Word and the administration of the sacraments, and in its solidarity with the poor and the oppressed. It proclaims that, in the eyes of the crucified and risen Christ, even the misfit, the unproductive and "colonialised" person is invited to share in the kingdom of Christ and experience in faith the *de facto* Lordship of Christ, both in his/her life and in the world. The Christian, who is *simul justus et peccator*, is a citizen of two kingdoms but of one world.

NOTES TO CHAPTER V

1 Peter L. Berger and Richard J. Neuhaus, *Against the World for the World* (New York: The Seabury Press, 1976), p. 158. "Hartford Theses" is the name given to the text of "An appeal for Theological Affirmation," which was issued on 26 January 1975, in Hartford, Connecticut. The eighteen (18) signatories of the affirmation included well-known Christian laypersons and theologians from the Protestant, Roman Catholic and Eastern Orthodox communities in North America. The summary of their affirmation reads thus: "The renewal of Christian witness and mission requires constant examination of the assumption shaping the Church's life. Today an apparent loss of a sense of the transcendent is undermining the Church's ability to address with clarity and courage the urgent tasks to which God calls it in the world. This loss is manifest in a number of pervasive themes. Many are superficially attractive, but upon closer examination we find these themes false and debilitating to the Church's life and work." Thirteen such false themes were listed; see *The Presbyterian Layman* (March 1975), 5. For an elaborate and lucid account of the "Hartford Theses," see Berger and Neuhaus, *Against the World for the World* .

2 Berger and Neuhaus, *Against the World for the World,* p. 158.

3 Among the factors of crucial importance in any consideration to use Marx's concept of alienation to explicate the past, present, and even future of Caribbean man and woman are: the obvious historical distance between Marx and today; the relative lack of industrialisation in the Caribbean vis-à-vis Marx's day (in western Europe), and certainly of other New World countries, North America being the example *par excellence*; various "official" brands of authentic Marxism; and finally, alienation, as used in Marx, which does not fully describe either the particular conditions of Caribbean man and woman, or the fundamental condition of a broken relationship between God and humankind in which humankind stands. In other words, the concept of original sin must be central to any theological explication of the condition of Caribbean man and woman, even, and precisely, where Marx's concept of alienation is used as a heuristic device.

4 William Watty, *From Shore to Shore* (Barbados: Cedar Press, 1981), p. 24, states: "The real question for us in the Caribbean is: What is the black man like, what are his values, what is his life-style and where is his commitment when he has overcome and is free at last?"

5 There is general agreement among scholars that economic considerations were primary in establishing and promoting human exploitation under slavery in the New World. See Sidney W. Mintz, *Caribbean Transformations* (Chicago: Aldine Publishing Co., 1974), pp. 63–64. Eric Williams, *Capitalism and Slavery* (Chapel Hill: The University of North Carolina Press, 1944), for example, in noting this point, goes even further in arguing that the abolition of the Atlantic slave trade, and of plantation slavery itself, in the New World, was prompted primarily by economic motives and, only secondarily, by humanitarian and Christian considerations.

6 Philip Mason, *Patterns of Dominance* (London: Oxford University Press, 1970), p. 274.

7 George Lamming, *The Pleasures of Exile* (London: M. Joseph, 1960), p. 60, quoted in *Slavery, Colonialism, and Racism,* ed. by Sidney W. Mintz (New York: W.W. Norton and Co., Inc., 1974), p. 45 (Mintz's emphasis).

8 V.S. Naipaul, *The Overcrowded Barracoon* (New York: Knopf, 1973), p. 254, quoted in Mintz, *Slavery,* p. 45.

9 G.W.F. Hegel, *The Phenomenology of Mind,* trans. by J.B. Baillie (London: 1931), pp. 234–237, and 237–240, respectively, quoted in Richard Norman, *Hegel's Phenomenology: A Philosophical Introduction* (London: Sussex University Press, 1976), p. 50.

10 Under the plantation system, the slaves were mere chattel. They did not own their labour, their product, nor their lives. They belonged totally to their master. Moreover, on the question of their

relation to their *species-being*, it was very evident that slaves were considered inferior human species. Community life was regulated by the plantocracy who were at liberty to break up "marriages" and family clusters according to the economic climate of the time.

[11] Dwarka Persaud, "Light and the Evolution of the Free Society: An Appraisal of Governor Light's Administration, 1838–1848," (unpublished B.A., History 401 thesis, University of Guyana, 24 May 1974), pp. 3–4, states: "When the momentous decision was made to abolish slavery, it was strongly felt that it would not be prudent to terminate the system unconditionally on 1 August 1834, but rather have a 'phasing-out' system of apprenticeship. Ostensibly and ideally, this provision was intended to re-educate and acclimatise the planters and the ex-slaves for their new roles as employers and employees in the 'free' society .... Its success depended almost entirely on the support of the plantocracy. Unfortunately, such support was withheld. Consequently, the British Parliament decided to terminate apprenticeship prematurely on 1 August 1838, two years before the original date for its termination."

[12] Hugh Tinker, *A New System of Slavery; the Export of Indian Labour Overseas 1830–1920* (London: Oxford University Press, 1974), provides a most informative and detailed study of the phenomenon of Indian indentureship which emerged after the failure of the apprenticeship system. Tinker, p. 383, states: "For slavery is both a system and an attitude of mind. Both the system and the attitude are still with us." See also, pp. 18–19. The irony of the persistence of slavery even after it had been declared illegal by an Act of the British Parliament is also well-illustrated in Alan H. Adamson, *Sugar Without Slaves: The Political Economy of British Guiana, 1838–1904* (New Haven: Yale University Press, 1972).

It is instructive to recall Marx's thesis that consciousness cannot be radically transformed by merely re-interpreting the world. Real, material transformation in the superstructure (and this includes ideas and consciousness as world view) will only be achieved through the revolutionary transformation of the socio-economic base of society. Despite the fact that history has not demonstrated the total accuracy of Marx's thesis, it is, nevertheless, of significance to remember that neither legislation nor coercion nor both can transform human consciousness overnight. Unfortunately, even Marxists suffer from such an insidious "loss of memory" which leads (and has led) to dehumanising and demonic consequences.

[13] See Mason, *Patterns of Dominance*, pp. 285–290.

[14] See Sidney Mintz, "The Rural Proletariat and the Problem of Rural Proletarian Consciousness," *Journal of Peasant Studies* , Vol. 1 (1974), 291–325.

[15] Eric Hobsbawm, *New York Review of Books* (February 22, 1973), 8, review of Irene L. Glendzier, *Franz Fanon: A Critical Study,* quoted in Mintz, *Slavery,* p. 46.

[16] Mintz, *Slavery,* p. 46.

[17] *Ibid.,* p. 47.

[18] V.S. Naipaul, *The Mimic Men* (London: Penguin Books, 1977), p. 8, in his characteristically cynical tone, writes of the colonial politician: "We lack order. Above all, we lack power, and we do not understand that we lack power. We mistake works and the acclamation of words of power; as soon as our bluff is called we are lost."

[19] David Lowenthal, "Race and Color in the West Indies," *Daedalus,* Vol. 96, No. 2 (Spring 1967), 580–581.

[20] For two excellent studies on the development and nature of Caribbean social structure, see Orlando Patterson, *The Sociology of Slavery* (London: MacGibbon and Kee, 1967); and Elsa V. Goveia, *Slave Society in the British Leeward Islands at the End of the Eighteenth Century* (London: Yale University Press, 1965).

[21] See Mason, *Patterns of Dominance*, pp. 278–279.

[22] *Ibid.,* p. 281.

[23] On the question of some of the stereotypes held by Africans and East Indians of each other, see

Mason, *Patterns of Dominance*, pp. 296–297. On the question of the European "officials' " attitudes to this conflict-ridden situation, see Paul Singh, *Guyana: Socialism in a Plural Society* (London: Fabian Society, 1972), p. 20, where he points out: "British constitutionalists have from time to time camouflaged the antagonisms that flared up repeatedly in the plural society. They propagated the popular concept that crown colony government provided for an equitable representation for different groups and that the attitude of the governor and chief administrative officials was one of impartiality to the various groups. They spared no pains to point out that they had no particular concern in wanting to promote the interest of any section of the population at the expense of the others, and they were well equipped to hold the scales evenly."

There is a measure of truth in such claims by colonial officials which must not be overlooked in the anti-colonial animosity that has been surfacing in the post-colonial era. At the same time, it must not be forgotten that the dominance of that minority group, not only in politics but in every significant aspect of West Indian life, conduced to the growth of such stereotypes as arose among the masses. The defining values operative in Caribbean society were imported from Europe, more specifically, Britain.

[24] Mintz, *Slavery*, p. 53.

[25] See Mason, *Patterns of Dominance*, pp. 290–294.

[26] J.S. Furnival, *Colonial Policy and Practice: A Comparative Study of Burma and Netherlands India* (London: Cambridge University Press, 1948); see also, M.G. Smith, *The Plural Society in the British West Indies* (Berkeley and Los Angeles: University of California, 1965).

[27] It is very distressing and perplexing to notice young children displaying hostility and suspicion towards children and older members of another ethnic group. Prejudice and stereotypes are easily picked up by children who observe the adults with whom they socialise. Though this phenomenon is by no means peculiar to the Caribbean, because of the "closeness" of social intercourse there, prejudice is acutely felt. We cannot go on blaming our history or those who are ethnically and culturally different from us for the continuation of the problem which this phenomenon represents. Breaking down walls of prejudice is one of the pressing tasks facing the church today.

[28] Singh, *Guyana: Socialism in a Plural Society*, p. 20.

[29] *Ibid.*

[30] *Ibid.*, p. 24.

[31] *Ibid.*

[32] Father Richard Ho Lung, "Perspectives on Caribbean Culture," interview with Monty Williams (published from a recording on tape), in *GISRA* (The Guyana Institute for Social Research and Action), Vol. 5, No. 4 (December 1974), 61.

[33] Naipaul, *The Mimic Men*, p. 8.

[34] Mintz, *Slavery*, pp. 47–48, perceptively points out: "From one perspective, of course, the Caribbean region is merely American—for all American societies are migrant societies, and all are composed in some measure of the descendants of strangers. But with several significant exceptions—the hispanophone societies in particular—the people of the Caribbean region are marked by the absence of a central tradition through which migrant populations could mediate their relationships to each other. The lack of just such a tradition has affected qualitatively the emergence of an ethnically based national consciousness and has required of Caribbean people a social innovativeness more in tune with the modern world than with the world of the eighteenth and nineteenth centuries. Neither perceived differences in physical type nor in ethnicity has been irrelevant in the development of that innovativeness, but such differences may well have intensified one variety of conciousness."

In North America, the ethic was derived from the Puritan religion. Thus, it is common to speak of American civil religion as an outgrowth of Puritan religion which began on North American soil with the arrival of the first settlers. For a seminal treatment of this theme, see Robert N. Bellah,

The Broken Covenant; American Civil Religion in Time of Trial (New York: The Seabury Press, 1975), especially, pp. 1–35.

    K.V. Parmasad, "By the Light of a Deya," *Tapia,* Vol. 22 (1971), p. 5, reminds his readers that an Afro-Caribbean culture is not *the* authentic culture of the East Indians in Trinidad. He recognises the need for a social order in Trinidad that transcends the alienated past. However, he insists that if the price of gaining such an identity and national spirit is the stripping of other ethnic groups of their uniquenesses, then such a national spirit is a misnomer, for it promotes alienation even further. It is very sobering to reflect upon the mission of the church in this complex and frustrating situation.

[35] Mintz, *Slavery,* p. 47; see also, Mintz, *Caribbean Transformations,* pp. 37–38.

[36] Mintz, *Slavery,* p. 47.

[37] Sehon Goodridge, *Politics and the Caribbean Church: A Confession of Guilt,* CADEC Study Paper No. 2 (Barbados, W.I.: Catholic News Printery, n.d.), p. 6.

[38] *Ibid.* On the question of the need for a Caribbean ideology for change and transformation so that the new, liberated Caribbean man and woman may emerge, see William G. Demas, *Change and Renewal in the Caribbean,* ed. by David I. Mitchell (Barbados, W.I.: Caribbean Conference of Churches Publishing House, n.d.).

[39] Goodridge, *Politics and the Caribbean Church,* pp. 6–7.

[40] Karl Marx and Frederick Engels, *The Communist Manifesto* (New York: International Publishers Co., Inc., 1948), p. 44.

[41] In spite of their different approaches to the task of theologisation in the Caribbean, these four writers reflect the growing spirit of ecumenism within the Caribbean church. Michael Campbell-Johnston, S.J., was one of the most important voices in the Roman Catholic Church on the question of social justice. Idris Hamid was a Presbyterian from Trinidad and Tobago, C.S. Reid a Jamaican Baptist, while Paul G.Singh is a Methodist layman from Guyana.

[42] The writings considered here are Paul G. Singh, "Marxian Socialism," (paper presented at a public meeting held at Redeemer Lutheran Church, Georgetown, Guyana, 16 November 1975), 1-10; Kortright Davis, ed., "The Christian-Socialist Dialogue," in *Moving into Freedom*, "Working Together with Christ" Series. No. 2, The Second CCC Assembly, Guyana, 1977 (Barbados: The Cedar Press, 1977); Paul G.Singh, "Christianity and Socialism: Towards a Reconciliation?" *Guyana Graphic*, 17 August 1975; Paul G. Singh, "With God and Marx: Towards a People's Democracy?" *Guyana Graphic*, 24 August 1975.

[43] Davis,"Christian-Socialist Dialogue," p. 81.

[44] *Ibid.*, pp. 81–86.

[45] Singh, "Towards a People's Democracy?" See also Davis, "Christian-Socialist Dialogue," p. 84.

[46] Singh, "Towards a People's Democracy?"

[47] *Ibid.*

[48] The following discussion is taken from the newspaper article, Michael Campbell-Johnston, "Basic Aspirations of Socialism are Profoundly Christian," *Guyana Graphic*, 10 August 1975.

[49] Reid's argument is extracted from the "U.T.C.W.I. Founders' Day Lecture;" see C.S. Reid, "A Christian Evaluation of Marxist Trends in the Caribbean," (n.d.), (mimeographed), 1–8.

[50] *Ibid.*, 7 (emphasis Reid's).

[51] *Ibid.*, 8.

[52] *Ibid.*, 6. See also, Watty, *From Shore to Shore*, p. 26.

[53] *Ibid.*, 6–7.

[54] *Ibid.*, 6.

[55] The argument developed here is based on three essays written by Idris Hamid: "Decolonializing

the Christian Faith: A Fresh Approach to the Christian Faith in the Context of the Caribbean," in *Fambli; The Church's Responsibility to the Family in the Caribbean,* A consultation conducted by CARIPLAN, ed. by Lilith Haynes (New York: Church World Service, 1972), pp. 152–172; *In Search of New Perspectives,* Caribbean Ecumenical Consultation for Development (Barbados, W.I.: CADEC, 1970), pp. 1–19; and "Theology and Caribbean Development," in *With Eyes Wide Open,* ed. by David I. Mitchell (Barbados, W.I.: CADEC, n.d.), pp. 120–133.

[56] Hamid, "Decolonializing the Christian Faith," p. 164. It is to be noted that Hamid writes as one who has grown up in the Caribbean. This does not mean that someone from the "outside" cannot write sympathetically and with deep insight about the experience of colonialism in the Caribbean.

[57] *Ibid.,* p. 154.

[58] Hamid, "Theology and Caribbean Development," p. 124.

[59] Hamid, "Decolonializing the Christian Faith," p. 155.

[60] *Ibid.,* pp. 153–154.

[61] Hamid, "Theology and Caribbean Development," p. 125.

[62] *Ibid.,* p. 126.

[63] *Ibid.,* p. 125.

[64] *Ibid.*

[65] *Ibid.* This conclusion is one of the primary assumptions in James Cone's analysis of black theology. A reading of any one of Cone's major works will indicate this. See, James H. Cone, *A Black Theology of Liberation* (Philadelphia: J. B. Lippincott Co., 1970); Cone, *God of the Oppressed* (London: SPCK, 1977); Cone, *The Spirituals and the Blues: An Interpretation* (New York: The Seabury Press, 1972).

[66] Hamid, "Theology and Caribbean Development," p. 125.

[67] Hamid, "Decolonializing the Christian Faith," p. 171.

[68] *Ibid.,* pp. 158–159.

[69] *Ibid.,* p. 159.

[70] See Hamid, *In Search of New Perspectives,* pp. 7–8.

[71] Hamid, "Decolonializing the Christian Faith," p. 159.

[72] Hamid, *In Search of New Perspectives,* p. 8.

[73] Langdon Gilkey, *Reaping the Whirlwind* (New York: The Seabury Press, 1976), p. 237.

[74] Hamid, "Decolonializing the Christian Faith," p. 165. See also, p. 164.

[75] *Ibid.,* p. 166.

[76] Watty, *From Shore to Shore,* pp. 27–28, correctly points to the acute need for the creation of a new community so that "disintegration"—"the peculiar predicament of the Caribbean"—might be overcome. See also, pp. 49–50.

[77] In accordance with the distinction between God and the future God gives and will give through Jesus Christ, it should be pointed out that the concepts of "in history" and "beyond history," the "already" and the "not yet," which are commonly used in modern eschatological theology to distinguish between the present and future liberation, cannot be read back into Luther's theology without qualification. Salvation and liberation from sin and the powers of evil are already present to the eyes of faith. Luther tells us: "We do not wait for forgiveness and all the graces as though we would not receive them until the life to come, rather, they are now present for us in faith, even though they are hidden and will be revealed only in the life to come." *Luther's Works* (WA), Vol. 17, Pt. 2, p. 229, as quoted in Paul Althaus, *The Theology of Martin Luther,* trans. by Robert C. Schultz (Philadelphia: Fortress Press, 1970), p. 404. Both the church and the individual Christian find that historical reality contradicts faith. Thus theology is always a theology of the cross and is always thoroughly eschatological. See Althaus, *Theology,* p. 404. These ideas have been

incorporated into the theology of the cross presented in our study.

[78] *The Book of Concord*, trans. and ed. by Theodore G. Tappert in collaboration with Jaroslav Pelikan, et. al. (Philadelphia: Fortress Press, 1959), p. 29.

[79] *Ibid.*, p. 30.

[80] Among the great number of works which discuss this theme from various, different, and, even, conflicting perspectives are: Leonardo Boff, *Jesus Christ Liberator: A Critical Christology for our Time,* trans. by Patrick Hughes (Maryknoll, New York: Orbis Books, 1978); Cone, *God of the Oppressed* ; Ignacio Ellacuría, *Freedom Made Flesh*, trans. by John Drury (Maryknoll, New York: Orbis Books, 1976); Ernst Käsemann, *Jesus Means Freedom,* trans. by Frank Clarke (Philadelphia: Fortress Press, 1977).

[81] John Macquarrie, "A Theology of Alienation," in *Alienation,* ed. by Frank Johnson (New York: Seminar Press, 1973), p. 320.

[82] Wolfhart Pannenberg, *What is Man?* trans. by Duane A. Priebe (Philadelphia: Fortress Press, 1970), p. 148.

[83] *Ibid.,* p. 117 (emphasis mine).

[84] *Ibid.*, p. 119.

[85] *Ibid.*, pp. 119–120.

[86] *Ibid.*, p. 37.

[87] *Ibid.*, p. 38 (emphases mine).

[88] *Ibid.*, p. 134.

[89] *Ibid.*, p. 148.

[90] *Ibid.*, p. 149.

[91] Franz Lau, "The Lutheran Doctrine of the Two Kingdoms," *Lutheran World* ,Vol. xii, No. 4 (1965), 355–356, points out that speaking about a *doctrine* of two kingdoms in Luther is misleading. He argues that the "doctrine" was more specifically a Reformation conception than just simply Luther's. There are grounds for "designating the doctrine of the two kingdoms as a common Christian teaching" which is "not entirely meaningless." However, its meaning "is possible only to a degree," i.e., to the extent which we are able to maintain the tensions by playing off its inherent contradictions against one another.

In Luther's writings, the two most significant works which help us to understand his view of ethics *sub cruce* in the world are: "Temporal Authority: To what extent it should be obeyed," in *Luther's Works,* American Ed., Vol. 45, "The Christian in Society," Pt. 2, trans by J.J. Schindel and ed. by Walther I. Brandt (Philadelphia: Muhlenberg Press, 1962), pp. 81–129; and "The Freedom of a Christian," trans. by W.A. Lambert, in *Three Treatises* (Philadelphia: Fortress Press, 1960), pp. 277–316.

From the vast corpus of writings on Luther's teaching on the two kingdoms, ethics and culture, politics and government, the following works are given special consideration in the development of our discussion here: Paul Althaus, *The Ethics of Martin Luther*, trans. and with a foreword by Robert C. Schultz (Philadelphia: Fortress Press, 1972); Heinrich Bornkamm, *Luther's Doctrine of the Two Kingdoms,* trans. by Karl H. Hertz (Philadelphia: Fortress Press, 1966); Carl E. Braaten, *The Flaming Center* (Philadelphia: Fortress Press, 1977), pp. 57–62; George W. Forell, *Faith Active in Love* (Minneapolis: Augsburg Publishing House, 1964); "The Political Use of the Law," in *Luther and Culture,* Martin Luther Lectures, Vol. iv, ed. by G.W. Forell, et.al. (Decorah, Iowa: Luther College Press, 1960), pp. 3–23; Douglas John Hall, *Lighten Our Darkness* (Philadelphia: The Westminster Press, 1976); Franz Lau, "The Lutheran Doctrine of the Two Kingdoms," pp. 335–372; and Carter Lindberg, "Theology and Politics: Luther the Radical and Muntzer the Reactionary," *Encounter*, Vol. 37, No. 4 (Autumn 1976), 356–371.

[92] Althaus, *Ethics of Martin Luther*, p. 5; see also, pp. 3,9.

[93] *Ibid.*, p. 5.

[94] The significance of Luther's use of scripture in his formulation of his doctrine of the two kingdoms cannot be overemphasised. Lau, "The Lutheran Doctrine of the Two Kingdoms," 358–359, writes: "The double antitheses, (anti-enthusiast and anti-scholastic), however, proceeds directly from Luther's study of Scripture and indicates that Luther is a Biblical theologian and allows his questions to be raised by Holy Scriptures. Luther's doctrine of the two kingdoms must be understood, in the first instance, on the basis of the fact that he could not come to terms with Holy Scripture except by means of his doctrine of the two kingdoms."

[95] *Luther's Works*, Vol. 45, p. 88; see also, Althaus, *Ethics of Martin Luther*, pp. 51–53, who points out that Luther's thought shows a shift from his earlier emphasis upon the opposition between the two kingdoms, to the positive role of the kingdom of the world which also expresses the goodness of God.

[96] *Luther's Works*, Vol. 45, p. 90.

[97] Bornkamm, *Luther's Doctrine of the Two Kingdoms*, p. 2.

[98] *Luther's Works*, Vol. 45, p. 91.

[99] Bornkamm, *Luther's Doctrine of the Two Kingdoms*, p. 17.

[100] *Ibid.*, p. 18.

[101] *Luther's Works*, Vol. 45, p. 92; see also, p. 105.

[102] *Ibid.*, p. 92; see also, p. 110, and Althaus, *Ethics of Martin Luther*, p. 55, on the kingdom of wrath.

[103] In his comments on Romans 13:1, Luther points out that the secular authority deals with external matters, not with matters of faith. "St. Paul is speaking of the governing authority. Now you have just heard that no one but God can have authority over souls. Hence, St. Paul cannot possibly be speaking of any obedience except where there can be corresponding authority. From this it follows that he is not speaking of faith, to the effect that temporal authority should have the right to command faith. He is speaking rather of external things, that they should be ordered and governed on earth." *Luther's Works,* Vol. 45, p. 110. See also, J.M. Porter, ed., *Luther Selected Political Writings* (Philadelphia: Fortress Press, 1974), p. 19.

[104] Lau,"The Lutheran Doctrine of the Two Kingdoms," 365.

[105] See Althaus, *Theology*, pp. 242–245, for a brief but clear description of Luther's teaching that the Christian is "simultaneously righteous and sinner."

[106] There are many nuances in Luther's use of *opus alienum* and *opus proprium* which we cannot take up here. However, for our purposes, it needs to be recognised that God's "proper" work is God's saving work through Christ and God's "alien" work is God's hidden work of continuing to preserve God's creation from ruin and chaos. The latter serves the former, for both constitute a unity in the twofold nature of God's love. See Althaus, *Theology*, pp. 120, 274–280.

[107] See Gustaf Wingren, *Creation and Law*, trans by Ross McKenzie (Edinburgh: Oliver and Boyd Ltd., 1961), pp. 149–173, 174–197, where he treats the use of the law in relation to the world and in relation to the conscience of the individual, respectively. "The article of the Creed which refers to Creation must precede the second article which deals with redemption, even when the Creation referred to is Creation in Christ. The order in which the two are given does not represent the sequence in our acquisition of knowledge concerning God, but the sequence in God's dealings with us." (p. 41).

[108] Bornkamm, *Luther's Doctrine of the Two Kingdoms*, p. 14.

[109] Althaus, *Ethics of Martin Luther*, p. 46.

[110] See Karl H.Hertz, ed., *Two Kingdoms and One World* (Minneapolis: Augsburg Publishing House, 1976), pp. 323–324.

[111] Hall, *Lighten our Darkness*, p. 152.

[112] Luther argues that the Christian's righteousness before God is not his but Christ's. It is therefore an "alien" righteousness under which the sinner "hides" through faith. Luther is therefore consistent in his description of the Christian as *simul justus et peccator*. See, Althaus, *Theology*, pp. 227–242.

[113] Hall, *Lighten our Darkness*, p. 152.

[114] See Regin Prenter, *Luther's Theology of the Cross*, ed. by Charles S. Anderson (Philadelphia: Fortress Press, 1971), pp. 3–7. "But a cross which is either only objective (outside of us) or only subjective (personal to us) is not the cross of Christ which is the means of our salvation. The deep truth of Luther's theology of the cross is that it views the cross on Golgotha and the cross which is laid upon us as one and the same." (p. 18)

[115] Bornkamm, *Luther's Doctrine of the Two Kingdoms*, p. 33.

[116] Care should be taken here lest the impression be given that the Christian is called to experience a cosmic battle within himself/herself. "Feeling" the tension is being aware of its reality through faith in Christ. But the Christian is assured that Christ has already defeated the powers of evil and will disclose that victory at the eschaton. The Christian is therefore at peace in the peace of God which the Holy Spirit effects.

[117] Bornkamm, *Luther's Doctrine of the Two Kingdoms*, p. 33.

[118] Lindberg, "Theology and Politics," 363.

[119] Bornkamm, *Luther's Doctrine of the Two Kingdoms*, p. 24.

[120] *Ibid.*, p. 35.

[121] Lindberg, "Theology and Politics," 371.

CONCLUSION

Marx's world view has functioned as a soteriological system by which humankind, not God, has the sole responsibility for the transformation of the very basis of society, the mode of production, and for the recreation and redirection of the forces of history so that they will result in the transcendence of alienation and continually conduce to humankind's creation and enjoyment of real human freedom.

Unfortunately, Marx is far from clear in his description of the kairos he envisions. He fails to maintain the indispensable tension between both the primacy of human freedom and the primacy of the forces of production in his argument for the eventual emergence of final communism from alienating capitalism. He is not fully empirical in his analysis of the capitalist mode of production and in his anticipation of its sure demise. Despite Marx's own feeling to the contrary, it is conclusive that his analysis of capitalism and of alienation of the worker is ethical in inspiration and intention. He considers that his non-ethical pronouncements stem from his actual discernment of certain laws of history.

Throughout both his early and mature writings, Marx's preoccupation is anthropology. He is convinced that his philosophy of humankind is far more humanising than any other philosophy, either religious or secular. His concern is real, living human beings and authentic historical, liberating *praxis-theoria*. The fundamental component of Marx's *Weltanschauung* is his radical reduction of all reality to human history, to an atheistic, anthropocentric, immanental reality where human beings are viewed as the final arbiters and standard of themselves and their future.

Marx's world view poses a crucial challenge to Christian theology. How might Christian theology continue to speak about God? How might it give due consideration to the legitimate criticisms of religion explicitly stated by Marx, not by opting for a Marxian hermeneutics or for a Marxian future vis-à-vis any version of the Christian hope, but precisely by arguing from an explicitly Biblical and theological base? Observing Marx's obvious and noble struggles on behalf of humankind, Christian theology finds itself faced with the task of once again explicating the faith so that the truth of God's transcendent and immanent concern for humanity is clearly and persuasively communicated. This is the task of an evangelical theology of the cross, which includes a radical concept of God. It is a return to the paradoxical revelation of God through the cross of Jesus Christ. Hope in history and hope beyond history, i.e., in the Absolute Future of God, are seen in the context of the cross and resurrection of Jesus. The last word of the cross is not despair and nihil, but hope, hope in the God of wrath and of love.

The God of the theology of the cross reveals godself, not in glory, triumph and power—according to the world's standards—but in shame, defeat and powerlessness, i.e., in the suffering and death of Jesus Christ. The Holy Spirit empowers the church to bear witness to the Divine liberation of humankind. The church insists that human nature is not the product of human effort but is Divinely given. When human beings raise the question of the tragedy of human existence, the church points them to the God of Jesus Christ who is the gracious God hidden in God's wrath. God, who is ultimately gracious, does not turn a blind eye nor a deaf ear to human suffering, pain and death. The Triune God suffers for the sake of humankind. Only through the God of the cross can human beings find real, human freedom. To ask human beings to liberate themselves is further enslaving and will lead to demonic consequences, as history has vividly demonstrated. Salvation and reconciliation are *sola gratia*.

In light of the message of justification by grace alone, human *praxis* is free and humanly fulfilling in relation to the neighbour. In other words, reconciled to God through faith in Jesus Christ, the Christian is free to serve his/her neighbour in love. Service of neighbour includes both individual and corporate action. It calls for both inner spiritual transformation and external transformation of the socio-economic, political (and other material) structures of human existence. It is especially in relation to external transformation that Christian theology can and does find significant grounds for dialogue and cooperation with Marxists. But this dialogue is grounded in the conviction that God in Christ has acted decisively and definitively for the sake of humankind. Like the Marxist, the Christian works on behalf of humankind. Unlike the Marxist, the Christian is motivated by obedience to the crucified and risen Lord, Jesus Christ. Such a motivation does not impair human dignity, nor is it subordinate to that of the Marxist's. On the contrary, it is a confession that humankind's "being" transcends humankind's own self-definition, for it is bound up with the suffering and crucified God.

We note that our concern, in response to the Marxian challenge, is not with the Christian-Marxist dialogue *per se*. In the context of our primary concern with the mission of the church in the Caribbean, we engage that dialogue only indirectly. Instead of concentrating primarily upon finding common ground for dialogue and cooperation with Marxists, we direct attention to the question of how the church in the Caribbean might continue to speak about God and confess that God is present in the world, creating hope in the resurrection of the dead and in the eschatological fulfilment of reconciliation through Christ.

Marx's appeal in the Caribbean is not founded on the presence of a proletariat in the region. The region is mainly agricultural, and certainly not industrialised on any such scale comparable to what Marx envisages when he views and analyses western European society and its future. There are pervasive plural divisions and forces within the societies in the region, but no advanced technological development. Marx's division of society into two fundamental classes—the capitalist and the worker—has limited relevance when applied to Caribbean societies. There is a notable and crucial absence of a Marxian proletarian consciousness among the Caribbean masses. In short, the Marxian prerequisites for the proletarian revolution are significantly absent.

However, in spite of the absence of the obvious prerequisites for the proletarian revolution, the situation in the Caribbean has been and still is very explosive. It is a situation which has arisen out of the economic, social, political and racial problems which plague Caribbean societies. The challenge to the church posed by these conditions does not arise out of the church's own failure *per se* to fulfil its social mission. Rather, it is the result of the failure of capitalism whose roots go back to the very formative years of Caribbean society which was founded upon the alienating plantation system. Under this system, a small European oligarchy enslaved and exploited a disproportionately larger non-European population. These were the conditions which formed Caribbean man's and woman's ambiguous mentality.

The alienation of Marx's worker and the alienation of Caribbean man and woman are not the same, though they share significant similarities, such as lack of ownership of the means of production and powerlessness in relation to the overall economic structures in society. Caribbean man and woman are enigmas. They are neither African nor East Indian, Portuguese nor Chinese, European nor North American. Moreover, to say that they are West Indians or *Caribbean* men and women—which points to their historical, cultural and geographical orientation—does not solve the problem but merely exacerbates the problem of the identity of Caribbean man and woman.

It is wishful thinking to argue, as Marx does, that the abolition of private ownership of the means of production will generate the radical proletarian changes in attitudes and behaviour of the masses . This criticism is not a dismissal of the acute need to end economic exploitation by large, impersonal corporations. It needs to be recognised, however, that the real symbolic power in communal ownership of the means of production, in Marx's terms, is mitigated by many factors, not least of all the inaccuracy and naivete of his utopian predictions based upon his obvious positive humanism. Ideas and consciousness as a whole—i.e., the superstructure—have an inherent life of their own in the sphere of human reality. Consciousness as superstructure is shaped and influenced by the socio-economic conditions in society. It is not derived solely from the base. Thus awareness of and dependence upon God is not the result of the alienated productive process. On the contrary, it results from the fact that the question of God is intrinsic to all reality and to the quest for authentic humanity.

The Caribbean voices we reviewed provide an ecumenical and pan-regional flavour to the debate. All four writers are acutely concerned with Caribbean man and woman. They are explicitly aware of the alienation of Caribbean man and woman and of the need to work for their real historical liberation. Singh, Campbell-Johnston, and Reid openly discuss the question of a Caribbean response to Marxism. Hamid echoes this concern, though there is no clearly stated reference to that particular problem. On the whole, in these Caribbean voices of the church, the three primary factors, which the church needs to consider in its confession of faith are present: Christian identity in Christ and the need for a kerygmatic, "servant" and sacramental theology; the Marxist/socialist way to human liberation and the building of the future utopia; and the alienated condition of Caribbean man and woman and their society.

Christian theology is primarily concerned with the first of these three factors. It is precisely this concern that leads to a critical consideration of the other two factors. The Christian message is revealed in the cross of Christ. It does not arise out of a speculative appraisal of the historical context in which the message is proclaimed and practised. When the church does not take the situation seriously, it runs the rise of proclaiming a docetic Incarnation. By the same token, when the situation shapes and gives content to the message of the gospel, the result is an ideology of glory.

Caribbean man's and woman's uniqueness should not be used to minimise or obscure their inherent commonality with all human beings who are separated from and reconciled by God. Caribbean man and woman are also fundamentally separated from God and can be ultimately reconciled to God, to themselves, and to their fellow human beings, through faith in Jesus Christ. Reconciliation here is not triumphalistic, for it is experienced *sub cruce*. The cross of Christ leads to the cross of the Christian. It is only through Jesus Christ that the kingdom of God has come and will come. Therefore, Caribbean man's and woman's salvation and reconciliation are also *sola gratia*.

If the church's existence and mission arise out of the activity of the Triune God in the definitive and decisive activity of God in the God-Man, Jesus Christ, then the church cannot avoid concrete, incarnate and loving action in society on behalf of humanity. Moreover, it cannot avoid pointing to the presence of transcendent hope in the world today. Concrete action alone, even in response to the Marxian or other challenge, without the accompanying proclamation of the presence of faith and hope in the midst of and beyond the results of human *praxis-theoria,* is in danger of reducing the church to the status of a social relief agency. Moreover, to reduce the church to the status of a social relief agency would not be the most loving thing to do for humankind. It does not constitute a fully radical and wholistic view of humankind. Indeed, it is not radical obedience to the God of Jesus Christ. The *Weltgeist* is not the Holy Spirit. Scriptural texts, such as Matthew 25:31–46— whether taken by themselves or in the context of the rest of scripture—do not legitimate such an exclusive interpretation of the church's mission in the world or in any particular society.

However, proclamation of faith and hope in God, when divorced from real, genuine and loving action, is a blatant distortion of the gospel. It leaves the impression that the message of the cross is just a speculative message among other messages and not the particular message that God the Son became incarnate and suffered and died and rose again for the salvation of the whole world even though this is a scandal. Accordingly, faith and hope are empty of meaning in the world, and the cross is no longer central to Christian theology.

The message of the love of God becoming incarnate which does not find expression in concrete action, including simple acts of kindness and radical acts for the transformation of structures which dehumanise human beings and allow for unchecked manipulation of human sin and greed in the lives of individuals, groups and society as a whole, will seem hollow and ineffectual. It is a distortion of the evangelical meaning of the powerlessness of God. In other words, the power of God expressed in the Divine powerlessness on the cross is distorted when it becomes the basis for Christian or so-called Christian societies or any individual or group, to enslave and dehumanise individuals, groups or societies. Such an ethic is not an ethic of the cross but of a theology (and ideology) of glory. Both the history of Christendom and of Marxism have repeatedly fallen victim to this distortion, which has led to demonic consequences. When such an ethic is practised by parties identifying themselves as Christian—and who are identified by their victims as such—God is presented as the promoter of injustice and oppression, and not as the One who supremely suffers on behalf of humankind. The church is made up of sinners, but to be sinful is not an excuse for inactivity, apathy or distorted activity. On the contrary, in the name of Jesus Christ, those very sinners, and this means *all* who are freed by the gospel, are called to engage in both individual and corporate liberating activity on behalf of the neighbour. By neighbour is meant those "who are of the household of faith," as well as those who are regarded as outside that household. In other words, the neighbour is both within and without the visible church. This is the way of Jesus who came for sinners.

Finally, it is sobering to note that Marx's philosophy, as a *Weltanschauung*, might easily gain a strong footing in society through the legitimate route of protest atheism. As a sociological institution, the church must be open to criticism, including the Marxian critique of ideology. However, the church must not allow itself to be manipulated by such criticisms. The church must remember that it is also a divine creation and that it is judged and forgiven by the law and the gospel, not by Marx's principle of ideology critique. Through Word and sacrament, which find simple and radical and, at best, ambiguous, fragmentary expression in concrete action among believers and in society, the church is called to be faithful to its Lord, Jesus Christ. In the face of the challenge of Marx's *Weltanschauung*, the church dares to proclaim Jesus Christ and him crucified, that God was in Christ reconciling the alienated world to God, the Triune Creator, that Christ will come again to judge the living and dead and to bring God's reign to completion. In the face of Marx's "wisdom," the church dares to proclaim a theology of the cross which is a scandal, but which is also the wisdom and power of God.

SELECT BIBLIOGRAPHY

BOOKS

Adamson, Alan H. *Sugar Without Slaves. The Polictical Economy of British Guiana, 1838–1904*. New Haven: Yale University Press, 1972.

Althaus, Paul. *The Ethics of Martin Luther*. Translated by Robert C. Schultz. Philadelphia: Fortress Press, 1972.

_____. *The Theology of Martin Luther*. Translated by Robert C. Schultz. Philadelphia: Fortress Press, 1970.

Altizer, Thomas J.J. *The Gospel of Christian Atheism*. London: Collins, 1967.

Alves, Rubem A. *A Theology of Human Hope*. St. Meinrad, Ind.: Abbey Press, 1975.

Anderson, Gerald H., ed. *Asian Voices in Christian Theology*. Maryknoll, N.Y.: Orbis Books, 1976.

Anderson, Gerald H. and Stransky, Thomas F., C.S.P., eds. *Mission Trends No. 4; Liberation Theologies in North America and Europe*. New York: Paulist Press, and Grand Rapids, Mich.: Wm. B. Eerdmans, Publishing Co., 1979.

Aptheker, Herbert, ed. *Marxism and Alienation*. New York: Humanities Press, 1965.

_____, ed. *The Urgency of Marxist-Christian Dialogue*. New York: Harper and Row Publishers, 1970.

Aron, Raymond. *Main Currents in Sociological Thought*. New York: Basic Books, Inc., Publishers, 1965.

Assmann, Hugo. *Practical Theology of Liberation*. Translated by Paul Burns, with a preface by Ernesto Cardenal, and an introduction by Gustavo Gutiérrez.

London: Search Press Ltd., 1975.

_____. *Theology for a Nomad Church*. Translated by Paul Burns. Maryknoll, N.Y.: Orbis Books, 1976.

Avineri, Schlomo. *The Social and Political Thought of Karl Marx*. Cambridge: Cambridge University Press, 1968.

Axelos, Kostas. *Alienation, Praxis, and Techné in the Thought of Karl Marx*. Translated by Ronald Bruzina. Austin: University of Texas Press, 1976.

Barth, Karl. *Protestant Theology in the Nineteenth Century*. Translated by Brian Cozens and John Bowden.. London: SCM Press Ltd., 1972.

Baumer, Franklin L. *Modern European Thought*. New York: The Macmillan Publishing Co., Inc., 1977.

Bell, Daniel. *The End of Ideology*. New York: Collier Books, 1961.

Bell, Wendell, ed. *The Democratic Revolution in the West Indies*. Cambridge, Mass.: Schenkman Publishing Co., Inc., 1967.

Bellah, Robert N. *The Broken Covenant; American Civil Religion in Time of Trial*. New York: The Seabury Press, 1975.

Berger, Peter L. *Facing Up to Modernity*. New York: Basic Books, Inc., Publishers, 1977.

Berger, P.L., and Neuhaus, R.J. *Against the World for the World*. New York: The Seabury Press, 1976.

Bernstein, Henry, ed. *Underdevelopment and Development; The Third World Today*. Selected Readings. London: Penguin Books, 1976.

Boff, Leonardo. *Jesus Christ Liberator: A Critical Christology for our Time*. Translated by Patrick Hughes. New York: Orbis Books, 1978.

_____. *Trinity and Society*. Translated by Paul Burns. Maryknoll, N.Y.: Orbis Books, 1988.

Boff, Leonardo and Boff, Clodovis. *Liberation Theology*. Translated by Robert R. Barr. San Francisco: Harper & Row, Publishers, 1986.

Bonhoeffer, Dietrich. *Letters and Papers from Prison*. Enlarged edition. Edited by Eberhard Bethge. Translated by Reginald Fuller, et. al. London: SCM Press, Ltd., 1976.

_____. *Doing Theology in a Revolutionary Situation*. Philadelphia: Fortress Press, 1975.

Bornkamm, Heinrich. *Luther's Doctrine of the Two Kingdoms*. Translated by Karl H. Hertz. Philadelphia: Fortress Press, 1966.

Braaten, Carl E. *The Flaming Center*. Philadelphia: Fortress Press, 1977.

_____. *The Future of God*. New York: Harper and Row, Publishers, 1969.

Braunschweig, Max. "The Philosophic Thought of the Young Marx." *Alienation*. Vol. 8. Edited by Gerald Sykes. New York: Basic Books, 1964.

Brosché, Fredrik. *Luther on Predestination. The Antinomy and Unity between Love and Wrath in Luther's Concept of God*. Stockholm: Liber Tryck, 1977.

Brown, Raymond E., S.J. *Jesus God and Man*. London: Geoffrey Chapman Publishers, 1968.

Brown, Robert McAfee. *Gustavo Gutiérrez: An Introduction to Liberation Theology*. Maryknoll, N.Y.: Orbis Books, 1990.

Brunner, Peter and Holm, Bernard J. *Luther in the Twentieth Century*. Martin Luther Lecture Series. Vol. 5. Decorah, Ia.: Luther College Press, 1961.

Burnham, Frederic B., McCoy, Charles S. and Meeks, M. Douglas, eds. *Love: The Foundation of Hope*. San Francisco: Harper & Row, Publishers, 1988.

Burns, Emile. *A Handbook of Marxism; Being a collection of extracts from the writings of Marx, Engels, and the greatest of their followers*. London: Victor Gollancz Ltd., 1935.

Cadorette, Curt. *From the Heart of the People*: *The Theology of Gustavo Gutiérrez*. Oak Park, Ill.: Meyer-Stone Books, 1988.

Cairns, David. *The Image of God in Man*. Fontana Library of Theology and Philosophy. London: Collins, 1973.

Cameron, Kenneth Neil. *Marx and Engels Today: A Modern Dialogue on Philosophy and History*. New York: Exposition Press, Inc., 1976.

Capps, Walter Holton. *Hope Against Hope*. Philadelphia: Fortress Press, 1976.

Cone, James H. *A Black Theology of Liberation*. Philadelphia: J.B. Lippincott Co., 1970.

_____. *Black Theology and Black Power*. New York: The Seabury Press, 1969.

_____. *God of the Oppressed*. London: SPCK, 1977.

_____. *The Spirituals and the Blues: An Interpretation*. New York: The Seabury Press, 1972.

Cook, Guillermo. *The Expectation of the Poor*. Maryknoll, N.Y.: Orbis Books, 1985.

Costas, Orlando E. *The Church and its Mission: A Shattering Critique from the Third World*. Wheaton, Ill.: Tyndale House Publishers, Inc., 1974.

Cousins, Ewert H., ed. *Hope and the Future of Man*. Philadelphia: Fortress

Press,1972.

Crassweller, Robert D. *The Caribbean Community; Changing Societies and U.S. Policy*. London: Pall Mall Press, 1972.

Cuthbert, Robert W. M. *Ecumenism and Development*. Bridgetown, Barbados: Caribbean Conference of Churches, 1986.

Davis, Kortright. *Emancipation Still Comin'*. Maryknoll, N.Y.: Orbis Books, 1990.

_____, ed. *Moving into Freedom*. "Working Together With Christ" Series. No. 2. The Second CCC Assembly, Guyana, 1977. Barbados, W.I.: The Cedar Press, 1977.

Dean, Thomas. *Post-Theistic Thinking: The Marxist-Christian Dialogue in Radical Perspective*. Philadelphia: Temple University Press, 1975.

Demas, William G. *Change and Renewal in the Caribbean*. Edited by David I. Mitchell. Barbados, W.I.: CCC Publ. House, n.d.

Despres, Leo A., ed. *Ethnicity and Resource Competition in Plural Societies*. The Hague: Moulton Publishers, 1975.

Dillenberger, John. *God Hidden and Revealed*. Philadelphia: Muhlenberg Press, 1953.

Dirscherl, Denis, S.J., ed. *Speaking of God*. Milwaukee: The Bruce Publishing Co., 1967

Dussel, Enrique. *History and the Theology of Liberation*. Translated by John Drury. Maryknoll, N.Y.: Orbis Books, 1976.

Ebeling, Gerhard. *Luther*. The Fontana Library of Theology and Philosophy. Translated by R.A. Wilson. London: Collins, 1975.

Ellacuría, Ignacio. *Freedom Made Flesh*. Translated by John Drury. Maryknoll, N.Y.: Orbis Books, 1976.

Ellis, Marc H. and Maduro, Otto, eds. *The Future of Liberation Theology*. Maryknoll, N.Y.: Orbis Books, 1989.

Ellul, Jacques. *Jesus and Marx: From Gospel to Ideology*. Translated by Joyce Main Hanks. Grand Rapids, Mich.: Wm. B. Eerdmans Publishing Co., 1988.

Engels, Frederick. *Ludwig Feuerbach and the Outcome of Classical Germany*. Edited by C.P. Dutt. (Translator not given) New York: International Publishers Co., Inc., 1941.

Erskine, Noel Leo. *Decolonizing Theology*. Maryknoll, N.Y.: Orbis Books, 1981.

Feuerbach, Ludwig. *The Essence of Faith According to Luther*. Translated by Melvin Cherno. New York: Harper and Row, Publishers, 1967.

Fierro, Alfredo. *The Militant Gospel*. London: SCM Press Ltd., 1977.

Fleischer, Helmut. *Marxism and History*. Translated by Eric Mosbacher. London: Allen Lane The Penguin Press, 1973.

Forde, Gerhard O. "Luther's Theology of the Cross" *Christian Dogmatics*. Carl E. Braaten and Robert W. Jenson, eds. Vol. 2. Philadelphia: Fortress Press, 1984, pp. 47-63

Forell, George W. *Faith Active in Love*. Minneapolis, Mn.: Augsburg Publishing House, 1964.

Forell, George W., et. al. *Luther and Culture*. Martin Luther Lectures. Vol. IV. Decorah, Ia.: Luther College Press, 1960.

Fromm, Erich. *Marx's Concept of Man*. New York: Frederick Unger Publishing Co., 1961.

Frostin, Per. *Materialismus Ideologie Religion: Die Materialistische Religionskritik Bei Karl Marx.* Munchen: Chr. Kaiser Verlag, 1978.

Furnival, J.S. *Colonial Policy and Practice: A Comparative Study of Burma and Netherlands India.* London: Cambridge University Press, 1948.

Garaudy, Roger. *Marxism in the Twentieth Century.* Translated by Rene Hague. London: Collins, 1970.

Gardavsky, Vitezslav. *God is Not Yet Dead.* Translated by Vivienne Menkes. London: Penguin Books, 1973.

Gardiner, Patrick, ed. *The Philosophy of History.* London: Oxford University Press, 1974.

_____, ed. *Theories of History.* Glencoe, Ill.: The Free Press, 1959.

Gilkey, Langdon. *Reaping the Whirlwind.* New York: The Seabury Press, 1976.

Girardi, Giulio. *Marxism and Christianity.* Translated by Kevin Traynor. New York: The Macmillan Publishing Co., Inc., 1968.

Gollwitzer, Helmut. *The Christian Faith and the Marxist Criticism of Religion.* Translated by David Cairns. Edinburgh: The Saint Andrew Press, 1970.

_____. *The Existence of God as Confessed by Faith.* Translated by J.W. Leitch. London: SCM Press Ltd., 1965.

Goodridge, Sehon S. *A Companion to Liberation Theology.* Bridgetown, Barbados: Cedar Press, 1984

_____. *Politics and the Caribbean Church: A Confession of Guilt.* Caribbean Ecumenical Consultation for Development. Study Paper No. 2. Barbados, W.I.: Catholic News, 1971.

Goveia, Elsa V. *Slave Society in the British Leeward Islands at the End of the*

274

Eighteenth Century. London: Yale University Press, 1965.

Gutiérrez, Gustavo. *The Power of the Poor in History*. Maryknoll, N.Y.: Orbis Books, 1983.

_____. *A Theology of Liberation*. Rev. ed. Translated and edited by Sister Caridad Inda and John Eagleson. Maryknoll, N.Y.: Orbis Books, 1988.

Hall, Douglas John. *Lighten Our Darkness; Towards an Indigenous Theology of the Cross*. Philadelphia: The Westminster Press, 1976.

Hamid, Idris. *A History of the Presbyterian Church in Trinidad; 1868–1968*. San Fernando, Trinidad: St. Andrew's Theological College, 1980.

_____. *In Search of New Perspectives*. Caribbean Ecumenical Consultation for Development. Barbados, W.I.: CADEC, 1970.

_____, ed. *Out of the Depths: A collection of papers presented at four missiology conferences held in Antigua, Guyana, Jamaica, and Trinidad in 1975*. San Fernando, Trinidad: Rahaman Printery Ltd., 1977.

Haynes, Lilith. *Fambli. The Church's Responsibility to the Family in the Caribbean: A consultation conducted by CARIPLAN*. New York: Church World Service, 1972.

Headley, John M. *Luther's View of Church History*. New Haven: Yale University Press, 1963.

Hertz, Karl H., ed. *Two Kingdoms and One World*. Minneapolis, Mn.: Augsburg Publishing House, 1976.

Herzog, Frederick. *Liberation Theology: Liberation in the Light of the Fourth Gospel*. New York: The Seabury Press, 1972.

Hill, William J. *The Three-Personed God*. Washington, D.C.: The Catholic University of America Press, 1982.

Hodgson, Peter C. *New Birth of Freedom*. Philadelphia: Fortress Press, 1976.

Hook, Sidney. *From Hegel to Marx*. London: Victor Gollancz Ltd., 1936.

Hyppolite, Jean. *Studies on Marx and Hegel*. Translated by John O'Neill. London: Heinemann Educational Books Ltd., 1969.

Jackson, T.A. *Dialectics*. New York: Burt Franklin, Lennox Hill Publ. and Distrib. Co., 1936.

Jenkins, David E. *The Contradiction of Christianity*. London: SCM Press Ltd., 1976.

_____. "What does salvation mean to Christians today?" *Living Faith and Ultimate Goals*. Edited by S. J. Samartha. Geneva: WCC, 1974.

John, P. M. *Marx on Alienation*. Columbia, Mo.: South Asia Books, 1976.

Johnson, Frank, ed. *Alienation*. New York: Seminar Press, 1973.

Jordan, Z.A. *The Evolution of Dialectical Materialism*. New York: St. Martin's Press, 1967.

Jüngel, Eberhard. *God as the Mystery of the World*. Translated by Darrell L. Guder. Grand Rapids, Mich.: Wm. B. Eerdmans Publishing Co., 1983.

Kamenka, Eugene. *The Ethical Foundations of Marxism*. London: Routledge and Kegan Paul, Ltd., 1962.

_____. *Marxism and Ethics*. 2nd ed. London: Macmillan Publishers, Ltd, 1970.

Kantonen, T.A. *Man in the Eyes of God: Human Existence in the Light of the Lutheran Confessions*. Lima, Ohio: C.S.S. Publishing Co., 1972.

Karris, Robert J., O.F.M. "Poor and Rich: The Lukan Sitz im Leben."
Perspectives on Luke-Acts. Edited by Charles H. Talbert. Edinburgh: T. and T.
Clark, Ltd., 1978.

Käsemann, Ernst. *Jesus Means Freedom*. Translated by Frank Clarke.
Philadelphia: Fortress Press, 1977.

Kerr, Hugh T. *A Compend of Luther's Theology*. Philadelphia: The Westminster
Press, 1966.

Kirk, J. Andrew. *Liberation Theology*. Atlanta: John Knox Press, 1979..

Kitamori, Kazoh. *Theology of the Pain of God*. Translated from the Japanese.
London: SCM Press Ltd., 1966.

Knight, Franklin W. *The Caribbean: The Genesis of a Fragmented Nationalism*.
New York: Oxford University Press, 1978.

Knight, Franklin W. and Palmer, Colin A., eds. *The Modern Caribbean*. Chapel
Hill, N.C.: The University of North Carolina Press, 1989.

Kolakowski, Leszek. *Main Currents of Marxism*. Vol. I: *The Founders* .
Translated by P.S. Falla. London: Oxford University Press, 1978.

_____. *Marxism and Beyond*. Translated by Jane Zielonko Peel. London:
Pall Mall Press, 1968.

Koren, Henry J. *Marx and the Authentic Man*. Pittsburgh: Duquesne University
Press, 1967.

Koyama, Kosuke. *No Handle on the Cross: An Asian Meditation on the Crucified
Mind*. London: SCM Press Ltd., 1976.

_____. *Waterbuffalo Theology*. London: SCM Press Ltd., 1974.

Labedz, Leopold. *Revisionism*. London: George Allen and Unwin Ltd., 1962.

Lapide, Pinchas and Moltmann, Jürgen. *Jewish Monotheism and Christian Trinitarian Doctrine*. Translated by Leonard Swidler. Philadelphia: Fortress Press, 1979.

Lash, Nicholas. *A Matter of Hope*. Notre Dame: University of Notre Dame Press, 1981.

Lehmann, Paul L. *Ideology and Incarnation*. Geneva: John Knox Association, 1962.

Lewis, Sybil and Matthews, Thomas G., eds. *Caribbean Integration. Papers on Social, Political and Economic Integration*. Third Caribbean Scholars' Conference. Georgetown, Guyana, April 4–9, 1966. Rio Piedras, P.R.: University of Puerto Rico, 1967.

The Library of Christian Classics. Vol. XVI. *Luther: Early Theological Works*. Translated and edited by James Atkinson. London: SCM Press Ltd., 1962.

_____. Vol. XVII. *Luther and Erasmus: Free Will and Salvation*. Translated and edited by E. Gordon Rupp and Philip S. Watson, et.al. London: SCM Press Ltd., 1969.

Livergood, Norman D. *Activity in Marx's Philosophy*. The Hague: Martinus Nijhoff, 1962.

Lobkowicz, Nicholas, ed. *Marx and the Western World*. Notre Dame: University of Notre Dame Press, 1967.

Lochman, Jan M. *Church in a Marxist Society*. London: SCM Press Ltd., 1970.

_____. *Encountering Marx*. Translated by H. Robertson. Philadelphia: Fortress Press, 1977.

Löwith, Karl. *From Hegel to Nietzsche*. Translated by David E. Green. New York: Rhinehart and Winston, Inc., 1964.

Luijpen, William A. *Theology as Anthropology.* Theological Series 12. Translated by Henry J. Koren. Duquesne Studies. Pittsburgh: Duquesne University Press, 1973.

Luther, Martin. *Luther's Works.* American ed. Edited by Jaroslav Pelikan, et. al. 54 vols. Philadelphia: Fortress Press/Muhlenberg Press; St. Louis: Concordia Publishing House, 1958.

_____. *Three Treatises.* Philadelphia: Fortress Press, 1960.

Lynch, William, S.S. *Christ and Prometheus.* Notre Dame: University of Notre Dame Press, 1970.

McGrath, Alister E. *Luther's Theology of the Cross.* Oxford: Basil Blackwell Ltd., 1985.

MacKinnon, Donald. *Explorations in Theology 5.* London: SCM Press Ltd., 1979.

McLellan, David. *Marx Before Marxism.* London: Macmillan Publishers, Ltd., 1970.

_____. *Marxism and Religion.* New York: Harper & Row, Publishers, 1987.

_____. *The Thought of Karl Marx: An Introduction.* London: Macmillan Publishers, Ltd., 1971.

_____. *The Young Hegelians and Karl Marx.* London: Macmillan Publishers, Ltd., 1969.

_____, ed. *Marx's Grundrisse.* London: Macmillan Publishers, Ltd., 1971.

McKelway, Alexander J. and Willis, E. David, eds. *The Context of Contemporary Theology.* Atlanta, Ga.: John Knox Press, 1974.

McMurtry, John. *The Structure of Marx's World-View*. Princeton: Princeton University Press, 1978.

Machovec, Milan. *A Marxist Looks at Jesus*. Translated from the German. Introduction by Peter Hebblethwaite. Philadelphia: Fortress Press, 1976.

Mandelbaum, Maurice. *History, Man, and Reason*. Baltimore: The Johns Hopkins Press, 1971.

Marcuse, Herbert. *From Luther to Popper*. Translated by Joris de Bres. London: Verso Edition, 1983.

Marx, Karl. *Early Texts*. Translated and edited by David McLellan. Oxford: Basil Blackwell, 1971.

_____. *Early Writings*. Translated and edited by T. B. Bottomore. Foreword by Erich Fromm. New York: McGraw-Hill Book Company, 1964.

_____. *Grundrisse. Foundations of the Critique of Political Economy*. Translated by Martin Nicolaus. Penguin Books. London: New Left Review, 1973.

_____. *Pre-Capitalist Economic Formations*. Translated by Jack Cohen. Edited and with an introduction by E.J. Hobsbawm. London: Lawrence and Wishart, 1978.

_____. *Selected Writings in Sociology and Social Philosophy*. Translated by T. B. Bottomore. Edited by T. B. Bottomore and Maximilien Rubel. London: C. A. Watts and Co. Ltd., 1963.

Marx, Karl and Engels, Frederick. *Collected Works*. Vol. 5. London: Lawrence and Wishart, 1976.

_____. *The Communist Manifesto*. Authorized English Translation. New

York: International Publishers Co., Inc., 1948.

_____. *Selected Works.* 2 Vols. Moscow: Foreign Languages Publishing House, 1951.

Mason, Philip. *Patterns of Dominance.* London: Oxford University Press, 1970.

Meeks, M. Douglas. *Origins of the Theology of Hope.* Foreword by Jürgen Moltmann. Philadelphia: Fortress Press, 1974.

Mészáros, István, ed. *Aspects of History and Class Consciousness.* London: Routledge and Kegan Paul, 1971.

_____. *Marx's Theory of Alienation.* London: The Merlin Press, Ltd., 1970.

Míguez Bonino, José. *Christians and Marxists.* Grand Rapids, Mich.: William B. Eerdmans Publishing Co., 1976.

Mintz, Sidney W. *Caribbean Transformations.* Chicago: Aldine Publishing Co.,1974.

_____, ed. *Slavery, Colonialism and Racism.* New York: W. W. Norton and Co., Inc., 1974.

Miranda, José Porfirio. *Communism and the Bible.* Translated by Robert R. Barr. Maryknoll, N.Y.: Orbis Books, 1982.

_____. *Marx and the Bible.* Translated by John Eagleson. Maryknoll, N.Y.: Orbis Books, 1974.

Mitchell, David I., ed. *With Eyes Wide Open.* A Collection of Papers by Caribbean Scholars on Caribbean Christian Concerns to Commemorate the Inaugural Assembly of the Caribbean Conference of Churches, Jamaica, Nov., 1973. Barbados, W. I.: CADEC, n.d.

Moltmann, Jürgen. *The Church in the Power of the Spirit.* Translated by Margaret

Kohl. New York: Harper and Row, Publishers, 1977.

_____. *The Crucified God.* Translated by John Bowden and R. A. Wilson. New York: Harper and Row, Publishers, 1974.

_____. *Experiences of God.* Translated by Margaret Kohl. Philadelphia: Fortress Press, 1980.

_____. *The Experiment Hope.* Edited, translated and with a foreword by M. Douglas Meeks. London: SCM Press Ltd., 1975.

_____. *The Future of Creation.* Translated by Margaret Kohl. Philadelphia: Fortress Press, 1979.

_____. *God in Creation.* Translated by Margaret Kohl. San Francisco: Harper & Row, Publishers, 1985.

_____. "The Christian Theology of Hope and its Bearing on Development." *In Search of a Theology of Development.* Translated by the WCC translation section. Lausanne: Imprimerie La Concorde, 1969.

_____. *Man.* Translated by John Sturdy. London: SPCK, 1974.

_____. *On Human Dignity.* Translated and with an introduction by M. Douglas Meeks. Philadelphia: Fortress Press, 1984.

_____. *The Passion for Life.* Translated by M. Douglas Meeks. Philadelphia: Fortress Press, 1973.

_____. *The Power of the Powerless.* Translated by Margaret Kohl. San Francisco: Harper & Row, Publishers, 1983.

_____. *Religion, Revolution, and the Future.* Translated by M. Douglas Meeks. New York: Charles Scribner's Sons, 1969.

_____. *Theology and Joy.* Translated by Reinhard Ulrich. London: SCM

Press Ltd., 1973.

_____. *Theology of Hope*. Translated by James W. Leitch. London: SCM Press Ltd., 1967.

_____. *The Trinity and the Kingdom*. Translated by Margaret Kohl. San Francisco: Harper & Row, Publishers, 1981.

Moltmann-Wendel, Elizabeth and Moltmann, Jürgen. *Humanity in God*. New York: The Pilgrim Press, 1983.

Morse, Christopher. *The Logic of Promise in Moltmann's Theology*. Philadelphia: Fortress Press, 1979.

Muckenhirn, Maryellen, ed. *The Future as the Presence of Shared Hope*. New York: Sheed and Ward, 1968.

Naipaul, V.S. *The Mimic Men*. London: Penguin Books, 1977.

Nelson, J. Robert, ed. *No Man is Alien*. Leiden: E.J. Brill, 1971.

Niebuhr, H. Richard. *Christ and Culture*. New York: Harper and Row, Publishers, 1975.

Nisbet, Robert A. *The Sociological Tradition*. London: Heinemann, 1966.

Norman, Richard. *Hegel's Phenomenology: A Philosophical Introduction*. London: Sussex University Press, 1976.

Norris, Russell B. *God, Marx, and the Future*. Philadelphia: Fortress Press, 1974.

Oestreicher, Paul, ed. *The Christian-Marxist Dialogue*. An International Symposium. London: Macmillan Publishers, Ltd., 1969.

Ogletree, Thomas W., ed. *Openings for Marxist-Christian Dialogue*. Nashville: Abingdon Press, 1968.

Ollman, Bertell. *Alienation.* London: Cambridge University Press, 1971.

Pannenberg, Wolfhart. *Jesus-God and Man.* Translated by Lewis L. Wilkins and Duane A. Priebe. London: SCM Press Ltd., 1968.

_____. *The Apostles' Creed In Light of Today's Questions.* Translated by Margaret Kohl. London: SCM Press Ltd., 1972.

_____. *The Idea of God and Human Freedom.* Translated by R.A. Wilson. Philadelphia: The Westminster Press, 1973.

_____. *Theology and the Kingdom of God.* Edited by Richard John Neuhaus.
Philadelphia: The Westminster Press, 1969.

_____. *What is Man?* Translated by Duane A. Priebe. Philadelphia: Fortress Press, 1970.

Patterson, Orlando. *The Sociology of Slavery.* London: MacGibbon and Kee, 1967.

Petulla, Joseph M. *Christian Political Theology: A Marxian Guide.* Maryknoll, N.Y.: Orbis Books, 1972.

Plamenatz, John. *Karl Marx's Philosophy of Man.* London: Oxford University Press, 1975.

Popper, K.R. *The Open Society and its Enemies.* Vol. II. *The Hide Tide of Prophecy: Hegel, Marx, and its Aftermath.* London: George Routledge and Sons, Ltd., 1945.

Porter, J. M., ed. *Luther Selected Political Writings.* Philadelphia: Fortress Press, 1974.

Prenter, Regin. *Creation and Redemption.* Translated by Theodor I. Jensen.

Philadelphia: Fortress Press, 1967.

_____. *Luther's Theology of the Cross*. Facet Books. Edited by Charles C. Anderson. Philadelphia: Fortress Press, 1971.

_____. *Spiritus Creator. Luther's Concept of the Holy Spirit*. Translated by John M. Jensen. Philadelphia: Fortress Press, 1953.

Quade, Quentin L., ed. *The Pope and Revolution*. Foreword by Richard John Neuhaus. Washington, D.C.: Ethics and Public Policy Center, 1982.

Robinson, N.H.G. *The Groundwork of Christian Ethics*. London: Collins, 1971.

Runyon, Theodore, ed. and trans. *Hope for the Church*. Nashville: Abingdon, 1979.

Rupp, Gordon. *The Righteousness of God*. London: Hodder and Stoughton, Ltd., 1953.

Sanderson, John. *An Interpretation of the Political Ideas of Marx and Engels*. London: Longmans, Green and Co., 1969.

Schacht, Richard. *Alienation*. With introductory essay by Walter Kaufmann. London: George Allen and Unwin Ltd., 1971.

Schillebeeckx, Edward. *Jesus. An Experiment in Christology*. Translated by Hubert Hoskins. Glasgow: Collins, 1979.

Segundo, Juan Luis. *Liberation of Theology*. Translated by John Drury. Maryknoll, N.Y.: Orbis Books, 1976.

Selinger, Martin. *The Marxist Conception of Ideology, A Critical Essay*. Cambridge: Cambridge University Press, 1977.

Selsam, Howard and Martel, Harry, eds. *Reader in Marxist Philosophy*. From the writings of Marx, Engels, and Lenin. New York: International Publishers Co.,

Inc., 1963.

Shaw, William H. *Marx's Theory of History*. Stanford: Stanford University Press, 1978.

Siggins, I.D.K. *Martin Luther's Doctrine of Christ*. New Haven: Yale University Press, 1970.

Siirala, Aarne. *Divine Humanness*. Translated by T.A. Kantonen. Philadelphia: Fortress Press, 1970.

Simon, Ulrich E. *A Theology of Auschwitz*. London: Victor Gollancz Ltd., 1967.

Singh, Paul. *Guyana: Socialism in a Plural Society*. London: Fabian Society, 1972.

Smith, M. G. *The Plural Society in the British West Indies*. Berkley and Los Angeles: University of California, 1965.

Smith, Ronald G., ed. *World Come of Age*. London: Collins, 1967.

Sobrino, Jon, S.J. *Christology at the Crossroads*. Translated by John Drury. London: SCM Press Ltd., 1978.

_____. *Jesus in Latin America*. Maryknoll, N.Y.: Orbis Books, 1987.

_____. *The True Church and the Poor*. Translated by Matthew J. O'Connell. Maryknoll, N.Y.: Orbis Books, 1984.

Staniloae, Dumitru. *The Victory of the Cross*. Fairacres, Oxford: SLG (The Sisters of the Love of God) Press, 1970.

Stojanovic, Svetozar. *Between Ideals and Reality. A Critique of Socialism and its Future*. Translated by Gerson S. Sher. New York: Oxford University Press, 1973.

Stone, Ronald H. *Realism and Hope.* Washington, D.C.: University Press of America, 1977.

Stumme, Wayne, ed. *Christians and the Many Faces of Marxism.* Minneapolis: Augsburg Publishing House, 1984.

Tappert, Theodore G., ed., in collaboration with Jaroslav Pelikan, et. al. Translated by Theodore G. Tappert. *The Book of Concord.* Philadelphia: Fortress Press, 1959.

Taylor, Charles. *Hegel.* Cambridge: Cambridge University Press, 1975.

Thielicke, Helmut. *The Hidden Question of God.* Translated by Geoffrey W. Bromiley. Grand Rapids, Mich.: William B. Eerdmans Publishing Co., 1977.

Tillich, Paul. *Love, Power, and Justice.* New York: Oxford University Press, 1974.
_____. *Systematic Theology.* 3 Vols. Chicago: University of Chicago Press, 1973.
_____. *The Protestant Era.* Abridged ed. Translated by James L. Adams. Chicago: University of Chicago Press, 1973.

Tinker, Hugh. *A New System of Slavery: The Export of Indian Labour Overseas 1830–1920.* London: Oxford University Press, 1974.

Tucker, Robert C. *Philosophy and Myth in Karl Marx.* 2nd rev. ed. London and New York: Cambridge University Press, 1972.

_____. *The Marxian Revolutionary Idea.* London: George Allen and Unwin Ltd., 1969.

von Campenhausen, Hans. *The Formation of the Christian Bible.* Translated by John A. Baker. London: Adam and Charles Black, 1972.

von Loewenich, Walther. *Luther's Theology of the Cross.* Translated by Herbert J.A. Bouman. Minneapolis, Mn.: Augsburg Publishing House, 1976.

Vree, Dale. *On Synthesizing Marxism and Christianity.* New York: John Wiley and Sons, 1976.

Wartofsky, Marx W. *Feuerbach.* London: Cambridge University Press, 1977.

Watson, Philip S. *Let God be God!* London: The Epworth Press, 1947.

Watty, William. *From Shore to Shore.* Barbados: Cedar Press, 1981.

Welch, Claude. *Protestant Thought in the Nineteenth Century.* Vol. I. 1790–1870. New Haven: Yale University Press, 1972.

Wetter, Gustav A. *Dialectical Materialism.* Translated by Peter Heath. London: Routledge and Kegan Paul, 1958.

Williams, Eric E. *Capitalism and Slavery.* Chapel Hill: The University of North Carolina, 1944.

_____. *From Columbus to Castro: The History of the Caribbean 1492–1969.* London: Andre Deutsch, 1970.

Wingren, Gustaf. *Creation and Law.* Translated by Ross McKenzie. Edinburgh: Oliver and Boyd, Ltd., 1961.

_____. *The Christian's Calling. Luther on Vocation.* Translated by Carl C. Rasmussen. Edinburgh and London: Oliver and Boyd, Ltd., 1958.

Winter, Derek. *Hope in Captivity. The Prophetic Church in Latin America.* London: Epworth Press, 1977.

Word & World (Justification and Justice). Vol. VII. No. 1. (Winter 1987).

Yoder, John H. *The Politics of Jesus.* Grand Rapids, Mich.: William B. Eerdmans Publishing Co., 1972.

PERIODICALS

Alves, Rubem. "The Seed of the Future: The Community of Hope." *International Review of Mission*. Vol. 63 (1974), 551–569.

Bell, Daniel. "The 'Rediscovery' of Alienation." *The Journal of Philosopy*. Vol. 56. No. 24. (Nov. 19, 1959), 933–952.

Bentley, James. "Prometheus versus Christ in the Christian-Marxist Dialogue." *The Journal of Theological Studies*. Vol. 29. Part 2 (October 1978), 483–494.

Bosch, David J. "Racism and Revolution: Response of the Churches in South Africa." *Occasional Bulletin of Missionary Research*. Vol. 3. Part 1 (1979), 13–19.

Braaten, Carl E. "A Trinitarian Theology of the Cross." (Review article on Jürgen Moltmann, *The Crucified God.) The Journal of Religion*. Vol. 56. No. 2 (April 1976), 113–121.

Braybrooke, David. "Diagnosis and Remedy in Marx's Doctrine of Alienation." *Social Research*. (Autumn 1958), 325–345.

Brown, Robert McAffe. "Reflections on Detroit." *Christianity and Crisis*, Vol. 35, No. 17 (October 27, 1975), 225–256.

Campbell-Johnston, Michael, S.J. "Basic Aspirations of Socialism are Profoundly Christian." *Guyana Graphic*. (10th August, 1975).

Carroll, M. Daniel. " 'Liberation Theology Comes of Age': Clarifying an Assessment. " *The Expository Times*. Vol. 98. No. 6. (March 1987), 170–171.

Castro, Fidel. "Christianity and the Revolution." *New Black-friars*. Vol. 59. No.

695 (April 1978), 152–165.

Conklin, Francis, S.J. "Some Aspects of the Marxian Philosophy of God." *The New Scholasticism*. Vol. 28 (1954), 38–57.

"Conversation from Bossey." *International Review of Mission*. Vol. 68. No. 270 (April 1979), 131–138.

Costas, O.E. "Conversion as a Complete Experience." *Gospel in Context*. (July 1978), 14–24.

Dahl, Nils A. "Is There a New Testament Basis for the Doctrine of the Two Kingdoms?" *Lutheran World*. Vol. 12. No. 4 (1965), 337–354.

Dussel, Enrique. "The Kingdom of God and the Poor." *International Review of Mission*. Vol. 18. No 270 (April 1979), 115–130.

Forstman, H. Jackson. "A Beggar's Faith." *Interpretation*. Vol. 30. No. 3 (July 1976), 262–270.

Frostin, Per. "Modern Marxist Critique of Religion—A Survey." *Lutheran World*. Vol. 20. No. 2 (1973), 141–154.

Garaudy, Roger. "As Marxists, We are Struggling on Behalf of Man." *Background Information*. For Church and Society. No. 34. Geneva: WCC (December 1965), 5–9.

Goodbridge, Sehon. *Political and the Caribbean Church: A Confession of Guilt*, CADEC, Study Paper No. 2. Barbados, W.I.: Catholic News Printery, n.d.

Halle, Louis J. "Marx's Religious Drama." *Encounter*. Vol. 25. No. 4 (October 1965), 29–37.

Hertz, Karl. "A Response to Hans Schwarz." *Lutheran Quarterly*. Vol. 27. No. 1 (February 1975), 76–79.

Herzog, Frederick. "Liberation Hermeneutic as Ideology Critique?" *Interpetation*. Vol. 23 (October 1974), 387–403.

Ho, David Y.F. "The Concept of Man in Mao Tse-tung Thought." *Psychiatry*. Vol. 41 (November 1978), 391–402.

Hodges, Donald Clark. "The Young Marx—A Reappraisal," *Philosophical and Phenomenological Research*. Vol. 27. No. 2 (December 1966), 219.

Hoffman, Paul E. "The Origin and Nature of Marxism as a Challenge to the Church." *Missionalia.*. Vol. 6. No. 2 (August 1978), 46–57.

Hyde, Douglas. "Liberating the Powerless Ones." *The Month*. (November 1978), 389–390.

Ishida, Joshiro. "Salvation, Mission and Humanization." *Lutheran World*. Vol. 18. Part 4 (1971), 370–375.

_____. "The Theology of Kazoh Kitamori." *Trinity Theological College Annual*. Vol.5 (1968), 18–22.

Jepsen, Alfred. "What can the Old Testament contribute to the discussion on the Doctrine of the Two Kingdoms?" *Lutheran World*. Vol. 12. No. 4 (1965) 325–336.

Jorgensen, Theodor. "Cultural, Christian and Lutheran Identity as a Christological Problem." *Africa Theological Journal*. Vol. 7. Part 1 (1978), 86–95.

Kappen, S. "The Marxian Concept of Man in the Indian Context." *Indian Journal of Theology*. Vol. 27. Nos. 3, 4 (July-December 1978), 123–136.

Käsemann, Ernst. "The Pauline Theology of the Cross." *Interpretation*. Vol. 24. No. 2 (April 1970), 151–177.

Keck, Leander. "The Son Who Creates Freedom." *Concilium*. Vol. 10. No. 1 (1974), 71–82.

Kurien, K. Matthew. "The Marxist Concept of Man." *The Indian Journal of Theology.* Vol. 27. Nos. 3,4 (July-December 1978), 112–122.

Langslet, Lars Roar. "Young Marx and Alienation in Western Debate." *Inquiry.* Vol. 6. No. 1 (Spring 1963), 3–17.

Lau, Franz. "The Lutheran Doctrine of the Two Kingdoms." *Lutheran World.* Vol. 12. No. 4 (1965), 355–372.

Lindberg, Carter. "Theology and Politics: Luther the Radical and Muntzer the Reactionary." *Encounter.* Vol. 37. No. 4 (Autumn 1976), 356–371.

Lochman, Jan M. "The Place of Prometheus." *Interpretation.* Vol. 32. No. 3 (July 1978), 242–254.

_____. "Towards an Ecumenical Account of Hope." *The Ecumenical Review.* Vol. 31. No. 1 (January 1979), 13–22.

Löffler, Paul. "The Reign of God has come in the Suffering Christ." *International Review of Mission.* Vol. 68. No. 270 (April 1979), 109–114.

Lowenthal, David. "Race and Color in the West Indies." *Daedalus.* Vol 96. No. 2 (Spring 1967), 580–626.

_____. "The Range and Variation of Caribbean Societies." *Annals of the New York Academy of Sciences.* (February 1960), 786–795.

Lowith, Karl. "Man's Self-Alienation in the Early Writings of Marx." *Social Research.* (1954), 204–230.

MacEoin, Gary. "Neocolonialism in Latin America." *Christian Century.* (2 June, 1971), 685–697.

McKenzie, Herman I. "Race and Class in Guyana." *Study Encounter.* Vol. 8. No. 4 (1972), 1–14.

McLellan, David. "Marx's View of the Unalienated Society." *The Review of Politics*. Vol. 31. No. 4 (October 1969), 459–465.

Massey, James A. "The Hegelians, the Pietists, and the Nature of Religion." *The Journal of Religion*. Vol. 58. No. 2 (April 1978), 108–129.

Mathias, T. A., S. J. "The Living God." *Indian Journal of Theology*. Vol. 18. Part 4 (1969), 246–258.

Mintz, Sidney W. "The Rural Proletariat and the Problem of Rural Proletarian Consciousness." *Journal of Peasant Studies*. 1 (1974), 291–325.

Neuhaus, Richard J. "Liberation Theology and the Captivities of Jesus." *Worldview*. Vol. 16 (June 1973), 41–48.

Olssen, E.A. "Marx and the Resurrection." *Journal of the History of Ideas*. Vol. 29. No. 1 (January-March 1968), 131–140.

O'Malley, Joseph J. "History and Man's 'Nature' in Marx." *The Review of Politics*. Vol. 28. No. 4 (October 1966), 508–527.

O'Neill, John. "The Concept of Estrangement in the Early and Later Writings of Karl Marx." *Philosophy and Phenomenological Research*. Vol. 25 (September 1964-June 1965), 64–84.

Parmasad, K.V. "By the Light of a Deya," *Tapia*, 22 (1971).

Parsons, Howard L. "The Prophetic Mission of Karl Marx," *The Journal of Theology*, Vol. 44 (1964), 57.

Patterson, Orlando. "Franz Fanon: My Hope and Hero." *New World Quarterly*. Vol. 2. Part 3 (May 1966), 93–95.

Persaud, Dwarka. "Light and the Evolution of the Free Society: An Appraisal of Governor Light's Administration, 1838-1848." Unpublished B.A., History 401

Thesis, University of Guyana, 1974.

Persaud, Winston. "The Article of Justification and the Theology of Liberation." *Currents in Theology and Mission*. Vol. 16. No. 5 (October 1987), 361–371.

Petrovic, Gajo. "Man as Economic Animal and Man as Praxis." *Inquiry*. Vol. 6. No. 2 (Spring 1963), 35–36.

Prien, Hans-Jurgen. "Liberation and Development in Latin America." *Lutheran World*. Vol. 20. No. 2 (1973), 114–132.

Reid, C.S. "A Christian Evaluation of Marxist Trends in the Caribbean." U.T.C.W.I. Founders' Day Lecture. (n.d.) (Mimeographed)

Rodney, Walter. "Contemporary Political Trends in the English-speaking Caribbean." *The Black Scholar* (September 1975), 15–21.

Rosen, Zvi. "The Influence of Bruno Bauer on Marx's Concept of Alienation." *Social Theory and Practice*. Vol. 1. Part 2 (1970), 50–60.

Schreiter, Robert J. "The Anonymous Christian and Christology." *Missiology: An International Review*. Vol. 1. No. 1 (January 1978), 29–52.

Schwarz, Hans. "Luther's Doctrine of the Two Kingdoms—Help or Hindrance for Social Change." *Lutheran Quarterly*. Vol. XXVII. No. 1 (February 1975), 59–75.

Seeman, Melvin. "On the Meaning of Alienation." *American Sociological Review*. Vol. 24 (1959), 783–791.

Siebert, Rudolf J. "The New Marxist Conception of Christianity: Hope Versus Positivism." *Anglican Theological Review*. Vol. 59. No. 3 (July 1977), 237–259.

Singh, Paul G. "Christianity and Socialism: Towards a Reconciliation?" *Guyana Graphic*. (17 August, 1975.)

_____. "Marxian Socialism." Lecture delivered in the Redeemer Lutheran Church Parish Hall, Georgetown, Guyana (November 1975.) (Mimeographed)

_____. "With God and Marx: Towards a People's Democracy?" *Guyana Graphic* (24 August, 1975.)

Suda, Max Josef. "The Critique of Religion in Karl Marx's *Capital*." *Journal of Ecumenical Studies*. Vol. 15 (Winter 1978), 15–28.

Taber, Charles R. "The Limits of Indigenization in Theology." *Missiology: An International Review*. Vol. 6. No. 1 (January 1978), 53–79.

Tidemann, Paul A. "A Christian Looks at Socialism." Lecture delivered in the Redeemer Lutheran Church Parish Hall, Georgetown, Guyana (23 November, 1975.) (Mimeographed)

van der Bent, Ano J. "Christian and Marxist Responses to the Challenge of Secularization and Secularism." *Journal of Ecumenical Studies*. Vol. 15. No. 1 (Winter 1978), 164.

Vercruysse, Jos. E., S.J. "Luther's Theology of the Cross at the Time of the Heidelberg Disputation." *Gregorianum*. Vol. 57. Fasc. 3 (1976), 523–548.

Verghese, Paul. "On God's Death." *Indian Journal of Theology*. Vol. 17. Part 4 (1968), 151–161.

van den Beld, A. "Karl Marx and the End of Religion." *Theology Today*. (July/August 1977), 66–71.

WCC EXCHANGE. No. 2 (May 1977) "The Confession of Faith of the Presbyterian-Reformed Church in Cuba." 1–20.

_____.No. 4 (September 1977) "Recent Important Books and Articles on the Christian-Marxist Encounter." 1–3.

295

_____. No. 4 (September 1977) "Theological Reflection on the Encounter of the Church with Marxism in Various Cultural Contexts." 1–21.

Weir, J. Emmette. "Liberation Theology Comes of Age." *The Expository Times.* Vol. 98. No. 1. (October 1986), 3–9.

Widjaja, Albert. "Beggerly Theology: A Search for a Perspective Towards Indigenous Theology." *South East Asia Journal of Theology.* Vol. 14. Part 2 (1973), 39–45.

Wigglesworth, Chris. "Which Way to Utopia: With Marx or Jesus?" *Evangelical Review of Theology.* Vol. 1 (October 1977), 95–107.

Yoder, John H. "Political Theology: Revolutionary Violence, Status Quo or …?" Collation of two lectures. *Sojourners.* (October 1975), 1–7.

_____. "Probing the Meaning of Liberation." *Sojourners.* 25 (September 1976).

Zimany, Roland D. "Enduring Values of Luther's Approach to Knowing God." *Lutheran Quarterly.* Vol. 27. No. 1 (February 1975), 6–26.

DATE DUE

MAY 1 9 2004			
OCT 1 7 2008			